MW00488379

"This much-needed book addresses re: teaching context. It offers down-to-earth, a in Christian higher education who want to cators. It offers concrete help for thinking about the task of teaching, rooted in sound theory and guided by clear thinking. Michael Lawson offers insight and guidance, not tricks, for educators serving in the context of Christian higher education. I am grateful that this book is available for both new and seasoned educators."

Perry G. Downs, professor emeritus of educational ministries, Trinity Evangelical Divinity School

"What a helpful book for new and future faculty members! This is a highly practical book that reflects a lifetime of experience of teaching in Christian higher education. Michael provides foundational principles and best practices across a wide range of critical aspects of teaching, including classroom management and learning assessment. It is a resource I want all of our doctoral students to read."

Kevin E. Lawson, director of Ph.D. and Ed.D. programs in educational studies, Talbot School of Theology, Biola University

"As someone who speaks or writes daily about the vocation of Christian schooling, I have found myself remarkably refreshed and reinvigorated after only an all-too-hasty reading of Michael Lawson's book *The Professor's Puzzle*. The tonic for my mind and heart began early with his differentiation between the Greeks' search for wisdom and a Christian's recognition of the source of wisdom. Written as if he were holding a conversation with his readers, Professor Lawson presents, then helps to solve, the puzzle that confounds every seriously thoughtful instructor: How do I help my students learn what is needful? I recommend this book to those who join me in a desire to inculcate into our teachers a desire for an intentional biblical worldview pedagogy that leads our students to love God more and appreciate his divine love for each of us."

D. Bruce Lockerbie, chairman, PAIDEIA, Inc., Stony Brook, New York; author, *The Way They Should Go; Thinking and Acting Like a Christian; A Christian Paideia; A Passion for Learning: A History of Christian Thought on Education*

"Dr. Lawson's book will make us all better educators. It is warm, well written, and draws you in. I've not read a more instructive treatment of the craft of becoming an effective educator. Reading it was like taking a long walk with an old friend in a place I love—academics. Sometimes it was hard to keep up and convicting. Sometimes I learned what I was embarrassed not to know. At all times I knew I was in good hands, being taught by someone who loves the topic and the student. This book could be the best tool in the kit. I wish I'd had it decades ago."

Beverly Lucas, former associate vice president for institutional effectiveness and accreditation and professor of Christian education, College of Biblical Studies, Houston, Texas

"Listen up, fellow Christian educators! *The Professor's Puzzle* is required reading for the guild. This hands-on, accessible text addresses our most critical issues with categorical precision. Dr. Michael Lawson, a master educator and practitioner, speaks from both classroom and administrative experience. Yet he does so with great pastoral skill. Make this the tool for your professional development—and your personal puzzle will radically improve."

Mark M. Yarbrough, vice president for academic affairs and academic dean, Dallas Theological Seminary

"I wish this book had been written thirty-five years ago when I stepped into a classroom for the first time as a teacher and wondered if the students were as terrified as I was. Whether summiting the lofty peaks of educational philosophy or hacking through the tangled underbrush of syllabi and institutional life, those who dare to believe that God can use them as a professor will find *The Professor's Puzzle* a trustworthy map, and Mike Lawson is the expert guide whom they need by their side. It's that good."

Mark Young, president, Denver Seminary

THE
PROFESSOR'S
PUZZLE

THE
PROFESSOR'S
PUZZLE

TEACHING
IN CHRISTIAN
ACADEMICS

B&H
ACADEMIC
NASHVILLE, TENNESSEE

MICHAEL S. LAWSON

The Professor's Puzzle: Teaching in Christian Academics

Copyright © 2015 by Michael Lawson

B&H Publishing Group
Nashville, Tennessee

ISBN: 978-1-4336-8410-4

Dewey Decimal Classification: 371.1
Subject Heading: TEACHERS—TRAINING \ TEACHING \
CHRISTIAN EDUCATION

Printed in the United States of America

DEDICATION

This book dedication seems like a very clumsy way to pay my intellectual debts. Having "run over" my manuscript one more time, I looked in life's rearview mirror. The sweet faces and dear names of those who gave me strength, wisdom, understanding, insight, and correction effortlessly appeared. As I age, the list of those who carried me to this time and place gets longer and longer. I absolve them all from any overstatements, understatements, misrepresentations, or foolishness found in this volume. And I thank them all for helping me grow up "in Christ."

I dedicate this book to . . .

the Lord Jesus, the greatest teacher of both method and content who ever lived, who came looking for me when I was not looking for him

Dr. Howard G. Hendricks, the best classroom teacher I ever observed, who believed in us students more deeply than we believed in ourselves

Dr. Kenneth O. Gangel, the best model of a Christian academician I ever worked for, who had the courage, patience, and persistence to lure me into academic ministry

Dr. Donald C. Campbell, a seminary president worthy of the term "emeritus," who knew me as a student at Dallas Theological Seminary but hired me anyway

CONTENTS

PREFACE

PUTTING THE *PROFESSOR'S PUZZLE* TOGETHER

A number of years ago I inherited a course named "Teaching in Christian Higher Education" from Dr. Kenn Gangel. Under his leadership, the course became required for all students in the Academic Ministry Track at Dallas Theological Seminary.[1] At that time, I spent the better part of a sabbatical completely dismantling and reassembling the course. The reassembly took into account a review of the literature designed to train young faculty. This book and particularly the puzzle reflect that research.

Since that time, a number of good books have emerged for professor enrichment but nothing to guide aspiring teachers through the necessary role adjustments. Historically, acquiring a PhD did not involve specific preparation for teaching. Everyone assumed mastery of content (evidenced by a PhD) qualified one to teach. But accrediting agencies continue to squeeze academic institutions for measurable

---

[1] The course is no longer required in the DTS curriculum.

student learning outcomes. This trend exposes the assumption's deficiency because professors must completely refocus on what students learn rather than their personal research. In spite of accrediting agencies, PhD training remains almost entirely focused on research.[2]

I designed the *Professor's Puzzle* to guide aspiring teachers through the initial shock of moving from the extended period of independent research required for their PhD to classroom teaching. I've added material because of the online explosion that catapulted the teaching profession into uncharted waters. That material appears in the chapters on planning, managing, evaluating, instructing, and relating. In an online platform, learning objectives remain the same, but teaching processes move from mostly "telling" toward "guided learning." This major recalibration leaves many experienced professors unable to adjust. Their faith in and reliance on the force of their personalities to communicate handicaps their efforts in a virtual environment. In fact, I have heard some declare the online environment off limits for their subject material. Of course that is nonsense. Online education is simply another form of distance education, which has been around at least since the apostle Paul wrote letters!

In addition, teachers in Christian secondary schools began to take my course. Their questions caused some material tweaks to account for older adolescent students. Many Christian secondary schools do not require the same educational certification as public schools. Consequently, some teachers come through the back door with little more than a fair understanding of their subjects. I hope this volume "putties up" some training cracks for these strategic educators. The students they represent deserve a truly Christian education, not just teaching from a Christian.

---

[2] I say "almost" as the last time I checked evangelical seminaries, no courses on teaching were required in PhD studies; but I don't check every day either.

Lastly, I bumped into a group of people hiding just below the surface. They bubbled up as soon as Dallas Seminary offered a new Doctor of Educational Ministry degree. A flurry of inquiries filled my e-mail inbox. Every kind of master's degree seemed to be knocking at our door. More often than not, their seminary degree was only remotely related to their teaching role. One common theme emerged; they already had teaching positions they could not leave. Their roles required more specific training in artful teaching and careful administration rather than the pure research offered in a PhD. They came from small Bible colleges, church-based Bible institutes, and mission schools. They represented every shape and size of school. I hope this book helps all those who enter the teaching profession through the back door feel welcome.

Many pieces of the *Professor's Puzzle* can be found in general education research publications. I have attempted to gather them all in one puzzle. Although Christian education relies heavily on general education research, I have leavened each and every piece with the yeast of Christian theology. After all, we have been in the teaching business from the very beginning. Some pieces need more yeast than others. Christian education is not merely public education with a devotion-plopped on top. If Christian theology does not permeate everything in our educational system—from the president's office to the janitor's closet—then I question whether we have the right to call it Christian.

One piece, "Institutional Realities," became part of the puzzle when I realized I could account for all the educational variations except institutional policies and politics. These realities often surprise and shock newcomers to the faculty. Higher education (and even lower education if there is such a thing) does not always reflect a rational universe. We do things because a major donor wants them done that way, we don't have enough money to do them the right way, the person in charge is the brother-in-law of the "Grand PooBah,". . . need I go on? Life is like that. The faster we adjust to the realities, the less stress we feel.

In preparation for this volume, I submitted an annotated outline. After reading it again, I decided it might serve readers well—especially if they decide not to read the book sequentially. If you are looking for immediate help with a problem, by all means go to the chapter that addresses your need. Before you lay the book down for too long, please read the chapter on philosophy. That chapter alerts you to my (hopefully) consistent perspective guiding my approach through each chapter. Here is the annotated summary representing each piece of the *Professor's Puzzle*.

Preface: *Putting the Professor's Puzzle Together* (see graphic on facing page)

This introduces the reader to the essential components of successful teaching found in the book. The book begins where Christian teaching ought to begin, with a proper philosophy and understanding of truth. With that background, the focus shifts to the thinking and planning that informs course design. The character formation of the teacher, lesson planning, presentation skills, and assessment also appear in appropriate chapters. This perspective enables the reader to plan a highly detailed course syllabus and lesson plans that thoughtfully coordinate and structure the students' learning experiences. All of this must be done from a distinctly Christian point of view.

Chapter 1—*A Philosophy for Christian Academic Education*

The word *Christian* transforms everything about education. For instance, if the goal of all *Christian* education is to love God more, then we ought to ask students at the end of every course, "Do you love God more, and, if so, how did this course contribute to that growth?" While I am not advocating a strictly devotional approach, I am advocating more

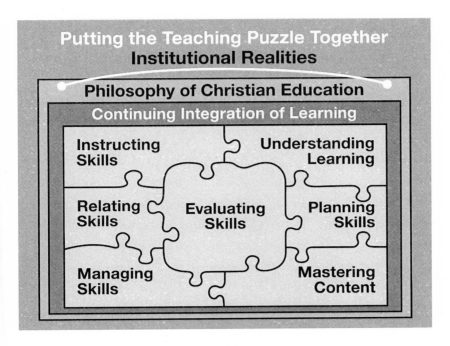

than content recall as the goal for *Christian* education. Also *Christian* ought to change the role of the teacher from adversary to advocate. The chapter graphics provide readers with a bit of structure for continuing development of their philosophy from a theological point of view.

Chapter 2—Helping Students and Professors Integrate Learning

A Christian worldview depends on an understanding that all learning is interconnected and interdependent. The compartmentalized approach that characterizes public education has influenced the Christian community to think more about particular subjects and less about how and why things fit together. A Christian approach to learning recognizes the larger picture of truth and enables students to fit individual subjects within that structure. In theological education, for instance, we often think of theology emerging from exegesis. But, sometimes we use theology to inform exegesis. These are interdependent and not unidirectional.

Chapter 3—Learning Theories for Practitioners

Depending on your categories, there are around fifty different theories.[3] Most teachers do not have time to wade through and evaluate the usefulness of each theory. This chapter will summarize the essence of ten significant theories and how they might be used. For example, Benjamin Bloom's taxonomy is universally accepted as the best guide to writing course objectives for cognitive information. In many Christian circles, certain theories are categorically rejected, but they often contain significant pieces of truth that help us understand the learning process.

Chapter 4—Planning Skills in Syllabus Design

At least six steps belong in syllabus design. However, a syllabus is no more than a description of the learning experiences planned for the students. Each of these experiences, from classroom activities to course requirements to assessment devices, must connect back to course objectives. Each course objective must find its expression clearly achieved in the experiences of the students. Ultimately, the course should be evaluated on the basis of whether the objectives were accomplished in the lives of the students. The plan should also take into account that classroom "learning" varies over a fifteen-week semester. A check list and a model example appear in appendix A.

---

[3] Accessed September 11, 2014, http://www.learning-theories.com.

Chapter 5—Mastering Content

Most students preparing to be scholar/teachers assume this is the only real criterion. In fact, everything in their PhD training points toward knowledge mastery as their exclusive goal. Contract renewals based on student evaluations often shock the unsuspecting new teachers. While teachers are expected to know their material, the current pressure in higher education as everywhere in education is to measure student learning outcomes. Teachers will need to reconsider strategies that help their students master the content or demonstrate an achievement of the course objectives.

Chapter 6—Managing Skills: The Classroom Experience

The successful classroom teacher must manage at least six different elements. While transfer of information dominates most classroom experiences, more powerful learning opportunities can be employed. The students themselves tend to be one of the most neglected resources in any classroom. The careful selection of appropriate methods makes the learning process a more active endeavor, which in turn leads to long-term memory. One helpful way of making that selection looks at the various components from the student's point of view.

Chapter 7—Evaluating Skills: Assessing Students, Courses, and Professors

Although testing remains a favorite assessment device among professors, there are many ways to make this single tool more effective. Depending on the course objectives and specific learning outcomes desired, testing may not provide an accurate measurement. In order to examine the results of learning, teachers need a tool chest stuffed with devices to assure the students and themselves that real learning occurred.

Chapter 8—Instructing Skills: Using Appropriate Variety

No book on teaching is complete without a chapter on instruction (read: lecturing). Some use the terms *teaching* and *instruction* (lecturing) interchangeably. Technically, instruction describes a professor's activity in giving information. Today teachers can provide information in a variety of ways. Students have direct access to an ever-growing information resource through technology. The role of the professor continues to shift away from just giving information to helping students evaluate information from a Christian perspective.

Chapter 9—Relating Skills: A Particularly Christian Idea

Of all the pieces in the *Professor's Puzzle*, this one displays the heart of Christian education best. Unlike the public sector, which may or may not care about the overall development of the students, Christian teachers should relish opportunities to engage the broader concerns of their students' lives and education. In addition, the Scriptures provide the healthiest guidelines for dealing with conflict and difference between teachers and students. From a theological point of view, Christian professors and students actually work within a family framework.

Chapter 10—Institutional Realities

Teachers must become students of the institution they serve. There are many mixed messages. For instance, the administration may emphasize time with students while the tenure review committee may only value publications. Or, at a different level, the teaching schedule and committee work may leave little time to improve teaching skills. What institutions say they value and what they actually celebrate and reward are often quite different. I have never seen a celebration of a professor's student appointment calendar. Most often, teachers will have to work very hard to stay student focused. Many decisions at the institutional level are driven more by finances than philosophy. Professors live within this constant tension. Working in a Christian institution provides both access and opportunity to minister to students. How a professor chooses to use those will in many ways measure his commitment to personal Christian goals. After all is said and done, it is not how he starts his teaching career but how he used it.

May God bless your every effort to represent the Savior to the students he chooses to entrust to you.

Michael S. Lawson
Dallas Theological Seminary

A PHILOSOPHY FOR CHRISTIAN ACADEMIC EDUCATION

"The fear of the LORD is the beginning of wisdom."
Psalm 111:10

Introduction

Plato did not invent philosophy (the love of wisdom), although his name has become synonymous with it. When we consider his teacher, Socrates, and his student, Aristotle, we find the Greek foundation stones of Western philosophy. In the East, thinkers like Guatama Buddha and Confucius also took leading roles in the search for wisdom, but they have not affected Western educational philosophies. A love of wisdom (philosophy) did not originate with philosophers or thinkers. The Bible traces an earlier and significantly different history for wisdom and those who love "her."

1

In the opening book of the Bible, Eve took the first misguided step in her pursuit of wisdom. But eating the fruit brought only the knowledge of good and evil, not the wisdom she sought. Obviously they are not the same thing. In contrast, Job traces the source of wisdom directly to God, not a particular fruit. In the New Testament, James echoes that thought and announces God's open promise to generously bestow wisdom on any who ask him in faith. Solomon sought wisdom above wealth, power, or vengeance, and Proverbs extols her virtues in chapter after chapter. The Old Testament encompasses a whole genre of material called "Wisdom literature," verifying her significance. Ultimately the apostle Paul painted a bold contrast between God's wisdom and Greek wisdom in the opening chapter of his Corinthian correspondence.

Fundamentally, Greek philosophers and the Bible differ in their starting places for wisdom. The great Greek thinkers struggled to explain the nature of reality as best they could in their *search* for wisdom. They used reason and logic, which they assumed existed to test ideas and perceptions. They questioned any notion that failed their rational tests. Their formulations attempted to account for both the visible (tangible) world and the invisible (intangible) world around them.[1] However, Greek philosophy ended where it began, with a *search*. Ultimately, the Greeks and those who followed after them could not escape the confines of their own logic.

On the other hand, the Bible begins with the *source* of wisdom, the Creator himself. He blessed the tabernacle craftsmen with wisdom. God's wisdom guided both Moses and Daniel. Solomon's unprecedented wisdom came as a gift from God. Ultimately, all the treasures of wisdom are bound up in Christ, the exact representation of the Father.

---

[1] Plato and Aristotle differed in their view of reality. Plato believed the perceived world of objects could be best understood through their ultimate forms. Aristotle believed the forms resided in the particulars of the perceived world.

And God grants generous portions of wisdom without criticism to those who ask in faith. Furthermore, God's wisdom doesn't only explain life; God's wisdom produces a life that "is first pure, then peace-loving, gentle, compliant, full of mercy and good fruits, without favoritism and hypocrisy" (Jas 3:17). Those who embrace God's wisdom live such lives.

Given the disparity between the Greek's *search* and the Bible's *source*, why do Christian scholars bother with Greek philosophers? Let me suggest four answers. First, Greeks set the philosophical agenda for Western thinkers. No one interacting with philosophy can ignore their questions. Second, Western theology organized itself to answer Greek philosophical questions.[2] Third, Augustine and Aquinas brought Christian thought to bear on Platonic and Aristotelian ideas respectively. The writings of these two ecclesiastical giants continue to influence Christian theology in the West. Fourth, many "modern" practices of education have roots deeply buried in Greek soil. For instance, Plato thought education ought to sort people into proper social positions. Education still tends to establish social status, even in Christian circles.

This chapter is not designed to provide a Christian philosophy. Instead, I hope to provide basic categories, questions, and comments to guide your construction of a personal philosophy of Christian education applied specifically to an academic setting. In order for us to think together, you need to know how I am using some key words. Of course, *Christian* refers to all Christ's teaching and character. I am particularly interested in his core values, which should permeate anything that bears his name. *Theology* refers to a comprehensive understanding of God based on both Scripture and creation. For clarity, I use the capitalized term *Philosophy* to refer to the Greeks and those who followed them, while the lower-case *philosophy* describes the wisest approach or best practice. *Education* encompasses the broadest scope of human learning

---

[2] Andrew Walls, *The Cross-cultural Process in Christian History* (Maryknoll, NY: Orbis Books, 2002), 79. This book belongs on your "must read" list.

and should be distinguished from academic schooling. Schooling only provides a portion of any person's overall education.[3] Therefore, a general philosophy of *Christian education* fits a wide variety of contexts totally, many of which are unrelated to schooling. But, *Christian* should modify everything associated with both education and schooling.

In the ancient world, education and religion were inseparable. Religion provided oxygen for the culturally rich structures in a society's general education. A son normally learned a trade at his father's side and there watched his father offer sacrifices designed to increase the family's success. The visible and invisible worlds intertwined. This understanding of reality in the West began to change as the Enlightenment's effects took hold. Eventually, educators separated general (scientific) education from religious (unverifiable by science) education. The university curriculum, once unified under theology, split into physical studies and metaphysical studies—with the latter deemed to have little practical value.

Today, children of the Enlightenment who come to faith in Christ need restructured thinking at the most basic level because Christian education stands in stark contrast to this dichotomy. Christian education offers a unified system. A genuinely Christian school recognizes the Creator in every subject and applies Christian values to every practice or policy.[4] I freely admit this is easier said than done. We do tend to "sprinkle" a little Christianity on inherited structures and practices rather than giving them a thorough cleansing with biblical theology. I am confident we can and must do better.

In addition, Christian education must account for two features never mentioned in the public sector. Western Philosophy has largely

---

[3] Children learn their mother tongue and many core values before schooling begins.

[4] The next chapter on integration will attempt to show why and how these come together.

abandoned the search for moral absolutes. Public education in a plu-
ralistic society mainly focuses on information. The Savior's teaching
mandate focuses on obedience rather than mere cognition as his final
objective. Plus, the Holy Spirit's activities among administrators, teachers, and students alter an ordinary school setting. We ought to expect
evidence of his work.

Developing a Philosophy of Christian Education

To develop a philosophy of Christian education, I offer a graphic of various categories that represents how someone might make an intellectual
journey beginning where he is and ending with a philosophy of Christian education in a specific context. Let your eyes work from the inside
out and then clockwise from "Theological" around the outer edge.

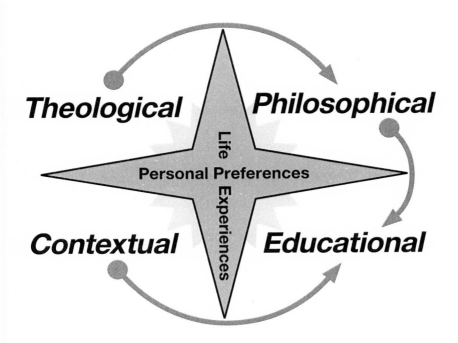

Here is how the graphic works:

1. I acknowledge the existential beginning of the journey. We never quite separate ourselves from personal experiences and preferences. We may affirm or react to them, but those experiences form an invisible hand that shapes us. For example, I have difficulty finding a place for testing in my schooling philosophy because I hated each and every test experience. As an educator, I understand how to use testing positively, as the chapter on evaluating skills will show. But I have never used testing in any course during almost thirty years of academic work. Those early experiences continue to shape my philosophy.

2. My aversion to testing demonstrates another significant point in a personal philosophy, the difference between an affirmed philosophy and an operational philosophy. Although I acknowledge a place for testing in my affirmed philosophy, I never make room for it in my courses. Bringing personal preferences into a philosophy is acceptable as long as we don't bind them on everyone else or damage students in the process. You might also want to be careful to modify your personal preferences to fit within the institution you serve.

3. Look again at the graphic working from the inside out and clockwise. Life experiences often precede our formulation of theological notions. In a perfect world, proper theology comes simultaneously with life experiences, interpreting them, and shaping our personal preferences.[5] In our current circumstances, we often accumulate a great many personal experiences before we formulate a reasonably comprehensive understanding of God. Our growing

---

[5] The only theologically correct, completely integrated system I know is the Old Testament Levitical system designed for the nation of Israel. The next chapter is dedicated to exploring an updated version of integration suitable for contemporary settings.

understanding should help us evaluate our personal experiences and preferences to see whether to modify our philosophy.

4. Next, our theology should address questions raised by Philosophy—especially if we find ourselves in Western cultures. I would change this section to address the categories of the dominant philosophy within a particular setting. For example, in the East I would look carefully at Mohammed, Confucius, Buddha, or Hindu thinkers dominating the setting. The important questions raised by the Greeks or others deserve Christian answers because Christianity works inside a comprehensive truth-based system. As Christian apologists have pointed out, the Bible gives the most complete and satisfying answers to those questions.

5. Now, our growing theological philosophy moves to inform educational issues and questions. Questions about the goals, curriculum, and participants in education find their best answers inside a theologically informed philosophical scaffold.

6. One last step applies our thinking to a specific context. Generally speaking, contexts can be formal, nonformal, or informal. Everyone recognizes that standard church-based educational endeavors differ radically from academic institutions bound up in proper credentialing, government regulation, and accreditation. Formal settings reflect the latter; nonformal reflect the former. Informal contexts also offer powerful educational opportunities when used intentionally.

Basically, then, our theology should answer Philosophical questions and address educational issues in specific contexts. This provides a rather orderly way to think through our constructing process. The starburst acknowledges the disorderly reality. Ideas about theology, Philosophy, education, and context come in erratic spasms at unpredictable times from unexpected sources as we move through time and space. We often have unassimilated bits and pieces orbiting in our minds. Significant time may elapse before we finally place them appropriately in our philosophies. So, the graphic reflects an ongoing process. While we gather and process ideas constantly, we often fail to evaluate them theologically. Or, conversely, when we add new theological ideas, we fail to adjust the educational processes we have constructed. So, the graphic emphasizes an essential point in Christian thinking. As our comprehension of God grows, we should adjust our ideas about philosophy, education, and context accordingly.

Look at the four major categories of the graphic.

Theology

Although Christian thinkers have applied their theology to Western philosophy for more than two thousand years, applying theology to educational processes is often a new experience. When theology is applied to education, it most often finds a home in what should be taught rather than how education ought to be experienced. Formal instruction about theology usually comes via individual courses of study, leaving students to somehow integrate the various courses into a comprehensive picture of God and his world. My seminary training ended before I ever began to draw the pieces into any kind of holistic understanding about God.[6] In fact, a substantial amount of time elapsed before the various bits and pieces congealed into a more coherent form. Only then did my view of God begin to seep into my educational philosophy. As I reexamined some formal theological categories from my training, a number of questions began to stir in my thinking. Here is a sample.

> *Bibliology:* If God used such a rich mixture of method in the
> Bible (drama, story, poetry, song, paradox, solemn occasion,

---

[6] Don't misunderstand; I recited and believed the creeds even before my conversion. However, a full understanding of God goes way beyond the creeds. I am still growing in my understanding.

festival, visions, dreams, animals, plants, food, etc.), why were my seminary professors so enamored with the lecture?

Theology proper: Should a love for God rather than a mere knowledge of God anchor the heart of an educational philosophy? If so, how do students move from mere cognition about him to an intimate relationship with him? What role does/ should a school have in this process?

Christology: Does competitive grading conflict with the Christological implications of Philippians 2? How should Jesus' example as a foot-washing servant affect faculty/student relationships?

Pneumatology: Do we undervalue the fruit of the Spirit when we applaud and reward cognitive achievements so highly? How can the fruit of the Spirit be accommodated in our assessment devices?

Soteriology: Where in our educational policies do we apply unmerited favor and make room for repentance, forgiveness, and restoration? Is Christian education for believers only? Do non-Christians have any place in Christian education?

My own personal dream is that no educational process escapes thorough theological evaluation, and every new policy clearly is designed to reflect appropriate theological underpinnings.

Philosophy

This chapter will not untangle all the Greek philosophical riddles but does acknowledge their influence and presence.[7] Rather than an apolo-

---

[7] If you want a straightforward, plain English approach to philosophy from a Christian point of view, I highly recommend George R. Knight,

getic, this chapter simply assumes the validity of Christian theology to answer these questions.

- *Origins* (cosmology): Where did we come from? How did we get here?
- *Purpose:* Why are we here? What unifying principles (if any) bind life together?
- *Reality* (ontology): Is what we experience real, a dream, or a shadow of something else? Is there an invisible reality? Does it impinge on the visible reality?
- *Truth:* Is there such a thing as unchanging absolute truth?
- *Knowledge* (epistemology): How do we or can we know anything?
- *Values* (axiology): Does anything transcend human opinion about what is good, beautiful, honorable, right, and so on?
- *Reason:* What role does reason have in human experience? Can we assume reason and logic are unaffected by emotion or personal preference?
- *History:* Is history a linear, circular, spiral, or random sequence of events?[8]

Could you write a four- or five-sentence answer to each of these affirming a Christian perspective? What would be the most important biblical passage you could reference for your position? You might want to reflect on the questions for a while before you gather an answer from the Bible's point of view.

Philosophy and Education: An Introduction in Christian Perspective (Berrien Springs, MI: Andrews University Press, 1998). For an extensive treatment of Western thinking from a Christian theologian/philosopher, I recommend the trilogy by Francis A. Schaeffer, *The Francis A. Schaeffer Trilogy: Three Essential Books in One Volume* (Wheaton, IL: Crossway, 1990).

[8] The questions shown are introductory rather than exhaustive.

Education

I encourage students to think through the theological implications of everything from formal classroom experiences to casual hallway encounters. Theology ought to escape from their textbooks and invade absolutely every living activity. Put another way, theology ought to help us make better decisions, not only articulate right definitions.[9] Given that perspective, look at the following educational questions. How can theology help us make better decisions about these issues?

- *Goals:* What are the goals of Christian education? In what way do these change in academic settings?
- *Learners:* Who are they, and what are their special needs? Do nonbelievers have a place in Christian education?
- *Curriculum:* What needs to be learned? When should it be learned? Do all subjects have a spiritual dimension and a connection to the Creator?
- *Teachers:* What are essential spiritual and academic qualifications? What role(s) should an educator play?
- *Learning theory:* How does learning take place? Do the planned educational experiences reflect sound learning theory?
- *Methodology:* What procedures will be used? Will the activities stimulate or subdue curiosity?
- *Measurements:* How will teaching/learning be demonstrated by the student and evaluated by the teacher? Will things other than cognitive data retention be evaluated?

---

[9] I am indebted once again to Andrew Walls for this thought that filled a painful cavity in my thinking. He believes the developing world church will bring forth fresh theological insights as they answer questions raised by their cultural context rather than Greek philosophical questions. For example, Hindus wonder why Christians eat God's creatures and show such disrespect for life. Buddhists cannot understand how loud modern Christian music promotes any reflective worship of any god. See *The Cross-cultural Process in Christian History.*

- *Rules:* What limits are established? In what ways will these procedures reflect Christian values?
- *Technology:* How does/will media affect education? What limits, if
  any, will be placed on the use of technology? How can technology
  be leveraged to advance learning?
- *Communication:* Should Christian education be conversational?
  What kind of relationship nurtures educational conversations?

Some of these questions have generic answers, but others require
a great deal of thinking and a specific context for a thorough answer.

Context

The graphic guiding our approach to a philosophy of Christian education applies theological answers to classic philosophical questions
in order to make wise decisions about educational choices in specific
contexts. In the history of education, a significant number of philosophies have been put forth. Each has merits and drawbacks. At various
times, Christian groups have embraced one or another while excluding all others. I find various contexts useful to demonstrate how we
alter philosophical emphases. In order to promote a conversation about
philosophy applied in context, I structure a hypothetical situation. You
might try it with several friends or colleagues. The discussion works
best in a group of four. Here are the scenario and the challenge:[10]

---

[10] Needless to say, this is not a comprehensive list, and these descriptions
are clearly oversimplified. But, they focus on central issues, which keeps the
conversation focused. I have found that the discussion and decision-mak-
ing process is more important than the actual percentage assigned. Other
options include: idealism, realism, progressivism, educational humanism,
reconstructionism, futurism, critical pedagogy, behaviorism, and Educational
Anarchism.

Welcome to the newly formed "Wegotittogether" Christian Philosophical Society. For several months, we have been postponing a discussion about our philosophical positions. Meanwhile, a number of groups have been pressing us for clear answers. You will see them listed below. In the interest of time, the executive officers narrowed the discussion focus to four leading philosophical positions. Please read each summary carefully. Then, after thoughtful and biblical reflection, assign a percentage of application for each educational context so that the total for the given group comes to 100 percent. You may use any percentage from 1 to 100, but we ask you not to use 25 percent. Please be prepared to discuss your choices at our next meeting.

PERENNIALISM

The goal of Christian education (CE) is to impart biblical knowledge. When people understand the truth, they will want to obey it. The mind is like a well; from its supply of clear pure truth can be drawn the answers to life's questions. Careless study may lead to contamination of the supply. Therefore, educators must organize lessons so the student can apprehend truth. Key verse: 2 Timothy 3:15–17

ESSENTIALISM

The goal of CE is to provide spiritual life-skills. Unless people develop for themselves the capacity to study the Bible, to pray, to worship, and to develop effective personal disciplines, they will always remain dependent on others for spiritual nourishment. The mind is like a workshop, therefore CE provides tools and equipment. Key verse: 2 Timothy 2:15

PRAGMATISM

The goal of CE is to stimulate corporate ministry. The great aim in life is not knowledge but obedience; most people already know more truth than they live. The mind is like a military command post where information is processed into strategic and tactical actions; therefore, CE should focus on discerning, developing, and exercising each person's spiritual gift. Key verse: James 1:22–25

EXISTENTIALISM

The goal of CE is to facilitate personal health. As caring undershepherds, educators should nourish the flock with special attention to the weak and hurting. The mind is like a plant; with proper care it can be vigorous and fruitful, but when neglected it shrivels and turns inward. Therefore, CE should be alert to identify and meet people's needs. Key verse: Hebrews 12:12–13

	Perennialism	Essentialism	Pragmatism	Existentialism	Total
The Episcobapterian Christian school (K-12)					
The Oldgeezers Sunday school class					
The Bestlooking Small Group					
The Totallybiblical Christian University					
The Missionest Bible School Ever					
The We'rethebest Theological Seminary					

(Students are asked to fill out the form first from their personal perspective then by group consensus.)

Now think carefully about why you made the choices you did. Did your allocations reflect some original personal preferences? Did any successful or unsuccessful educational experiences (without any real reference to theology) influence your decisions? As you explored your choices with others in your group, what changes occurred in your thinking? How did other views modify your own? Did your understanding of the purpose for each context alter your allocations significantly? Did the formal or nonformal context affect your assigned percentages? This exercise intentionally demonstrates how certain contexts alter our approaches. If you compared the group choices of five or six groups, the results might surprise you—at least they always surprise me. Just because you have a philosophy of Christian education does not mean everyone agrees with your priorities.

This volume is not designed to address church-based, nonformal educational processes.[11] However, it is designed to explore academic models of education, whether they are formal or nonformal, and the number of these latter models seems to be exploding. Is it fair to say that almost every church, parachurch, or mission agency is involved with one or more of these? If so, I suspect thousands of nonformal institutes are operating spasmodically throughout Africa, Asia, and Latin America. I also applaud their development stateside because not everyone needs an undergraduate or graduate degree. But many desire training beyond the sermon and Sunday school in order to permeate every corner of society with Jesus' teaching.

These intensive modular courses of nonformal institutes often range in duration from two to three days to one week. Some involve distance learning experiences combined with face-to-face interactions. They

---

[11] For an extended discussion of that challenge, see Michael S. Lawson and Robert J. Choun, *Directing Christian Education: The Changing Role of the Christian Education Specialist* (Chicago: Moody Press, 1992).

often target local leaders and address specific concerns. Although structured and focused, they differ from formal schooling in several ways:

- They may offer some kind of certificate but do not lead to an accredited degree.
- The measurements of learning tend to be anecdotal rather than standardized.[12]
- The prerequisites for the students who attend are minimal if they exist at all.
- The courses stand alone rather than inside a curriculum.
- Faculty credentialing is often less specific.

Pause with me for only a moment to think through the amazing advantages of these nonformal models of academic Christian education. My colleague Dr. Ramesh Richard presented the following graphic at a faculty retreat some years ago. As I think through this graphic, the reality of the world's population grips me.

No one knows exactly how many people live on planet earth. For purposes of our discussion, let us assume the world population clock represents a reasonable approximation.[13] Today, as I write this chapter, the world population sits at somewhere more than 7 billion. If the graphic and population are roughly accurate, then only 630 million people make more than $10,000 a year while 6.37 billion live on less.

The latter number also represents people with limited access to education of any kind, let alone a Christian education. Even a philosophy of Christian higher education must take Jesus' teaching mandate in Matthew 28 seriously. Those trained in Christian higher education tend to minister to the upper 9 percent. My post as a faculty member

---

[12] Success is often measured by comments of appreciation during or after the course rather than submission of course papers or testing.

[13] World Population Clock, accessed May 4, 2015, http://www.world ometers.info/world-population.

World Population/Income

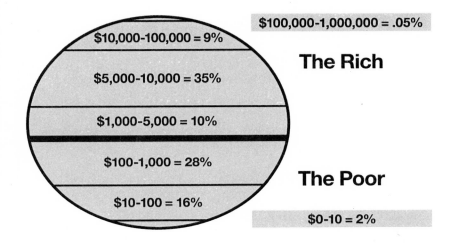

$100,000-1,000,000 = .05%

$10,000-100,000 = 9%

The Rich

$5,000-10,000 = 35%

$1,000-5,000 = 10%

$100-1,000 = 28%

The Poor

$10-100 = 16%

$0-10 = 2%

of Dallas Theological Seminary does not excuse me from Jesus' global vision. What strategy do we have for teaching 7 billion people? Christian higher education is certainly not up to the task by itself. But non-formal Bible institutes, training centers, and distance learning offer a promising infrastructure. I encourage their development wherever I go.[14] I hope you have a place for these in both your affirmed and operational philosophy. Most of the work in these settings offers little or no financial remuneration. What an honor to give away the training Jesus has entrusted to us!

Students add a special contextual modifier. Students vary within and between academic settings. The serious bachelor-level students at the Yanjing Theological Seminary differ from the playful bachelor-level students at the Greek Bible Institute. What master's-level students at the Freie Theologische Hochschule in Germany expect

---

[14] I am also in favor of planting churches, but this volume focuses on academic teaching.

from their teacher varies greatly from the master's-level students at the Hindustan Bible Institute in India. The research preoccupation of PhD students differs from the ministry concerns of DMin or DEd-Min students. These examples highlight how issues of culture, language, prior training, and future roles of students affect the context. A competent educational philosophy should embrace and account for these differences.

Outside the American context, the minority status of Christians often frames Christian education differently. For example,

- A Jordanian student said, "We are too small to divide the Christian community as you do in the West. Here there are Christians and Muslims. Your ecclesiastical divisions do not work well here."
- An Indonesian student said, "Do not pray our persecutions cease. Because we are persecuted, we are also richly blessed with many miracles."
- A Chinese student said, "Pray that we will be a good testimony to our government and a benefit to our society."
- A Haitian student asked, "How do we teach our people to avoid the witchdoctors and not return to them when God doesn't answer their prayers as they expected?"

These students seek an education that addresses their specific cultural concerns from a uniquely Christian perspective.

As our discussion of context concludes, let me offer one last word about formal, nonformal, and informal settings for education. Of the three, informal has the most power, especially if there is a strong relationship between the teacher and the student. More often than not, casual conversations catch people at a moment of learning readiness. While we see these moments in the ministry of Jesus, we often fail to grasp their significance in our own interpersonal encounters. Perhaps our words will not be used to complete an academic assignment or pass a test, but they might be the very words a student needs to move forward in his living walk with God. In my philosophy of Christian education, the teacher is always "on," redeeming each and every opportunity.

A Philosophy of Christian Education in an Academic Setting

Up to this point we have been thinking about our philosophy of Christian education in a general sense, noticing the variations caused by context. These various contexts modify the understanding and application of a Christian education. A course taught on the Gospel of John in an air-conditioned Dallas classroom will take a different turn under a humid Haitian thatched roof. Miraculously, Christian education actually flows into each and every context—but not always in the same way or with the same results. Sometimes it flows smoothly, and other times, well, let us just say it's bumpy.

We turn now to the various parts within a school's philosophy. Each of the parts has its own work of the Holy Spirit. Whether he is inspiring Scripture, bearing fruit, building community, comforting, or teaching, our dependence on his activity creates an essential unifying feature of a distinctly Christian philosophy. Truly, his name and work modifies everything we say about a philosophy of Christian education.

For the remainder of this chapter, I offer a series of categories and questions you might use to begin shaping your philosophy. I will suggest some answers in this chapter for the first four. The only way I know to illustrate these honestly is to reference my personal practices. If you find something you like, I probably borrowed it from a really good book, a professor I admired, a successful colleague, Jesus' interactions in the Gospels, or even one of my students. The last six questions have whole chapters later in the book. Ultimately, of course, you are creating your own personal philosophy. Here are the questions:

1. *Goals:* What are the goals of Christian education? Do these change in an academic institution?

2. *Learners:* Who are they and what are their special needs? Do nonbelievers have a place in Christian education? (See chap. 9, "Relating Skills.")

3. *Curriculum:* What needs to be learned? When should it be learned? (See chaps. 2, "Helping Students and Professors Integrate Learning," and 5, "Mastering Content.")

4. *Teachers:* What are essential spiritual and academic qualifications? What roles should educators play? (See chaps. 2, "Helping Students and Professors Integrate Learning," and 5, "Mastering Content.")

5. *Learning theory:* How does learning take place? Do the planned educational experiences reflect sound learning theory? (See chap. 3, "Learning Theories for Practitioners.")

6. *Methodologies:* What procedures will be used? Will the activities stimulate or suppress curiosity? (See chaps. 6, "Managing Skills," and 8, "Instructing Skills.")

7. *Measurements:* How will teaching/learning be demonstrated by the student and evaluated by the teacher? Will things besides cognitive data retention be assessed? (See chap. 7, "Evaluating Skills.")

8. *Rules:* What limits should be established? In what ways will procedures reflect Christian values? (See chap. 10, "Institutional Realities.")

9. *Technology:* How does/will media affect education? What limits, if any, will be placed on technology? (See chaps. 4, "Planning Skills in Syllabus Design"; 6, "Managing Skills"; and 8, "Instructing Skills.")

10. *Communication:* Should Christian education be conversational? What kind of relationship encourages educational conversations? (See chap. 9, "Relating Skills.")

Now, let's look in more detail at the first four categories and questions.

Goals: What Are the Goals of Christian Education?

Clear measurable goals are essential guides to any philosophy. Without these, we cannot know whether we have accomplished anything, or even the wrong thing. The central goal for Christian education ought to be a love for God. Jesus said this is the greatest commandment (Matt 22:34–40). No matter where I am, who attends, or what I intend to say, I am always asking myself, *How will this help them love God more?* If I cannot answer that question with some degree of precision, why am I doing it? This central question must be asked repeatedly and used to influence our educational design.

While I am much in favor of a deep emotional attachment to God, love for him means acting with patience and kindness toward family, friends, and even enemies.[15] Every lesson, every course ought to move us in some way toward that goal. The very fact that Jesus repeats his command to love one another five times in the Upper Room Discourse ought to galvanize this as the central goal for Christian education. Loving God with our minds ought to include using the knowledge we gain to make decisions that consistently reflect his values. Everything in Christian education should orbit around a love for God in such a way that no one could ever doubt it as the central goal.

I worry that endless school lectures have dulled students' capacity for personal reflection about their love for God. I wonder whether teachers or students make the connection between the material at hand and a love for God. Sometimes I prod students in this direction by asking, "In what way did this learning experience help you love God more?" I ask teachers to evaluate each class and course the same way.

---

[15] I often use the first two words of Paul's definition because impatience is relatively easy to detect, and unkindness is always measured by the victim's experience.

The teaching mandate of Jesus contains an educational feature unlike any other in the history of education. The acid test in Jesus' educational system requires obedience to Jesus' teaching rather than mere cognition or recall of his teaching. Our teaching must be organized so that no one loses focus on ways to obey his teaching. While I am not convinced we have organized theological or Christian university education in this way, I am content to see it change one lesson, one course, one student, or one teacher at a time.

The New Testament describes a fully grown disciple as "mature." Various passages emphasize different features of maturity. In the question about curriculum, we will examine these features a little further. However, they must always be wrapped in the first and Great Commandment and the second that is like it.

Now, think briefly about the secondary questions. Do the goals change in an academic institution? Christian schools at every level must keep the central goal clearly in view. Although schools cannot guarantee results, everything in them ought to consistently point in the same direction. Academics, athletics, and the arts must see themselves contributing to rather than competing for the central position. How are these educational goals visible throughout the daily routines of schooling? Students should easily point to a variety of activities that contribute to their movement toward a love for God if the school advertises a Christian education. And, every effort ought to be made to eliminate mixed messages.

Learners: Who Are They, and What Are Their Needs?

Numerous complaints have come to me over the past three decades about another young (always male) seminary graduate who has escaped to inflict a seminary-level education on poor unsuspecting adolescents. These graduates have no training in adolescent development, nor do the churches require that before hiring. These churches fail to look inside a degree program to make sure their new hire has appropriate training. Moreover, these young graduates fail to give thought to the learning readiness of their students. I find faculty members making similar mistakes in introductory courses when they ask students to wrestle with issues the experts have not resolved in twenty years of research. So, what is my point?

A philosophy of Christian education should recognize that we teach students, not merely subjects. In a Christian worldview, one size does not fit all when students are involved. Some need prodding, some need inspiring, some need encouraging, and some need comforting—blending all of these with instruction. Students arrive in classrooms with varying levels of background preparation. Christian teachers in churches and seminaries may need to adjust material to appropriately fit their students. Sometimes, the longer we teach the more difficult it becomes to remember how little beginning students really know or understand. Perhaps several examples from my own experience will help clarify why identifying the specific needs of students is so important. In each of these cases more thinking about who the students were and what they needed was definitely in order. If you are tempted to skip lightly over these, pause long enough to read the last one.

- *Location:* Seminary in India

  Subject: Faculty Training on Assessment

  Problem: Faculty complain that students refuse to do exegetical papers.

  What I learned: Students were not taught how to do an exegetical paper or what an exegetical paper was supposed to look like or provided with examples. Most of these students would leave the seminary, walking to their village ministry. They would not take a Greek text with them or the commentaries available only in the library. The faculty agreed it was very unlikely that those who returned to the villages (the majority of their students) would ever do another exegetical paper. So why were the students required to do Greek exegetical papers rather than Hindi exegetical papers from the only Bible they will have? Because these professors were teaching the subjects they had been taught in the way they had been taught (in England) during their training without any reference to the students in front of them.

- *Location:* Central Haiti

  Subject: Learning Theory for Christian Schoolteachers

  Problem: Christian schoolteachers in Haiti need only to pass a grade to teach it. Most of them had not graduated from high school, not to mention college.

  What I learned: These sweet dedicated teachers needed a lot less theory and a lot more time to process a few ideas that would work in their tiny village schools. I often had to rely on their thinking to find an application and then recruit the group to evaluate and modify it for immediate use upon their return to teaching.

- *Location:* Tyumen, Siberia

  Subject: Small Group Process for Church Pastors

  Problem: The organizer who selected the subject did not ask the pastors what subject would help them most.

  What I learned: These bivocational pastors had no formal training beyond high school. They gladly came to sponsored training events because the hotel was very nice and the food was better than what they had at home. They listened politely to the typically rich American pastor give his sermonized teaching but found little value for their tiny rural Siberian ministry. At least, that is what they shared with me. When they finally believed that I cared more about them than the subject, they asked me if I could help them with their sermons. Their only tool was their Russian Bible. The remainder of the week was dedicated to learning how to read and study their Russian Bible in preparation for a weekly sermon.

- *Location:* Central Mexico

  Subject: None. This was a strictly social visit with Manuel Arenas.

  Problem: How to design an appropriate and affordable Bible school for poor Totonac Indian pastors.

  What I learned: Living life below Mexican poverty line standards is harsh to say the least. Designing a Bible institute for those students who do required some creative turns. While students attended classes orbiting around biblical and theological subjects, they spent afternoons learning the latest processes to grow turkeys, goats, vegetables, and fruit trees. Their agricultural efforts cut food costs while at school to almost zero and gave them precious insights to share back home. Totonacs depend on the sale of agricultural products for cash. Upon graduation, pastors returned to their villages with seed, small plants, breeding stock of goats and turkeys, along with Bible training. They brought both spiritual and financial value home. This was integration at its finest!

One of the great temptations for teachers is to look at a classroom full of students and assume they all are clamoring for the lesson they have prepared that day. Everyone focuses on the person doing the talking, allowing teachers to forget the individual stresses each student brings to the learning experience. Regulations may require physical presence, but their minds and hearts may be on their parent's pending divorce, a beloved family member's cancer, a personal financial crisis, or a myriad of other issues. So, teach your lesson but look deeply into the eyes of your students for indications of distraction and follow up. Try to associate the material at hand with something meaningful in the students' life experiences. Whatever else is true as a Christian teacher, you represent the Lord Christ and his boundless compassion.

Now consider the secondary question. Where do nonbelievers fit in a Christian education? At first blush, we might answer, "Christian education ought to be for Christians." While that may be a good answer, it does not correspond to reality. For quite a long time, Christian schools of various shapes and sizes have opened their doors to nonbelievers. One Christian school in the Philippines has 80 percent Buddhist children; another in Hong Kong enrolls substantial numbers of international diplomatic core children representing a smorgasbord of religions. A New Orleans seminary has an extension in Louisiana's Angola prison that allows anyone to attend, and of course Christian colleges, while requiring a faith commitment from faculty, usually have an open-door policy for students. Perhaps Christian education should play a larger role in helping nonbelievers understand Jesus' teaching and clearing up misconceptions.

Curriculum: What Needs to Be Learned?

Jesus made it clear that he wanted us to teach everything he taught. Most believe that encompasses the whole biblical corpus because his life and teaching documented in the Gospels and fully explained in the Epistles forge inseparable links with the Old Testament. We certainly expect Christians to have some sense of biblical theology and Christian history.[16] Teaching this part of the curriculum must lead to obedience, as simple knowledge about the Bible was never what Jesus intended. Ignoring obedience as an essential part of the curriculum is not an option for the teacher or the student. Christian teaching comes with serious expectations. Any course dealing with biblical material ought to feature a distinctive call to obedience for teacher and student rather than mere cognitive manipulation of information. The call to obedience for nonbelievers begins with a fundamental trust in Jesus. Without basic trust in the Savior, they lack both motivation for obedience and the Spirit's power to obey.

---

[16] I appreciate Walls's distinction between church history and Christian history.

As the New Testament unfolds, growing to *maturity* represents a major objective. Various passages reflect the different components that lead to maturity. Because curriculum by necessity is broken into smaller pieces, teachers need to help students connect what they are learning to why they are learning it. Too often the questions of why were answered long ago in a land far away and the reasons have been long forgotten. Although nonbelievers may accumulate a great deal of biblical information (as did the scribes and Pharisees), they cannot move toward maturity without the Spirit's enablement.

As you reflect on maturity's components, connect elements of the curriculum to one or more of these. Once again, if what we are doing does not really lead students to maturity, why are we doing it? Here are the references along with my sense of their application to curriculum.

- Ephesians 4:9–14 suggests gifted teachers prepare Christians for works of service and ministry, promote unity among believers, and stabilize faith. So Christian education culminates in service.
- Philippians 2:12–16 suggests mature Christians have a forward-looking heavenly perspective and ought to live up to whatever truth they have.[17] So Christian education encourages students to embrace an eternal perspective on life as lived.
- Hebrews 5:14 and 6:1 suggest mature Christians can handle advanced teaching and have practice making good decisions. So Christian education enables students to grapple more effectively with daily decisions.
- James 1:4 and 3:2 identify endurance as a key producer of maturity evidenced by the ability not to stumble in what one says. James 3:1 warns teachers of stricter judgment in this regard. So

---

[17] Christians who did not have a completed canon were still expected to move to maturity by acting on what they knew.

Christian education helps students understand and cope with difficult circumstances.

These four offer many anchor points for the various subjects within a theological education. However, teachers must help students make the connections. My professors in the business school at the University of North Texas began every course demonstrating how management, economics, statistics, accounting, or law was both an art and a science. This was their attempt to help students integrate the courses. While their efforts were largely wasted on me, I do believe as Christians we need to constantly reorient students to the ultimate goals of their education and how the material at hand moves them toward those goals.

The larger and more difficult question comes from what we commonly refer to as "general education." This category includes subjects like math, language, history, science, social studies, and so forth. What business does Christian education have with these subjects? Prior to the Enlightenment, Christians would not have asked this question. Now is a good time to reassert God's claim on everything knowable. Omnipresence normally has a technically defined theological meaning. But there is a sense in which the term fits a Christian philosophy of curriculum because every subject of inquiry has theological origins and significance. Christ is present in every subject, and we must teach students how to see him. God can be found as the Creator of substance for scientific inquiry, originator and confounder of languages, superintendent of history, and the philosophical foundation for predictable mathematics. Name your subject; each finds its origin in him. Somehow, Christian education let the theological significance of these subjects slip away while relegating theology to a class, department, or special school.

Now think about the secondary question. When should it be learned? From the beginning of schooling, God's presence in and authorship of everything being taught should be made clear. But schooling can be so stressful and pressured that much of God's presence is lost along the way. Jesus provided an educational mantra when he said, "I still have many things to tell you, but you can't bear them now" (John 16:12). The amount and sequence of learning needs careful consideration. How many of us were told to learn something because we "will need it someday" only to discover we didn't need it except to win at Trivial Pursuit?

I'm also concerned that so much of what was once learned in college has now been pushed down into the lower grades. The competitive nature of parents and schools often promote this. This has also occurred in theological education where seminary graduates teach exactly the same graduate level course to their undergraduate students in Bible colleges.[18] Sometimes students become victims rather than beneficiaries of an education. A healthy view of curriculum provides foundation and motivation for lifelong learning.

Teachers: What Are Essential Spiritual and Academic Qualifications?

Christian education demands more from its teachers than any other form of education. Students expect their Christian teachers will know their subjects and practice the Christian faith. No matter what the subject, we are always in the business of making disciples of Jesus Christ. We cannot escape our responsibility as living examples of what we want our students to become. Loving God must find its living expression in the teacher first, then in the student. Or, in the scary words of Jesus, the student "will be like his teacher" (Luke 6:40). If we want them to be filled with the Holy Spirit, they should at least experience the Spirit's sweet fruit during their encounters with us.

---

[18] In one case, the young teacher used his professor's syllabus without bothering to remove his professor's name.

The age of specialization places Christian teachers in a precarious position. The tendency in advanced studies is to know more and more about less and less. We may become so immersed in our subject area that we fail to see ourselves as only one piece within the student's larger educational experience. Some of my professors thought their course was the only one I was taking (or perhaps needed to take) that semester. If our training primarily came through the public sector, we may lack sufficient theological foundations to properly orient students. Neither of these concerns can be corrected without intentional effort.

Is there a reason why pastor and teacher are linked in Ephesians 4? Is there a reason that Jesus' apostolic commission of Peter repeatedly focused on shepherding? Yes, I know that teaching is listed independently in Romans 12 and 1 Corinthians 12. Is it possible to completely detach pastoring from teaching in the Christian sense? Students consistently want their teachers to be interested in them as persons, and those educators who are amplify the impact of their teaching.

What does Jesus' role as foot washer have to say to those who teach others on his behalf? And, if Jesus only does what he sees the Father doing, what excuse remains for us to act aloof? I raise this here because we inherit a tradition that typically distances teachers from students. There are great temptations to intellectual pride, professional competition, and/or inflated self-worth in the teaching profession. The words we use to describe our activities define us. Will any of the following activities characterize you?

- Coaching
- Mentoring
- Modeling
- Instructing
- Evaluating
- Guiding
- Illustrating

- Motivating
- Counseling
- Serving

Just before Jesus' example in the kenosis (self-emptying) passage, the apostle Paul admonished his readers, and by application, all of us, with these words: "Do nothing out of rivalry or conceit, but in humility consider others as more important than yourselves. Everyone should look out not only for his own interests, but also for the interests of others" (Phil 2:3–4). What if professors and teachers really considered students as more important than themselves? Here I appeal to the difference between our affirmed and operational philosophies. If we affirm their significance, then we must treat students as significant. I honestly believe this should distinguish Christian education from every other offering.

Conclusion

The basic purpose of this chapter was to furnish you with categories, questions, and comments to guide you through the process of creating a personal philosophy of Christian education in an academic setting. On page five I offered a graphic with those categories. In our discussion, I raised a lot of questions and offered a few comments. Of course, this whole professor's puzzle reflects my personal philosophy. Given the complex nature of a true philosophy of Christian education, my students have driven me to summarize my philosophy for them. The following graphic represents my best effort. I hope it helps keep you centered on the task God is entrusting to you.

Our operating philosophy of Christian education reflects what we really believe to be true and always guides our decisions and practices. May we attempt to collect and formulate the wisest approaches to education that consistently reflect Christian values. And, at the core of those values, may the fear of the Lord guide our wise choices. Whether I am planning a course, actively engaged with students in a classroom, or sitting alone evaluating their work, I try to remain aware that God holds me accountable for what I do to students. If, "The fear of the Lord is the beginning of wisdom," then I cannot construct a reasonable philosophy of Christian education without keeping this consideration before me at all times.

HELPING STUDENTS AND PROFESSORS INTEGRATE LEARNING

"All truth is God's truth."
Frank Gaebelein[1]

This chapter deals with Christian education particularly as it addresses schooling. If I were writing to church educators, this would take a decidedly different turn. I have chosen to describe the problem in an unusual way in an effort to simplify the discussion. If you feel I oversimplify the problem, please refer to one or more of the competent authors cited in the discussion. Their insights approach integration from various angles and provide wonderfully detailed but lengthy perspectives.

---

[1] Frank E. Gaebelein, "The Pattern of God's Truth," *Bibliotheca Sacra*, 111.441 (1954): 71.

The Problem

Life confronts everyone with a combination of harsh and pleasant experiences. Humans need a meaningful explanation that makes some sense of these two disparaging realities. Sickness, disease, death, war, rape, theft, slavery, poverty, hunger, greed, murder, and birth defects (among others) contrast vividly with young couples preparing for marriage, newborn babies, spring flowers, cool breezes, songbirds, sunsets, star-filled skies, fresh water, sweet fruit, and, personally, I include my wife's chicken and dumplings. Because these various experiences come at us in convoluted fashion, life's realities may resemble our old friend Humpty Dumpty.

> Humpty Dumpty sat on a wall.
> Humpty Dumpty had a great fall.
> All the king's horses and all the king's men
> Couldn't put Humpty Dumpty together again.

Rather than a single reality, life may appear as simply a bunch of broken pieces! A good quality Christian education should explain how all life's pieces fit together. Putting Humpty Dumpty's pieces together again is precisely our problem with integrating learning.

No matter where we are born in the world, we grow up with some explanation of how the pieces fit together. Perhaps you grew up as I did, seldom thinking about the distasteful pieces. In college, the pernicious insistence on relativism by some university professors forced me to reexamine my views of right and wrong, good and evil, harsh and pleasant realities. My views were loosely cobbled together from a solid, hard-working, mildly Christian, middle-class Texas family. Religion had its proper place on Sunday morning. The rest of the week was mine to do with as I pleased as long as I didn't break the law. Wrongdoers were punished and hard work always rewarded. No one close to me got seriously ill or died except for an uncle in a different city whose funeral

I was not allowed to attend. My grandparents died before I was born or while I was too small to remember. Vacation was once a year almost always in Colorado. We were the belly button of the middle class. I can remember the first divorced couple I met as a teenager. Even my aunt who was estranged from her husband remained married to and supported him until he died. I also remember the first time I heard of a professional athlete breaking his contract. I had no categories for broken marriages or broken contracts. Otherwise, my world was nicely organized, and all the pieces seemed to fit.

University professors challenged my neat categories. Were the laws that seemed so essential to maintaining order merely social conveniences? If, as these professors claimed, evolution was true and survival of the fittest the doctrine to believe, then things were as they should be. People who had money and power deserved it. People who wanted it would have to outsmart or overpower them. That made sense. So why were some of those same professors clamoring for "social justice" as though something was wrong? That did not make sense. Of course many adherents of materialist evolution try to untangle themselves from its uncomfortable social implications by talking loudly about human rights. Whenever I pressed for the source of human rights, the conversation got louder and filled with multisyllable words but no real reasons. They covered the lack of rationale with more volume. At least that is how it seemed to me.

My sophomoric wrestling took a decidedly different turn when God graciously confronted me with his Son's sacrifice for my sin and generous offer to be my Lord. I had been taught that Jesus died for the sin of the world, but it never occurred to me that I needed it—after all, I was native-born Texan! "All have sinned and fallen short of the glory of God" really shocked me. I gladly accepted his atonement and simultaneously yielded my life to him as Lord. Not only did I now have a Lord for my life but for all of life and life's pieces. Clearly, as Creator and

Redeemer, he could organize the pieces! I did not put all the pieces of Humpty Dumpty together that day, nor do I have all his pieces together today. But my growing biblical construct of Humpty Dumpty looks decidedly better than that of many friends who seem to leave numerous large pieces lying around.

Most of the world believes an explanation of life's reality consists of interrelated visible and invisible pieces.[2] They would probably also say we cannot really understand the visible pieces without understanding the invisible pieces. People hold these explanations very tightly. From childhood, respected parents teach and emphasize these explanations. Extended family, friends, neighbors, and sometimes whole cultures embrace essentially the same views and reinforce the explanations. Some cultures threaten death for anyone who thinks otherwise. Many, if not most, of life's pieces seem to fit. Those that do not are simply held as items to wonder about but not at the expense of damaging the whole explanation. The explanations go largely unchallenged even when alternative explanations are offered.

A friend told me how African tribal women received training in hygiene so they could work in a health clinic. These wonderful ladies learned to wash utensils, hands, clothing, and bedding so as not to spread disease. But when asked why people got sick, they responded, "Someone put a curse on them." They were happy to do what they were taught, but repeating procedures did not change the explanation for how the pieces fit together when it comes to sickness.

These explanations vary from place to place and may actually contradict one another. What explanation could ever reconcile the Hindu's innumerable gods who each control only individual pieces and the Muslim's Allah who they claim controls them all? The border between Pakistan and India is not like the one between the United States and

---

[2] I am using visible and invisible to stand for the material and immaterial parts of reality.

Canada. Pakistan and India represent oil and water in their explanations of life and reality. They can be stirred, but they can never be blended. The tensions there will never go away because they lie deep beneath their soils of explanation.

While I do not agree with the Hindu and Muslim explanations, I do respect the fact that they try to account for very important pieces to Humpty Dumpty. Invisible pieces like a purpose for life, good and evil, life after death, and spiritual forces all find a place in their explanations of life's reality. Sometimes pieces of their explanations surface in unexpected places. Disney's *Lion King* presents one such example. Mufasa, the lion king, offers the "Circle of Life" as an explanation to his young son, Simba, who will one day be king, according to the story, and needs to understand what the position means.

> Mufasa: "Everything you see exists together in a delicate balance. As king, you must understand that balance and respect all the creatures from the crawling ants to the leaping antelopes."

> Simba: "But dad, don't we eat the antelopes?"

> Mufasa: "Yes, Simba, but let me explain. When we die, our bodies become the grass and the antelope eats the grass. And so, we are all connected in the great circle of life."[3]

The deliciously resonate voice of James Earl Jones as Mufasa rumbles out the words so convincingly no one thinks to question the explanation. But, does the circle of life truly explain reality? Does the antelope like this explanation? The antelope dies an excruciatingly violent and painful death, while the lion dies of old age. How did the antelope end up in such a precarious position in the circle? Why can't he choose a

---

[3] *The Lion King*, Platinum Edition DVD: Walt Disney Productions, 2003 release.

different place in the circle? Does the circle of life seem fair to all its members? Of course *The Lion King* is a children's movie with a childish explanation, but I have living relatives who embrace this explanation.

For ever so long in the West, the history of explanations worked with a whole set of life's pieces. Some were harsh while others were pleasant, but they all belonged to life and needed explaining. The rules changed during the Enlightenment (which did not substantially affect Africa, India, Pakistan, Turkey, Iran, Iraq, Saudi Arabia, Kuwait, Egypt, China, Japan, most of Mexico, Central and South America. Need I go on?).[4] Certain Western thinkers of that era decided to separate life's pieces into visible and invisible categories. Moreover, they simply dismissed the invisible pieces and anyone who holds to them as irrelevant. This numerically tiny but vocal group of people promoted their point of view as the only rational explanation. Today, that view has become the dominant explanation in public universities.

Some of my university professors held that dominant view. Even though no one knows exactly how many visible pieces exist, nor is able to account for the extreme diversity of pieces or consciously holds all the known visible pieces at any one time, these individuals still proudly proclaim to have assembled Humpty Dumpty. I contend they have either Humpty or Dumpty, but not both. Their explanation only describes what they experience. They cannot criticize what has been nor prescribe what should be. They lack the invisible pieces of fixed values, ultimate purpose, and final hope to work with.

Sometimes people think Christians overstate the consequences of the naturalist case. But actual testimony from committed philosophical naturalists suggests the Christian critique is accurate. Philip Ryken cites one scientist who expands his materialist point of view: "Gone is

---

[4] Andrew Walls even refers to the Reformation as only "the European controversies of the sixteenth century" in *The Cross-cultural Process in Christian History* (Maryknoll, NY: Orbis Books, 2002), 39.

purpose," writes the Oxford chemist Peter Atkins. "Gone is the after-life, gone is the soul, gone is protection through prayer, gone is design, gone is false comfort. All that is left is an exhilarating loneliness and the recognition that through science we can come to an understanding of ourselves and this glorious cosmos."[5] Ryken concludes, "According to this culturally dominant creation story [evolutionary naturalism], the only purpose we have is whatever purpose we find for ourselves."[6] Frankly, this sounds to me like someone who just scooped up a glass of seawater and declares there are no whales in the ocean! While I am sure Peter Atkins is a smart man, he can hardly claim to have drawn his conclusions having evaluated every available piece of information.

Once in a while someone in that group breaks ranks, like Jeffrey M. Schwartz.[7] Schwartz teaches and conducts brain research at UCLA. His research not only opens the door to the possibility of invisible pieces; it demonstrates that at least one invisible piece (the mind) affects and changes a visible piece (the brain). He documents how the activity of the invisible mind changes the visible brain in both chemistry and wiring. His work with OCD patients clears new ground for extending the conversation about visible and invisible pieces. His views are considered radical, unacceptable, and nearly heretical in brain research circles. He makes no claim about God, but his encounters with various colleagues echoes my own experience when calling a culturally dominant view into question.

Of course, Christians have always had numerous groups of prominent scientists with strong Christian faith who do not adhere to the

---

[5] Philip Graham Ryken, *Christian Worldview: A Student's Guide* (Wheaton, IL: Crossway, 2013), 49–50. The citation can be found at Peter Atkins, "Science and Religion: Rack or Featherbed: The Uncomfortable Supremacy of Science," *Science Progress* 83 (2000): 28–31.

[6] Ibid.

[7] Jeffrey M. Schwartz and Sharon Begley, *The Mind and the Brain: Neuroplasticity and the Power of Mental Force* (New York: HarperCollins, 2002).

culturally dominant explanation.[8] These women and men recognize the insufficient nature of visible pieces to explain all of life. Organizations like the Christian Medical Society, Creation Research Society, and American Scientific Affiliation, to mention a few, represent these reputable scholars. But in spite of strength and credibility, their voices do not prevail in the public universities or even in some previously Christian universities. Consequently, an overwhelming majority of people in America and Europe are educated in a system that simply ignores the invisible pieces of Humpty Dumpty. And, by being taught to ignore a whole category of pieces, students assume those pieces have no real value or impact on the visible pieces.

This dominant explanation affects us in at least two ways: (1) as teachers, the deficiency of the dominant explanation may characterize our previous training and affect our understanding; and (2) students arrive in our schools and courses with varying degrees of exposure to or belief in the deficient system. To make matters worse, not only does public education ignore a whole category of pieces, but education's curricular structure tends to be quite compartmentalized. Once past the early grades where a single teacher teaches everything, disciplines tend to take divergent paths. So, even the visible pieces remain isolated and unconnected to one another.

My own training illustrates the deficiency of prior training. I came to Christ in 1963, and upon graduation from North Texas State University, entered seminary in 1965. Christian education as a major appealed to me. At the time, I thought in terms of two educational categories: general education and Christian education or, if you prefer, secular and

---

[8] In books like John Clover Marsma, ed., *Behind the Dim Unknown* (New York: G.P. Putnam & Sons, 1966), "Twenty six notable scientists, from twenty fields of natural and physical science—all monotheists—discuss the unsolved (and probably unsolvable) problems within their own fields and explain why they believe in God" (quoted from back cover).

sacred education. Language arts, math, history, social studies, and so forth, were clearly part of general (secular) education. In my understanding, Christian education gave attention to matters of the spiritual life as taught in the Bible and was chiefly done through church or parachurch ministries. The notion that Christian education approached and explained all learning was undoubtedly presented to me but probably got crowded out by too many other pressing issues. My comprehension of integrated learning came much later. In essence, I didn't really care how subjects in general education were learned or who taught them because I was focused on Christian education at church. This chapter offers evidence that a needed change took place in me.

My students illustrate the second way our current educational system affects us as Christian teachers. All my students are Christians as far as I know, yet they come with a wide variety of educational backgrounds. A good many only have Christianity dusted on the edges of their education, if at all. Their public university engrained the dominant explanation with the possible exception that they may now hold to a creationist point of view. Of course, some students come from Christian homes or schools, but they are a small minority in comparison. Even those with Christian school experience often lack a complete picture of Humpty Dumpty, with all his pieces. While they benefitted from a high-quality education in subjects taught by Christian teachers, they experienced a compartmentalized curriculum lacking an integrated whole. Their GPAs demonstrate how well they did in one subject after another, but they rarely understand how those subjects interrelate with one another or to the whole. Neither can they explain how their general education pieces interface with their current experience in theological education. I know; I ask them. Many (though not all) of my best students find the notion of integrated learning a novel idea.

Integration begins with Christian teachers who have a clear understanding that visible and invisible pieces not only fit back together but actually interconnect with one another. In other words, reality has both visible and invisible parts. Subjects in any curriculum are interconnected and interrelated. A true Christian education must take students as they come and guide them into as full an explanation of as many pieces as possible. In the end, students should have a fair notion of what God intended Humpty Dumpty (life) to look like. Or, in contemporary jargon, they have a proper worldview. Our task as Christian teachers shows where our piece (whatever course we teach) fits among all the curriculum pieces in their education and then shows how both visible and invisible pieces help us make sense out of life's experiences. I assume this is almost never done for the student in our compartmentalized approach to education because we address worldview issues in their master's degree. The average entering age of students at our seminary is around thirty-two. For most of them, our program represents their first exposure to shaping a Christian worldview or attempting to understand how Humpty Dumpty goes together.

Our Challenge

Because integrating learning occurs at various interconnected levels, I have framed the educational challenge by connecting four levels in the following way:

> "An integrated *life*
> should be taught through an integrated *curriculum*
> in order to reflect the integrated nature of *truth*
> found ultimately in *God* himself."

Note how the statement works from life toward God. Another approach is to work from God's revelation of himself in Scripture and creation back to life as integrated experience. In that case, the statement reads as follows:

> "*God* himself reveals
> the integrated nature of *truth*
> which should be taught through an integrated *curriculum*
> to produce an integrated *life*."

Modern education simply assumes students will take the various subjects in their education and somehow assemble a meaningful explanation. Christian education has tended to do the same thing. For the most part, integrating learning remains the unassisted task of the student. In my training at university and seminary, I had only one course that even attempted to synthesize anything. That course examined systematic theology and attempted to integrate its numerous components into a whole. The course was helpful but obviously limited in scope.

If we want students to know more than the answers to Trivial Pursuit, Christian education must teach them where each piece fits and how the visible and invisible pieces interrelate. What does Humpty Dumpty look like when he is "together again"? As teachers, we need to know where and how our courses fit within the whole. A coherent outlook on life (worldview) and a consistent practice of Christian living (integrated life) should be the products of a truly Christian education.

Integrated Life

Helping students develop a consistent outlook and integrated life begins with an appreciation for God's interest in all areas of learning. In Genesis, the Creator reflects on his work and exclaims, "It is good!" Just as students learn about famous writers, artists, and designers by studying their work, they must also learn about God by studying his work in creation and Scripture. The intricate design and attention to detail display his interest in every minute feature. As students learn to give attention to design and detail, they imitate God. The creation's immense magnitude and intimidating displays of power provide appropriate context for inflated human egos. Scientists are slowly learning about the interconnected and interdependent nature of the whole created order.

Students might conclude that humans simply occupy another place in the long list of life-forms except for God's appointment of humans as stewards of creation. While adults should conclude God exists by simply observing the creation, they could not conclude their responsibility for the creation without Scripture. As Christians, we take that responsibility seriously and believe God holds us accountable for what we do with and to his creation. His interests extend from the cattle of Nineveh to the sparrow that drops from the sky. God wants students to care as much about his creation as he does.

Christian education orients students to God's ownership of the world around them and their responsibility. God's world is not ours to do with as we please. Christian education also helps students take responsibility for their education as they develop God-given abilities. Their skills and insights will be needed in the body of Christ and ultimately in his kingdom. Those whose education integrates learning not only know their place in the creation but also come to understand their places in their countries, states, cities, neighborhoods, and families.

With its prevailing materialistic worldview, public education pushes students toward a more utilitarian objective. College students most often choose their studies with jobs or careers in mind. Career days for students in secondary education emphasize courses where students have achieved some success to point to possible future career choices. Seminary students are not exempt from a utilitarian approach to their theological education. I am often asked, "If I pick your department, what kinds of jobs are available, do you know basic salary ranges, which parts of the country offer the best opportunities, and what would my whole career path look like?" While we must give some attention to those details and how God works with his children through them, we must not neglect the larger goals of Christian education to love and obey God. We should be helping students sort through and put the pieces of life together so they don't look like a freshly fallen Humpty Dumpty. If Christian education does not point students toward a more integrated life, who will?

At its heart, Christian education revolves around Christ himself, the model of an integrated life. He experienced life as an integrated whole rather than a movement into and out of the spiritual realm. Sometimes we either forget or fail to point out that Jesus was skilled in

- Language arts: he used sentence structure and word choices to demonstrate his deity.
- Ancient history: he used Sodom and Gomorrah as an illustration.
- Public reading: he often read Scripture in the synagogue.
- Rhetoric: he went about the country preaching and teaching.
- Woodworking: he was known as a carpenter.
- Regional news: he reflected on two recent events to illustrate a theological point.
- Wine making: the governor of the feast noted the unusually high quality of the wine Christ made.
- Cooking: the only meal we assume he personally prepared was grilled fish.
- Local customs: he knew Jews and Samaritans do not talk to one another.
- Roman law: he recognized imperial taxes.
- Jewish tradition: he noted the tithing of dill and cumin.
- Social obligations: he knew when his feet had been neglected in the customary washing.
- Family responsibilities: even on the cross he was concerned about his mother.

- Biblical theology: he knew the requirements for making a new covenant in biblical terms.
- Mosaic law: he corrected a misrepresentation of Moses' command by noting the difference between command and permission.

Jesus seamlessly blended the visible and invisible into everything he did. All of his activities reflect his attachment to and reflection of the Father. He gives thanks before he eats, he forgives sin as part of healing, he prays all night before selecting the Twelve, he declares prophetic Scripture fulfilled after reading a section, he obeys his parents while affirming his loyalty to his Father's business, and he considers discussing theology a normal activity. There was no compartmentalizing or incongruity in Christ's earthly life.

Among other things, when the Word became flesh, Jesus cemented his words to his actions. The theological, philosophical, and practical implications of that event fill whole libraries. As multiple witnesses unfolded his life, Jesus' actions so consistently mirrored his teaching that he declared, "If you don't believe my words at least believe my works" or "I am . . . the truth." He added to his declaration in John 14:6, "and the life." He is both the truth and the life. Not only did Jesus reflect consistency between words and action; he demonstrated consistency through each area of life. He asked, "Who convicts me of sin?" This consistency runs the length of his life. Jesus was as merciful creating wine for a wedding in Cana as he was forgiving a thief while dying on a cross.

In his letter, James reaffirmed this consistency with his reminder to both listen to and do the Word and not to show favoritism to the rich over the poor. James would not need to give his instruction if Christians did not experience a constant tension between what they affirm and what they do. Which of us as teachers does not find ourselves drawn to those students who admire us and offended by those who criticize us? We find ourselves consistently inconsistent. One of the goals of a high-quality Christian education ought to be modeling for students the consistent integration of words and actions, or an integrated life.

While Jesus lived an integrated experience fusing the visible with the invisible, he was no Pollyanna. His Beatitudes clearly define "the good" in terms of activities and character qualities. They are not only good in some abstract sense; they bring a personal blessing and a promise to those who practice them. His pronouncements are good, wholesome, and healthful. No one challenges the value of the Beatitudes. In contrast, he acknowledged and forgave individual sin, condemned leaders for overburdening people, and acknowledged the presence of evil beings interfacing with human life. He made point-blank statements about the reality of eternal life, death, hell, and heaven. He expects people to make daily choices based on those realities.

Of course the task of integrating learning does not belong to the school alone. The Christian family remains the primary conduit for transmitting the faith from one generation to the next.[9] The family provides the best place to sort through values like blessing or cursing, thanksgiving or ingratitude, praise or grumbling, service to others or self-promotion. Children develop best when healthy families work together with competent schools and vibrant churches. In my opinion, it is easier to compensate for poor schooling than dysfunctional families. But parents entrust a great deal of a child's intellectual development to the school.

If the school provides a truly Christian education, students learn how to evaluate and choose based on the interconnections, interrelationships, and interdependencies of life's realities. Students can almost unconsciously construct a worldview if teacher after teacher connects her subject back to God. And, because everything (except evil) connects

---

[9] Michael J. Anthony and Michelle Anthony, eds., *A Theology for Family Ministry* (Nashville: B&H, 2011).

back to God, every subject teaches something about God. In essence, students learn how to love God with their minds as they see the interdisciplinary connections and probe deeper into each one.

Teachers must see their task as much more than instruction in subjects. In order to do that, some will need to overcome their own training. Many of us were pressed into the details of our discipline as we worked toward our advanced degrees. So, when we turn from those studies to teach back at introductory levels, we must resist the temptation to focus on those same details that have become so familiar to us. If we want our students to integrate their learning, we will need to periodically orient them within a theological framework and model integration through intentionally referencing other disciplines. In that way, students will watch integration in action. We want their education to paint a clear picture of where their integrated life fits within God's world and purpose.

Integrated Curriculum

"An integrated *life*
should be taught through an integrated *curriculum*
in order to reflect the integrated nature of *truth*
found ultimately in *God* himself."

The approach to a discussion about integration depends on whom one is addressing when the discussion begins. This section finds us standing before school colleagues committed to and engaged in Christian education. Whether secondary or postsecondary education, they labor inside established curriculums. Curriculums are rarely built from the ground up, and curriculum revisions are mostly cosmetic. I do not intend to be unkind, but having survived several curriculum revisions, actual class sessions change little. Sometimes a professor will modify a course objective or tweak an assignment to show compliance. My sense of the reality may be oversimplified, but teachers and professors with established courses reluctantly abandon what appears successful to them.

So, this section seeks to help everyone work with what is. No curriculum can teach everything, but it will teach something. And hopefully, when the last class dismisses, the subjects within the curriculum will have helped students integrate their learning.

Leaders of the Reformation understood education to be a priority. At the time, education was normally reserved for nobility or the financially blessed. The reformers worked hard to press schooling outward to embrace those less fortunate. They envisioned schools for children and youth to prepare them for adult responsibilities. As leaders, they held a consistently unified theological orientation to knowledge. The languages of the Bible and the Bible itself formed the curricular core. Every subject had a proper place within a Christian worldview. There was no bifurcation of things to be apprehended by faith and things to be apprehended by physical investigation. Every teacher from that era was first trained in Scripture and language.

One of the early formulations of integrated Christian education came from John Amos Comenius, "the founder of modern education."[10] Comenius, along with many others, believed all knowledge (*pansophic*) could be accumulated and taught. He viewed knowledge as an interconnected whole to be taught to both genders of youth who would thus be "trained in all things necessary for the present and for the future of life."[11] The expected result of teaching an integrated curriculum was an integrated life.

---

[10] Michael J. Anthony, ed., *Evangelical Dictionary of Christian Education* (Grand Rapids: Baker Academic, 2001), 159–60.

[11] Ibid. (Obviously, a lot less was presented in the schools of the sixteenth century.)

No one of that era anticipated the explosion of information that would follow or the separation of truth into categories. From their Christian point of view, all knowledge was interconnected; subjects were merely a conventional device for breaking down the whole into more manageable parts. The history of education in the West demonstrates what occurs without an integrated orientation. Today, public education looks like an examination of Humpty Dumpty's pieces without any reference to what a whole Humpty Dumpty might look like. Students take geography that is not connected to math that is not connected to language that is not connected to history that is not connected to social studies. You get the idea. Subjects are not connected to one another or any true organizing principle unless you consider the random chance of the evolutionary hypothesis an organizing principle.

The average Christian teacher in a high school, college, or seminary can do little to change that public school picture. When a student moves from the public sector into a Christian institution, an ideal curriculum should reveal both the central connection to God and the interdisciplinary connections among the subjects. School documents such as catalogs and syllabi should articulate these connections in writing. Because teachers are the face of a curriculum, those who work inside a curriculum must help students build the connections among the subjects and also back to the Creator. The beginning of every semester offers an ideal opportunity to verbally reinforce those connections. These need not be elongated speeches. A paragraph or two punctuated by a pause may be all that is needed. Teachers can also look through their teaching schedules for opportunities to reinforce these ideas. Students may not totally understand all the implications of integrating their learning, but they should experience a consistent pattern of comments from multiple teachers during their journey through a semester and a curriculum.

Students are not the only ones migrating from the public sector into Christian education. Often, Christian schools recruit teachers who have not thought about integration on any level. Their training left them with bifurcated categories of truth and subject-driven specialties. Their public education helped them become subject proficient but deficient in theological training or orientation. For those who lack a thorough theological grounding, seminaries and Bible schools are extending themselves into the community like never before. Extension sites and online courses pockmark the landscape like craters on the moon. Theological education has never been more accessible on either undergraduate or graduate levels. Those whose training left them theologically deficient can and should merge back into the conversation by extending their training and using their newfound theological sieve to evaluate their discipline. Even though a degree has been conferred, we should not consider ourselves to be fully trained until we have solid theological understanding (not only an evangelical affirmation) and a thoroughly integrated perspective. This is indeed a great day for Christian education if we seize our opportunities.

The journey toward an understanding of integration need not be made alone. Many have been on the road ahead of us. Their writings can bring us along quickly. Some of us owe the next generation a more integrated education than we received. While most of us can quickly name several authors of English literature, authors of integrating learning may be much more difficult to recollect. The following authors represent modern thinking on the subject. Because no one has written the final word on integration, each one approaches the subject from a slightly different angle. You will note how the discussion changes as the authors address different audiences.

- *The Whole Truth: Classroom Strategies for Biblical Integration* by Mark Eckel.[12] Eckel's extended bibliography of websites, books, and articles along with his practical exercises to reshape classroom experiences make this volume both extremely practical and unique. He is primarily addressing secondary schoolteachers.

- *Renewing Minds: Serving Church and Society through Christian Higher Education* by David S. Dockery[13] and *Conceiving the Christian College* by Duane Litfin.[14] Dockery draws us away from our detailed discipline orientation and toward our ongoing objective in Christian education. In addition to his extensive bibliography, Dockery provides a list of Christian associations relevant to various disciplines. Litfin focuses on key issues surrounding integration in Christian colleges. They are primarily addressing Christian college faculty and administration.

- *Faith and Learning on the Edge: A Bold New Look at Religion in Higher Education* by David Claerbaut.[15] Claerbaut makes a persuasive apologetic for an integration of faith into learning and then discusses the implications of integration for science, humanities, and the arts.

- *The Integration of Faith and Learning: A Worldview Approach* by Robert A. Harris.[16] Harris develops his discussion of integration from a broad perspective engaging multiple worldviews. He writes

---

[12] Mark Eckel, *The Whole Truth: Classroom Strategies for Biblical Integration* (Maitland, FL: Xulon Press, 2003).

[13] David Dockery, *Renewing Minds: Serving Church and Society through Christian Higher Education* (Nashville: B&H, 2008).

[14] Duane Litfin, *Conceiving the Christian College* (Grand Rapids: Eerdmans, 2004).

[15] David Claerbaut, *Faith and Learning on the Edge: A Bold New Look at Religion in Higher Education* (Grand Rapids: Zondervan, 2004).

[16] Robert A. Harris, *The Integration of Faith and Learning: A Worldview Approach* (Eugene, OR: Wipf and Stock, 2004).

directly to students whose primary educational experience has been in the public arena.

If I were dean or principal, I would pick one of these and ask each faculty member to read a chapter(s) and create a summary presentation for the rest of us to discuss. The integration of learning is a significant issue that all too easily slides under the table. If we allow that to occur, we will lose the unique contribution Christian education offers students of an integrated curriculum.

Integrated Truth

"An integrated *life*
should be taught through an integrated *curriculum*
in order to reflect the integrated nature of *truth*
found ultimately in *God* himself."

The Christian community has not stuttered in her declaration about the unity of truth. Jesus' words stamped an indelible and continuing impression on Christian thinkers from the beginning. They understood at once that he was the glue needed to put the pieces together as well as the model for what they look like when together. All the lofty discussions about truth suddenly had a much-needed sorting device. The impact of a unified system of truth was not lost on our forefathers. They staked out a claim on truth that extended well beyond the pages of Scripture to each and every piece of life, drawing it irresistibly back to its proper place. Listen to these leaders as they speak for themselves:

Justin Martyr: "Whatever has been uttered aright by any man
in any place belongs to us Christians; for, next to God, we
worship and love the Logos which is from the unbegotten and
ineffable God."

Augustine: "Every good and true Christian should understand that wherever he may find truth, it is his Lord's."

Rabbanus Maurus: "The seven liberal arts of the philosophers, which Christians should learn for their utility and advantage, we have, as I think sufficiently discussed. We have this yet to add. When those who are called philosophers, have in their expositions or in their writings, uttered perchance some truth, which agrees with our faith, we should not handle it timidly, but rather take it as from its unlawful possessors and apply it to our own use."

Desiderius Erasmus: "All studies, philosophy, rhetoric are followed for this one object, that we may know Christ and honor him. This is the end of all learning and eloquence."[17]

In fact this section should need little discussion except so many Christians have no exposure to these voices. They grew up without having them emphasized in their Christian education or entered the Christian faith without an awareness of their legacies. Few Protestant churches give even modest attention to historical matters. Even in seminary, I have bright students question the need for Christian history in their education. Some of my students have been so deeply influenced by the bifurcation of truth that they categorically deny any such unity exists. Nor was I successful in persuading them in spite of all Christian tradition and thinking to the contrary. The dominant explanation plus a compartmentalized educational curriculum created an insurmountable mental barrier for them.

If Christianity offers a unified perspective on truth, then whatever is taught ought to be anchored to, informed by, and integrated with that

---

[17] I am greatly indebted to D. Bruce Lockerbie who collected and published all these quotes and so much more in his volume *A Passion for Learning* (Chicago: Moody Press, 1994), 49, 79, 109, opposite the contents.

truth. The way students progress through the curriculum ought to help them move toward a unified perspective on truth. Students ought to know how each piece contributes to each other piece and the whole. If they enter theological education, they need to understand how theology wraps its arms around their so-called general education and embraces everything. Students often feel like the little metal ball in the pinball game, bouncing from one course to another for no apparent reason.

Throughout this section, I have been trying to show the necessity of educational integration. If, as we affirm, God is one, then truth as a reflection of God must also be a unified whole. Truth remains stable even as God remains stable although our understanding of it and him may be imperfect. Our curriculum should guide students toward an understanding of truth and God. Although every curriculum is artificially assembled, it ought to consistently reflect truth as a unified whole, not an arbitrary selection of subject materials. The way we teach our individual subjects ought to reveal the interconnections with other subjects. If this is genuinely important, then it must be explained, modeled, emphasized, and reinforced. Otherwise, it will slip by much like it did in my own experience. This may require a level of sophistication for teachers that goes beyond technical proficiency. In reality, we have not only isolated subjects from one another but also separated general education from theological education. Consequently, truth comes to students like pieces of Humpty Dumpty. Some ultimately figure out the connections; others never do.

Truth must ultimately correspond to and explain reality. The Bible is the only book that adequately deals with the existence of evil, the paradoxical nature of humans, an ultimate resolution of injustice, and the human heart's longing for immortality. Today, if you want answers to these issues, you must pursue a theological education by attending a seminary. Theology, once known as "the Queen of the sciences," finds herself discreetly hidden from public view. Those who speak of theology are sequestered to "special" schools. A better approach would be to have theology woven into the very fabric of everything a student studies in Christian education. After all, God continues to explain himself through both the creation and his living Word.

Unfortunately, theological education even neglects a full exploration of both sources of revelation. Seminaries work hard at exploring aspects about God through biblical research and systematic schemas. Yet everything we have learned or can learn in general education reveals something wonderful about the Creator. Courses exploring God's character from the contributions of natural revelation simply do not exist. Carisa Ash highlights this discrepancy in her PhD dissertation. She traces the affirmations of evangelical theology. Everyone agrees that God reveals himself in both special revelation (the Bible) and natural revelation (all those subjects normally included in general education). Both are sources of truth. Yet those who write theologies normally cite only the Bible. Few, if any, writers give equal space to both sources of truth.[18] This may be because a PhD in theology does not start with, include, or conclude with any academic training in the created order. In any case, a great deal about God goes unexplored or unconnected to him by those who champion his study.

Christian education may need to reassess and reassign its resources if it is to regain its central role in education circles and the society at large. We have unlimited access to the truth bound up in a Person and reflected in everything he has said and done.

---

[18] Carisa Ash, unpublished PhD dissertation, *A Critical Examination of the Doctrine of Revelation in Evangelical Theology* (Dallas Theological Seminary, 2011).

God Himself

The God of the Bible, unlike Muhammad's god or any other god, reveals himself in order to invite intimacy with those who bear his image. He created a predictable and visible universe so that wherever man looks he discovers something true and wonderful. Through his written revelation, he discloses certain invisible truths that expand man's understanding of reality. Ultimately, he completely reveals himself through the Lord, Jesus Christ. In fact, Jesus says so in his high priestly prayer in John 17. The whole purpose for created and written revelation is for man to understand and enjoy everything about God. Only in a combined understanding of these two do we have the final plan for putting Humpty Dumpty together again.

Whether we refer to the great *shema*, the first and greatest commandment, or Paul's living sacrifice, no life can be considered fully integrated until every facet aligns with God. That is another way of saying "righteous." The God of the Bible has no duplicity, no shadow of turning, and no hint of evil. As his image bearers, our education ought to help us reflect his beauty, majesty, creativity, compassion, responsibility, ethics, joy, justice, delight, and everything he wishes to manifest through us.

Conclusion

In my educational readings about integration, I find Frank Gaebelein's work the most compact and understandable. "All truth is God's truth" sums up our Christian position. The context for his now famous quote is as follows:

> For Christian education, therefore, to adopt as its unifying
> principle Christ and the Bible means nothing short of the
> recognition that *all truth is God's truth*. It is no accident that St.
> Paul, setting before the Philippian church the subject matter

of Christian thinking, writes: "Finally brethren, whatsoever
things are true . . . think on these things" (Phil 4:8). He knew
that Christian truth embraces all truth, and that nothing true is
outside the scope of Christianity.[19]

Although we have a clear affirmation, we have not yet pursued
integration as far as we can and should. Earlier in those same lectures,
Gaebelein explains the extensive implications of an integrated approach
to Christian education. "Nevertheless, in respect to a thorough-going
integration of Christ and the Bible with the whole institution, with all
departments of study, with all kinds of student activities, with all phases
of administration, there remains much land to be taken."[20]

I submit to you that whether Humpty Dumpty ever fell off a wall
remains a subject of literary investigation. However, I am absolutely
sure we and our educational system did! If we are to pull ourselves
back together again, we need a fully operational integrated approach
to Christian education. Should we carelessly neglect a single area, our
omission would indicate an area where God has no interest. We do bear
a responsibility for making sure this piece of the professor's puzzle fits
snugly into place.

---

[19] Gaebelein, "The Pattern of God's Truth," 71.
[20] Ibid., 69.

LEARNING THEORIES FOR PRACTITIONERS

"Learning not teaching is at the heart of Christian Education."
Eugene Trester[1]

In days gone by, professors assumed their role in teaching ceased when they stopped talking. When, how, or if students learned was not their concern.[2] That is no longer the case. As accrediting agencies continue to push accountability for student learning, a working knowledge of learning theory becomes more essential. But the field of learning theory lies cluttered with ideas, some helpful and others just confusing. One

---

[1] Kenneth Gangel cites Eugene Trester ("Biblical Andragogy," *The Bible Today*, September 1982: 293), in *The Christian Educator's Handbook on Teaching* (Grand Rapids: Baker, 1988), 160.

[2] Christian professors should always be concerned about their students' learning. However, the university model of scholarly unapproachable professors tempts some to forget who they represent.

research site lists around fifty different learning theories.[3] In fact, to this date, no one has actually synthesized what we know about learning or created an integrated comprehensive model.

One way I have introduced this problem envisions watching a baseball game through a wooden fence with a few small knot holes scattered over a bit of distance. One knot hole provides only a view of the batter. Is baseball only about a man with a bat? Another hole provides only a view of a man throwing the ball. Is baseball only about a man throwing a ball? A third hole shows just a man catching a ball. Is baseball all about catching a ball? Even when we put all three together, we have still not talked about running bases, the strike zone, intentional walks, pitch count, and so much more. Over years of struggling to wrap my arms around learning theory, I have arrived at several workable guidelines. Here are those that serve me best.

- Theories provide more insight at the macro than the micro level. Their ability to explain how humans learn begins to break down the more you press the details and explore the exceptions.
- Humans' adaptive capacity makes pure research difficult. Learners unconsciously compensate for deficiencies, which makes them a moving target for research.
- Learning disorders are normally studied but rarely exist in isolation. Social context plays a larger role in enabling or hindering learning than most people expect.
- Individual learning histories affect all learning theory research. Previous success or failure predisposes students to approach the next task with either confidence or apprehension. Those attitudes, in turn, either facilitate or hinder their learning.
- Most theories focus on schooling, which works well for a book like this but hardly explains the whole learning experience of humans.

---

[3] See http://www.learning-theories.com, accessed May 6, 2015.

For instance, the most difficult of all learning experiences, language acquisition, occurs before formal schooling begins. We have some notions about how but no explanations for why children work so hard at this challenging task.

For the purposes of this volume's intended reader, I selected my personal "top ten" learning theories. Noticeably absent from the list are theories that tend to focus on children because this volume looks toward those who teach high school and above. Nor have I included the notorious behaviorist theories although I believe they, too, in some ways provide helpful insight into learning. The following list provides an outline for the remainder of the chapter.[4]

1. *Learning Domains* help specify learning objectives for various kinds of learning in both syllabus design and lesson plans.
2. *Advanced Organizers* create frameworks for new learning through connections to known content and synthetic summaries.
3. *Brain Research* emphasizes user-friendly learning experiences because real learning is very complex work.
4. *Time on Task* challenges teachers to provide multiple learning strategies so students spend adequate time accomplishing the objectives.
5. *Hierarchy of Need* isolates both inhibiting and motivating factors that affect student readiness to learn.
6. *Learning Styles* categorize preferred approaches to learning as well as learning cycles that enhance long-term memory.
7. *Multiple Intelligences* explains why certain kinds of learning appear easier for particular individuals but not everyone.
8. *Cooperative Learning* demonstrates the power of groups to both shape and enhance the learning task.

---

[4] An outstanding and more comprehensive introduction to learning theory can be found in Rick Yount's *Created to Learn*, 3rd ed. (Nashville: B&H, 2010).

9. *Andragogy* demonstrates how adults approach learning using personal agendas and life experiences in contrast with children or youth.
10. *Motivation* is always the one true key to learning but is often ignored as a responsibility of the teacher.

Learning Domains[5]

Essentially, learning domains differentiate three kinds of learning. The "cognitive" domain explains how people work with information. Benjamin Bloom's taxonomy has almost become synonymous with this domain. The "affective" domain examines how people develop values and attitudes.[6] David Krathwohl outlines the basic processes based on his research. The "psychomotor" domain studies how people acquire physical skills.[7]

Of the three, the cognitive domain has certainly received the most publicity. Almost everyone in schooling tips their hat to Bloom's taxonomy and rightfully so. Much of schooling deals with acquiring and processing information. Unfortunately, many school systems around the world still rely on recall (the lowest level in his hierarchy) as both their educational goal and evidence of real learning. Bloom's taxonomy

---

[5] One website summarizes the taxonomies of Krathwohl and Bloom: accessed May 4, 2015, http://thesecondprinciple.com/instructional-design/threedomainsoflearnin/.

[6] Sometimes authors include words such as "feelings" to describe the affective domain. But in my experience, values and attitudes shape feelings.

[7] The conative domain sometimes becomes the third. Researchers here study human "actions, reactions, and interactions" as one author suggested (see Kolbe.com). In other words, this domain researches choice, decision making, and actual volition, or what makes a person choose one action over another.

moves students through various phases of information processing. Here is his original list:[8]

1. Knowledge (recall)
2. Comprehension (understanding)
3. Application (use)
4. Analysis (breaking down into parts)
5. Synthesis (reassembly)
6. Evaluation (discernment about value)

Only reading the six levels alerts us that, as educators, we may really want more than simple recall. Perhaps we also really want understanding. Are we happy with understanding without the ability to use information? Should the student use the information without being able to break the information into its various pieces? Can the student reassemble the various pieces into meaningful wholes? Is the student able to evaluate the significance of various opinions about the information or the relative importance of the information?

For those of us designing educational experiences, Bloom's taxonomy provides a more precise way of thinking about our objectives. When used properly, the taxonomy helps guide us through both syllabus design and lesson planning. (See chaps. 4, 5, and 6.)

The most intriguing domain for Christian educators should be the affective domain. The exploration of core values and operating attitudes preoccupies the thoughts of New Testament writers.[9] True Christian

---

[8] Accessed May 4, 2015, http://www.nwlink.com/~donclark/hrd/bloom.html. Later, "Creating" (as in adding new knowledge) was added to the top of the hierarchy.

[9] Philippians 2 describes the mysterious hypostatic union. Theologians spend a great deal of time precisely describing this union without distorting it toward Christ's humanity or deity. But the whole point of the description provides a model attitude of humility. In my experience, theological students devote precious little time to reflecting on or practicing this attitude.

education always sees information as the first step toward attitude or value adjustment. Whatever we guide students to investigate, the results ought to move us closer to God and his perspective. Yet, most of what we call Christian education dedicates itself to accurate transmission of information. If Christian education pays any attention to the affective domain, it is compartmentalized to chapel, spiritual formation, spiritual life, devotions, accountability groups, character development, and so on. This segregation of information from values and attitudes creates an awkward and unacceptable dichotomy for the Christian faith.

In an ideal world, every course regardless of subject matter would integrate an appropriate examination of values and attitudes. Though public universities teach math or language without reference to God, this does not mean Christians should. We exist in a created order where everything points to a Creator. For example, math relies on reason and predictability, but it also contains infinity and mystery.[10] We need reason and predictability to function in everyday life.[11] Teachers should carefully consider how their subjects intersect with Christian values and attitudes. Krathwohl's research provides some extremely helpful ways to carefully think through this domain. His taxonomy guides the planner through possible stages. The following list shows Krathwohl's categories but the descriptive phrases (*in italics*) are mine.

- Receiving—*acknowledging a new value or attitude exists*
- Responding—*complies with the attitude or value*
- Valuing—*personally embraces the value or attitude*
- Organizing—*arranges the value or attitude among other existing values or attitudes*
- Characterizing—*exhibits the value or attitude routinely*

---

[10] Pi has no finite answer; irrational numbers have a mysterious incapacity to be represented by a fraction.

[11] Evolution requires a random (unpredictable) universe.

Once we have decided which value or attitude our information addresses, we then need to choose at which level we want the students to work. We must do more than only tell students which attitudes they need to possess. As Christian educators, we need to guide their thinking in such a way that they seriously consider the personal implications of particular values or attitudes. The ultimate goal should always be to guide students to reflect a Christlike character, embracing a comprehensive array of his values and attitudes.

The psychomotor domain refers to any learning that requires a particular physical skill (as opposed to a cognitive skill). This domain is not usually considered a vibrant part of Christian education. Things like recreational skills, artistic skills, and musical skills come under this domain. Once again, these skills are often taught without any reference to God at all. But from a Christian point of view, they reflect a uniquely wonderful part of God's image although they do not often appear in a list of God's attributes. Moreover, attitudes such as patience, endurance, and attentiveness—along with values such as beauty, excellence, and creativity—seem intimately bound up with these skills. Bloom's taxonomy serves to introduce us to the processes used in skill development. Here is his list:[12]

- Imitation—observing someone else
- Manipulation—trying the skill
- Precision—becoming proficient at the skill
- Articulation—adapt and integrate the skill
- Naturalization—automatic mastery of the skill

Although many skills find their way into Christian education curriculums, proficiency rather than character development often overshadows the other objectives. Neither skill proficiency nor cognitive

---

[12] Accessed May 4, 2015, http://www.businessballs.com/blooms taxonomyoflearningdomains.htm#bloom%27s%20psychomotor%20domain.

mastery provides adequate Christian goals. However, both do provide exceptional opportunities for integrating character development into the curriculum. Both should utilize and include the processes of the affective domain to move students toward that objective.

Any responsible design of a syllabus or lesson plan will indicate an understanding of the learning domains because they are almost universally accepted as the proper beginning place. We will visit them again in the chapters to come.

Advanced Organizers[13]

David Ausubel generally receives the credit for articulating the Advanced Organizers Theory. Technically speaking, an advanced organizer helps a student connect his current reality with new information.[14] The stronger the connection between a student's current knowledge and the new information, the more likely the learning will transfer into long-term memory and use. The most difficult things to remember long term are those things that have no relationship to anything else in the student's experience.

A variety of items are frequently confused with advanced organizers. For instance, students may receive an outline of the upcoming lesson. If the outline does not connect to something a student already understands, it may be helpful for note taking, but it is not a true advanced organizer. An example of a true advanced organizer in language acquisition might be a list of commonly used English prepositions alongside a list of their counterparts in the language to be learned. Then, where the new language uses a particular preposition differently, the student can be pressed to remember the possible new usage.

---

[13] David P. Ausubel, *Educational Psychology: A Cognitive View* (New York: Holt, Rinehart, & Winston, 1968).

[14] Accessed May 4, 2015, http://topr.online.ucf.edu/index.php?title =Advance_Organizer&oldid=2468.

The last example presupposes the student knows how the prepositions function in English. This is not always a good assumption. A classmate of mine struggled to phonetically pronounce new Greek words. He had been taught the "word guess" method of reading, so all the exercises related to sounding out words were completely meaningless to him. Once he heard the word sounded out, he could associate the sound with what he saw on the page. But he could never sound out a new word.

Thinking through appropriate advanced organizers pushes teachers to figure out exactly what their students really know and connect it to the new learning in strong charts, diagrams, or other summaries.

Brain Research

The brain research field divides itself unevenly between those who assert that the brain and the mind are exactly the same and those who assert they are quite different. The former clearly outnumber the latter. Those who view the mind and the brain as two words for the same thing generally see the world from an evolutionary materialistic perspective; therefore, the brain/mind is a complex combination of cells, chemicals, and electrical impulses and no more. Critics of this view complain that in that case criminals cannot be charged with any human responsibility because they were simply responding to internal electro chemical impulses. Even though this is the prevailing view, the consequences of this view are not widely touted because society would degenerate into anarchy if people were not held accountable for their actions.

One prominent researcher who views the mind and the brain as distinct also proceeds from an evolutionary perspective but chooses to leave room for an immaterial (and unexplainable) part of man.[15] Jeffrey

---

[15] Jeffrey M. Schwartz and Sharon Begley, *The Mind and The Brain: Neuroplasticity and the Power of Mental Force* (New York: HarperCollins, 2002).

Schwartz's interest in Buddhist transcendental meditation led him to explore the power of the mind when treating his obsessive-compulsive disorder patients. When the compulsive thought became conscious, he asked his patients to refocus their minds on a more positive activity. So, instead of obsessing about washing their hands one more time, they were to think about watering the flowers or some other pleasant and constructive behavior. Admittedly, this requires a great deal of mental energy from these patients. Not only did his patients get much better results than other therapies, but his research discovered that the brain actually "rewired" itself with new chemical/electrical patterns. His book cited previously traces a bit of the history of the debate in this field as well as presenting his findings.[16] His work opens a wonderful door for extended discussions among scientists, philosophers, and theologians.

In my opinion, Schwartz's work has profound implications for those of us in Christian education. By making room for an immaterial part of man, this prominent scientist has invited us into the conversation. By being more informed about brain processes, we can be a bit more patient with the complex nature of real learning. While I obviously do not believe the Bible speaks directly to Schwartz's research, I do believe the Bible speaks forcefully and often to his notion of focused thinking.

For instance, Christians often pray along with the psalmist, "May the words of my mouth and the meditation of my heart be acceptable to You, LORD, my rock and my Redeemer" (Ps 19:14). The psalmist lifts up the blessed man in Psalm 1, whose "delight is in the LORD's instruction, and he meditates on it day and night." The apostle Paul urges believers to engage in a broad range of wholesome thinking in Philippians 4:6–9. And, I am persuaded that the "renewing of your mind" Paul mentioned

---

[16] Of course his evolutionary Buddhist approach is highly individualistic and does not provide any definitive social structure for differentiating evil from good or acknowledging any form of final justice if evil truly exists.

in Romans 12:2 begins with reflecting on and embracing the breathtaking mercies of God explained in chapters 1–11.

We would not need these admonitions if the brain did these things automatically. So, our task as teachers is to find new ways to creatively focus our students' thinking on godly attitudes and values. Perhaps Schwartz is right and, over time, the brain creates new networks that conform to the mind's directions.

Time on Task

The discussion about time on task began with John Carroll's "A Model of School Learning," linking learning to time.[17] This theory refocuses the classroom away from the activity of the teacher and onto the activity of the students. The research demonstrates that the more students actively engage in the learning task at hand, the stronger the learning. The challenge becomes keeping the learners interested and engaged in the learning task without becoming bored.

When I have only one session to teach learning styles, I generally plan several classroom activities. First, I give the students a verbal overview with PowerPoint slide support. Next I provide a short article summarizing learning styles written by my friend Marlene LeFever. While reading the article, I ask them to choose the learning style that best represents their approaches. This combination of a directed reading with a forced-choice exercise keeps the students engaged in the process. Once their choices have been made, I ask for a show of hands and tabulate the results as we move through the four styles. I ask them to notice how many people differ from them to emphasize the diversity even in a small classroom. These last moments are critical because teachers tend

---

[17] Accessed May 4, 2015, http://feaweb.org/time-on-task-a-teaching-strategy-that-accelerates-learning.

to teach from their own learning style and ignore the other three.[18] The session concludes with a question-and-answer segment. Students spend the entire hour working with one theory in five different ways (listening/viewing, reading, evaluating, voting, and question/answer). Some will later go online to take one of the many available learning style assessments, which reinforces the learning even more.

In essence, time on task emphasizes students' processing of material whether in or out of class. In order for students to remain engaged with the material over a lengthy amount of time, they need interesting activities along with intermediate indications of success. Those who construct video games utilize both of these to their advantage.[19]

Secondary and postsecondary education teachers tend to work in subjects of personal interest or aptitude. These two factors often make it difficult for them to understand students with little or no personal interest or aptitude for their favorite subject. If a teacher wants to move beyond content recall, he needs to think and plan on behalf of those with less interest or aptitude. In fact, master teachers almost lure students into their subject material and provide enough variety along the way to maintain their interest. These teachers utilize time on task to the students' advantage.

Hierarchy of Needs[20]

Abraham Maslow's *Motivation and Personality* introduced the "Hierarchy of Needs."[21] As a psychologist, Maslow sought to explain individual

---

[18] Accessed August 24, 2014, http://www.ltsn-01.ac.uk/static/uploads/workshop_resources/178/178_Learning_styles_and_disciplinary_difference.pdf.

[19] A student who taught gaming design shared this with me.

[20] Accessed August 24, 2014, http://www.maslow.com. Go there for more information.

[21] Abraham H. Maslow, *Motivation and Personality* (New York: Harper, 1954).

variations in motivation and development. Business and educational leaders quickly adapted his hierarchy to their settings, seeking to motivate both employees and students. The easiest way to grasp an overview of his hierarchy is to view it in chart form. My representation of his hierarchy follows:

Maslow's Hierarchy of Needs

Need for Self Actualization

Esteem Needs
1. Need for Self-esteem

2. Need for Esteem of Others

Love & Belongingness Needs

Safety Needs

Physiological Needs

Originally, Maslow demonstrated that individuals could not move to higher needs and aspirations until the lower needs were met. His highest level represents an individual who has reached his full potential and is deeply satisfied with his achievements. However, people cannot move toward that goal until they have moved successfully through the lower levels. The bottom level simply represents such basics as food, clothing, and shelter. Those who find themselves in war zones are preoccupied with basic survival found at the lower two levels. When life returns to relative safety and physical needs become easily met, then humans can work on the next three levels.

As educators applied the model to schooling, all kinds of seemingly unrelated issues surfaced. Children who performed poorly in school were not simply lazy. Perhaps through no fault of their own, they suffered from things like

- Poor nutrition
- Lack of sleep
- Intimidation on school buses or playgrounds
- Abuse at home

If issues like these are not resolved in childhood, they are simply carried forward into whatever levels of schooling come next. In addition, students may fail to develop true self-esteem because of a lack of acceptance among school peers or careless comments from thoughtless teachers. A large variety of experiences outside the classroom have direct bearing on student performance inside the classroom. The cumulative effect of a combination of these experiences can prohibit people from achieving their full potential. In almost thirty years of teaching graduate students, I have encountered too many perfectly capable students without the courage to accept the next educational challenge. Inevitably, they have failed to work through one or more of the midranges in Maslow's hierarchy.

As Christian educators, we may need to help a student overcome some previous deficiency in order to excel in the subjects we teach. This responsibility may not be detailed in our job description, but it ought to surface if we apply "Christian" to our role as teacher.

Learning Styles

Of all the learning theories, this one has become the most popular in Christian circles. No doubt Marlene LeFever contributed to its popularity with her book, *Learning Styles: Reaching Everyone God Gave*

You.[22] However, the term "learning styles" covers at least three different approaches.

One approach views learning through three different sensory preferences.[23] Accordingly, each student has a dominant sensory preference. Some students are auditory learners. They have powerful listening skills and do well with verbally presented materials. Other students are visual learners. Their visual skills help them do well with graphic materials. Finally, tactile-kinesthetic learners with manipulative skills shine when bodily movements or manipulation is required.

A very different approach views learning as a cycle (see next page). "The core of the model is a simple description of the learning cycle—of how experience is translated into concepts, which, in turn, are used as guides in the choice of new experiences. Learning is conceived as a four-stage cycle."[24]

The third approach focuses a bit more on individual learning preferences based on Bernice McCarthy's 4MAT system.[25] She and her colleagues create whole courses based upon her learning style research. Her website deserves a visit, as it provides a wide array of assessment and training materials. One part of the 4MAT system identifies four different kinds of learners. LeFever focuses on those learners in her article and book cited previously. McCarthy's four learner labels are

---

[22] Marlene LeFever, *Learning Styles: Reaching Everyone God Gave You* (Colorado Springs: David C. Cook, 1995).

[23] See http://www.nwlink.com/~donclark/hrd/styles/vakt.html.

[24] David A. Kolb, "Learning Styles and Disciplinary Differences" in *The Modern American College: Responding to the New Realities of Diverse Students and a Changing Society*, Arthur W. Chickering and Associates (San Francisco: Jossey-Bass, 1981), 235; accessed August 24, 2014, http://www.ltsn-01.ac.uk/static/uploads/workshop_resources/178/178_Learning_styles_and_disciplinary_difference.pdf. The graphic on p. 74 is my reconstruction of the illustration in Kolb's chapter.

[25] Accessed August 24, 2014, http://www.aboutlearning.com.

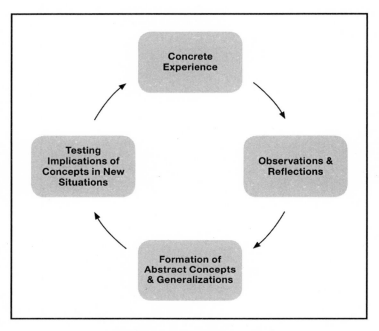

My Construct of Kolb's Cycle

Innovative, Analytic (or abstract), Concrete, and Dynamic (or Random). We all tend to be combinations of these four with one or two being dominant in our learning preferences. I have oversimplified her categories with the following descriptions:

- Innovative learners prefer interpersonal learning contexts. While they enjoy listening to experts, they then want to talk about what they and their classmates heard.
- Analytic (or abstract) learners prefer isolated learning contexts. After they hear an expert, they then want time to personally think through the material. Immediate conversations interrupt this process and are not valued.
- Concrete learners need immediate persuasion that the material has a useful purpose in order to listen to the expert. They prefer to quickly utilize what they have heard.

- Dynamic (or random) learners enjoy experimenting with material. They want to consult an expert only when something stumps them. They are easily distracted in long lectures and struggle to stay focused. This style best describes my personal preference.

When students take a learning style inventory, they gain helpful insights into why they differ from their classmates and why they prefer certain learning experiences. They may also be motivated to work harder on some of the compensating skills needed to excel. One interesting corollary notes how teachers tend to teach to their preferred learning style. So, when educators take a teaching style inventory, they become aware of their overemphasis and neglect. They may also be willing to work harder to include experiences for those of the other styles.

Multiple Intelligences

For many years, the standard IQ (intelligence quotient) test was thought to be a relatively accurate measure of human intelligence. In essence, the test sought to ask and answer the question "How smart are you?" and assumed human intelligence could be quantifiably measured through objective testing. Howard Gardner of Harvard University turned the question around by asking "How are you smart?"[26] Armed with this question, he has since identified and described eight different kinds of intelligence:

1. Visual-spatial intelligence
2. Linguistic-verbal intelligence
3. Mathematical intelligence
4. Kinesthetic intelligence
5. Musical intelligence

---

[26] Howard Gardner, *Frames of Mind: The Theory of Multiple Intelligences* (New York: Basic Books, 1983).

6.   Interpersonal intelligence
7.   Intrapersonal intelligence
8.   Naturalistic intelligence

He has also proposed the possible addition of a ninth type that he refers to as "existential intelligence."[27]

Educators find Gardner's theory particularly helpful in explaining why certain students quickly learn certain subjects but find other subjects more difficult. In Gardner's list, notice how linguistic-verbal and mathematical dominate the schooling experience. These two form the basis of almost all academic evaluation students receive in the formative years. Many children develop a lasting negative opinion of their intellectual capabilities based on their grades in these two areas. Social norms may reinforce these opinions. For instance, when school budgets get tight, art (visual-spatial), music (musical), and athletic (kinesthetic) programs suffer first. Further, children who excel at athletics must also perform reasonably well in language and math in order to participate in school-sponsored competitive athletic programs. However, the reverse is not true.

Anecdotal examples of the next three abound. A bank executive once told me he preferred to hire *B* students as bank tellers. He reasoned that an *A* student had not socialized enough in college to be a bank teller. He assumed the *B* student spent more time socializing and would have developed better essential interpersonal skills. The teller must project warmth and trustworthiness as he handles people's money. His smile and demeanor becomes the face of the bank.

In contrast, those with intrapersonal intelligence are more personally reflective. They sense some of their own inner conflicts. King David revealed this "intelligence" when he repeatedly addressed his own soul

---

[27] Accessed May 4, 2015, http://psychology.about.com/od/profilesal/p /howard-gardner.htm.

in the Psalms.[28] We take comfort in David's expressions. His personal reflection often expressed eloquently what we want to say.

Unlike any of the others, the naturalistic intelligence appears among those who possess unusual abilities with plants and animals. I visited an area in South Carolina dominated by tobacco farming. The farmers I met all followed one man's lead. The day he began cultivating his field, they fired up their tractors and did the same. The day he planted, they planted. The day he began harvest, they began harvest. The man had a sense about seasons, weather, soil, and tobacco plants that gave him consistently better results. No one including the man himself seemed to know why. But, no one varied from his pattern either.

As with virtually every learning theorist, Howard Gardner has his critics.[29] They complain about things like the lack of empirical research or defining intelligence too broadly. These and other charges may or may not be valid. Yet, something about his theory seems so self-evident that his theory enjoys great popularity with educators. He certainly broadens the conversation about human intelligence and makes room for greater diversity in our thinking and hopefully more patience with our learners.

Cooperative Learning

"Do your own work!" echoes through my every memory of school. If you needed to learn something, well, you were on your own. Only once during high school do I remember helping another student study for an exam. Though I studied a few times with other students in college, every project, paper, and test followed the same old rule. "Do your own work!"

---

[28] Psalms 57; 103.
[29] Jeffrey A. Schaler, *Howard Gardner Under Fire: The Rebel Psychologist Faces His Critics* (Peru, IL: Open Court Publishing, 2006).

My first encounter with a project that was produced by a group and was evaluated as a group occurred in a graduate course with Dr. Howard Hendricks. I was so sure I had misunderstood that I kept asking follow up questions: "You mean we can select our own group? How will you know who did which portion? So, we all receive the same grade for the whole project even if we only worked on part of it?" The memory of that conversation and his patient answers remain vivid to this day. That encounter contradicted every school experience I had up to that point.

Serious research into cooperative learning began sometime during the early 1960s. Several prominent leaders who began their research about that time trace their beginning through Morton Deutsch to Kurt Lewin.[30] Also, because of their extensive research, publishing, and training workshops, it is difficult to find materials without some reference to Johnson and Johnson. Their work, along with that of many others, demonstrates a consistent pattern of improved performance resulting from properly crafted cooperative learning experiences.[31] The US Department of Education summarizes this theory's significance:

> **WHAT ELSE DOES THE RESEARCH SAY?** More than 70 major studies—by federally sponsored research centers, field-initiated investigations, (sic) and local districts examining their own practices—have demonstrated cooperative learning's effectiveness on a range of outcomes: **Student achievement:** When two necessary key elements—*group goals* and *individual accountability*—are used together, the effects on achievement are consistently positive.[32]

---

[30] David W. Johnson, Roger T. Johnson, and Edythe Johnson Holubec, *Cooperation in the Classroom*, rev. ed. (Edina, MN: Interaction, 1998).

[31] Shlomo Sharan, ed., *Handbook of Cooperative Learning Methods* (Westport, CT: Greenwood Press, 1994).

[32] Accessed August 24, 2014, http://www2.ed.gov/pubs/OR/Consumer Guides/cooplear.html.

If I had only one theory to master and implement in my teaching, this would be the one. Yet, I inevitably get more resistance to this theory than any other when I teach students preparing for an academic career in Christian institutions. While individualism and competitive grading remain firmly entrenched in the university model of education, why do we as Christians honor them in our institutions? Cooperative learning provides the most wholesome opportunity to achieve so many of our Christian objectives.

- Where else can students "build each other up" in academics (1 Thessalonians 5)?
- How else can students "look out not only for [their] own interests, but also for the interests of others" (Philippians 2)?
- When can students fulfill their obligations to all the "one another" and "each other" passages of the New Testament?
- Is there not a lesson for academics in the fact that Jesus sent his disciples out two by two (and don't forget we all claim to be making his disciples)?
- Is there no lesson for academics in the multiple names always surrounding the apostles?

Here are several basic ways students can engage in cooperative learning as a part of their learning. Cooperative learning teams can . . .

- Create test questions.
- Prepare test review guide sheets.
- Debrief test answers.
- Create grading criteria for projects.
- Provide peer review for work.
- Help sick or injured members keep up.[33]

---

[33] Condensed from Susan Prescott, "Cooperation and Motivation," *Cooperative Learning and College Teaching* 3, no. 1 (Fall 1992).

In addition, courageous teachers might experiment with team test taking. At first blush, this seems like academic blasphemy. Examine the following suggestions carefully and see whether one or more of these might fit somewhere in your semester plan. Perhaps you give only one of your tests in teams.

Cooperative team testing options include when individuals take the test without help from the group, but . . .

- Final score is increased if the whole group performs above a certain level.
- Final score is calculated with X% based on individual score and Y% based on group average.
- Final score is calculated by group average.
- Final score is calculated with part from the test and part from a collaborative skills score.
- Only one member's test is graded and the whole group gets the same grade.
- The whole group takes one test together.

Tests where the group takes all or part of the test together seem counter-intuitive. However, the process of decision making about particular answers is often more complicated than it appears. More options for test taking will be discussed in the chapter on assessments.

In one faculty development workshop, a professor challenged the notion that collaborative learning could work in his preaching courses. As we explored several options, he decided to have the group prepare one sermon together but only one (randomly selected) would preach. This served several purposes, but the most important one was audience involvement. The student preacher knew that his team was really pulling for him in the experience. This essential confidence builder helped in the early stages of training. In addition, it softened some competitive feelings—and yes, budding preachers are competitive. Too many times, competition (a truly American tradition) actually works against our goals in Christian education.

Andragogy

Malcolm Knowles's name is most often associated with this learning theory.[34] Knowles uses the term "andragogy" to contrast with "pedagogy," which had almost become synonymous with principles of teaching. Historically, "pedagogy" referred to the teaching of children. Knowles sought to point out significant differences between children and adults as they approached learning. When taken seriously, those differences should affect our teaching strategies. He based his approach on six major differences. One handy summary explains them like this:

1. *The need to know*—Adults need to know why they need to learn something before undertaking to learn it.
2. *The learner's self-concept*—Adults have a self-concept of being responsible for their own decisions, for their own lives. Once they have arrived at that self-concept they develop a deep psychological need to be seen by others and treated by others as being capable of self-direction.
3. *The role of the learner's experience*—Adults come into educational activity with both a greater volume and a different quality of experience from youths.
4. *Readiness to learn*—Adults become ready to learn those things they need to know and be able to do in order to cope effectively with their real-life situation.

---

[34] Malcolm Knowles, *The Modern Practice of Adult Education: Andragogy versus Pedagogy* (Englewood Cliffs, NJ: Prentice Hall, 1970); accessed August 24, 2014, http://www.cumc.columbia.edu/dept/medicine/hospitalists/downloads/cc4_articles/Education%20Theory/Andragogy.pdf. Knowles published a great many works that have survived numerous revisions and updates.

5. *Orientation to learning*—In contrast to the subject-centered orientation to learning of children and youth (at least in school), adults are life-centered (or task-centered or problem-centered) in their orientation to learning.

6. *Motivation*—While adults are responsive to some external motivators (better jobs, promotions, higher salaries, and the like), the most potent motivators are internal pressures (the desire for increased job satisfaction, self-esteem, quality of life and the like). (Knowles 1990, pp. 57-63)[35]

The whole idea of adult education increases in significance as students move through secondary education into graduate institutions. In the 1960s, almost all my seminary classmates had just emerged from college. Today, our average entering age is around thirty-three.[36] Students with an additional ten years of life experience evaluate learning in very different ways. In one semester, my two interns were both older than me. One had retired as an Air Force pilot, and the other had supervised a nuclear power plant! I assure you their questions and my assessments took a totally different tone.

Education in America has morphed into a continuing lifelong process. Significant numbers of adults return to complete or advance their educational degrees. They often use these to change careers or improve their positions. The explosion of online educational opportunities seems unabated at the moment as more and more adults explore ways to expand and enrich their education.

Churches are discovering that many adults want a structured non-formal educational experience. They genuinely desire to know more about the Bible they carry and the God they worship. So, some churches

---

[35] Accessed August 24, 2014, http://academic.regis.edu/ed205/Knowles.pdf.

[36] Michael S. Lawson, "Look Who's Going to Seminary," *Christianity Today*, 1997.

establish their own Bible institutes.[37] Almost immediately these non-formal schools face quality expectations from their adult learners just as Knowles' anticipated.

- Before adults memorize anything, they will need to know why they need it. Otherwise, they prefer to look it up when and only when they need it. They may acknowledge the teacher thinks it is important, but unless persuaded, they give only minimal attention.
- Adults want teachers who treat everyone in the classroom with dignity and respect. They will no longer endure demeaning educational environments. They value their own and others' questions and opinions.
- Adults view expert presentations through their personal experiential lens. They even enjoy hearing how others' experiences affect their understanding of new material.[38]
- Adults return to formal and nonformal learning experiences fresh from a wrestling match with life. They are eager for anything that helps them with the issues they face daily.
- Adults bring their own agendas to the learning environment. When I ask students why they are taking my course, the honest young ones always admit, "because it's required." Older students tell me what they hope I address as we go through the course together.
- Adults willingly give unusual amounts of energy to learning when teachers tap their internal motivations. These vary from adult to adult as we will see in the next section.

---

[37] Within weeks of Dallas Seminary's announcement of a new doctor of educational ministries degree, inquiries came from so many church-based Bible institutes that we created a cohort for these applicants. This need took us by surprise.

[38] One older student (an international oil executive) told me he preferred the online classes because he got to read everyone else's papers.

If adult learning theory points us in any direction, it is away from a one-size-fits-all model of education. Adults determine to fit learning into their life experiences. While we do not want to create a completely utilitarian approach, we should be ready to demonstrate personal relevance.

Motivation[39]

If there is one key to learning, it is clearly motivation. Motivation does not explain how people learn, but it always explains why people learn. In fact, humans can compensate for a wide variety of personal or environmental deficiencies if they are highly motivated. Some individuals, whom I characterize as "predatory learners," have overcome seemingly insurmountable obstacles in order to learn. Helen Keller's name appears at the top of my list. No one questions the essential role of Anne Sullivan. She opened Helen's darkness through her gentle touch. But Helen's insatiable desire to learn led her to become the first deaf/blind person to complete a bachelor's degree. She became a leading advocate for others who were considered uneducatable at the time.

Internal motivation always provides the strongest incentive. However, a teacher does not always have easy access to a student's internal motivator. As teachers, we always work from the outside with our attempts to stimulate internal motivation. Early in my training, Dr. Howard Hendricks listed ten different keys he felt opened the door to internal motivation. Over the past forty-plus years, I have verified his list. So while the following list is his, the explanations are mine.

---

[39] While this section appears largely anecdotal, there is plenty of research on motivation. In fact, almost every learning theory speaks to the issue in one way or another. One excellent research-based text is Raymond J. Wlodkowski's *Enhancing Adult Motivation to Learn*, rev. ed. (San Francisco: Jossey-Bass, 1999). His summary suggests sixty different but quite practical motivational strategies specifically tailored to teaching.

First, look carefully at his caveat:[40]

Everyone can be motivated!
BUT
NOT at the same time
NOT in the same way
NOT by the same person

As teachers looking at a room full of faces, we easily overlook how students may be physically present but emotionally absent. Our best efforts fall on deaf ears because of stresses beyond our view. This is simply not the right time for the lesson we have prepared. Secondly, while adults may be quite susceptible to certain kinds of motivation, they may also be very resistive. Not everything we plan works with everyone we teach. Lastly, always remember, everyone has fans and critics. Those who like you tolerate your worst lessons, while those who dislike you will criticize your best ones. With our caveat firmly in place, look at this list of possible motivators.

1. We can motivate by creating a need. The two kinds of needs are felt and real. Felt needs exist at the conscious level, while real needs exist at the unconscious level. If what you plan to teach meets a conscious level (felt) need, you have little work to do. But, if it meets an unconscious level (real) need, then the unconscious but very real need must be brought to the conscious level.

As a brand-new believer, I was invited by a friend from Campus Crusade to join him on his weekly visit to the men's dorm. He explained that he did not have anybody to go with him, so I went. The first young man invited us in to talk about Jesus Christ. Imagine my surprise when my friend said, "Mike has just become a Christian. Mike, tell him what happened." Verbal paralysis overwhelmed me in that moment, and I

---

[40] Condensed from Howard G. Hendricks, *Teaching to Change Lives* (Sisters, OR: Multnomah Press, 1987).

cannot remember what I even said to that young man. I do remember exactly what I said to my friend later, and it was not with a happy tone of voice either. He then asked if I would like to join his class on "How to share your testimony." I did not have a need for that class before our visit; I certainly did afterward.

2. We can motivate by giving responsibility with accountability. Adults in particular appreciate taking responsibility for their education. They are familiar with this in the workplace. They are given a task and expected to perform it along with proper periodic supervision.

When I teach the class dealing with Christian higher education, I often announce that students will grade each other's papers. My young adult students love the idea. But when I add, "and I will grade your grading!" somehow their enthusiasm diminishes a bit. I do this because grading papers often remains a hidden responsibility for aspiring teachers. When even adult students are given responsibility without any accountability, they often do not take the responsibility seriously.

3. We can motivate by sustaining student interest over time. Although gaining attention is relatively easy, sustaining interest is not. Sustained interest is achieved when lessons and semesters have a proper balance between receiving information and processing information.

Of all the courses I teach, the "History and Philosophy of Christian Education" has the most potential to embalm students. The challenge of sustaining interest motivated me to enlist the services of my Rubber Ducky, create a Middle Ages game, present student dramas of Renaissance philosophers teaching courses like drivers education, and develop a match-the-quote class exercise to separate the ideas of Plato and Aristotle. In May 2012, three seniors, whose grades had already been submitted, shocked me by attending the last class. I felt extremely honored by their presence and said so. They rewarded my efforts to sustain their interest, and as a class we assembled a beginning philosophy of Christian education together.

4. We can motivate by structuring the learning experience. The idea is to break the learning into small enough pieces that accomplishing the early tasks creates the confidence to undertake larger challenges.

Retrieving comes natural for Labrador puppies. Returning the "dummy" thrown to the other side of a backyard seems like fun. They rarely tire of playing that game. Of course, finding a "dummy" in tall grass presents a more difficult challenge. So, trainers often seed a field with multiple "dummies." The young dog always finds a "dummy" and comes to believe he always can find it. Eventually, all of this provides the confidence to continue searching for a wounded duck or pheasant that has seemingly disappeared. Failing to find the fowl is not an option in the dog's mind. If the trainer concludes the bird cannot be found, he will have to go get the dog since he has never "not found" what he was sent after. Should we (especially in Christian education) not plan more for our students' success than their failure?

5. We can motivate by providing recognition, encouragement, and approval. Teachers have an especially powerful position in the minds of students. Their opinion about whether or not a student can perform a challenging task really matters and can help students persist in the learning task.

Names like Jaime Escalante and Marva Collins ought to be emblazoned in every classroom as reminders of the power of encouragement and believing in your students. Who really believed that East Los Angeles (largely Hispanic) kids could learn calculus when they normally performed poorly on low-level math tests? Jaime Escalante! The movie *Stand and Deliver* wonderfully depicts his motivational style. His record of students passing advanced placement calculus speaks for itself. Who really believed that inner-city (largely African American) kids could learn anything? Marva Collins! In fact, admission to her school required being expelled from their respective public schools. Her track record of Rhodes Scholar graduates speaks for itself.

6. We can motivate by dissolving emotional blocks. If students enter your class having been damaged in previous schooling experiences, they may approach it with great apprehension. Fear is not the best motivator. Learning increases as fear decreases.

I tend to walk out among my students—especially when I want to encourage a dialogue. Having paused after explaining the syllabus assignments on the first day, I asked if there were any questions. I thought I saw movement to my left, turned, looked directly at the student I thought had moved, and asked, "Yes, what is it?" Speechless, stunned, and paralyzed describe his terrorized reaction. He finally managed to stammer out, "I . . . I . . . I . . . didn't have a question." He looked so pitiful that I reached over and touched his shoulder and said, "It's OK. Don't worry. I haven't eaten a student in weeks!" The laughter from the class brought needed relief to their poor classmate. No one should enter anything called Christian education fearing personal humiliation or intimidation—especially from a Christian teacher.

7. We can motivate by fostering wholesome competition. I am not speaking about competition between students. Here we want to challenge each student to give his best effort, which means that at times he will exceed even his own best expectations.

A group of playful Greek students in Athens had just turned in their papers to me. I suspected they had not taken the task seriously. Listening to their jokes and laughter confirmed my suspicions. I began the class by thanking them for their effort on the project, using every sincere tone of voice I could muster. I reflected on Colossians 3:23 that challenges us with, "Whatever you do, do it enthusiastically, as something done for the Lord and not for men." I continued, "Of course evaluating papers you would submit to the Lord Jesus is a sobering responsibility, but I am looking forward to it." After reinforcing the thought from Colossians with several more comments, I excused myself to retrieve something I needed for the class hour. Of course the papers remained conspicuously on my teaching desk. But upon my return, the papers had mysteriously disappeared. The class leader (and there is always one) shyly asked if they could have a little more time to "refresh" their work. Even then I probably didn't get their very best efforts, but I did get a better product and an opportunity to teach an important piece of our theology.

8. We can motivate by intensifying interpersonal relationships. Even a small interest genuinely expressed by a teacher creates huge internal motivation with students. You may not be the greatest instructor in the subject matter assigned to you, but you will be irreplaceable in the life of each student with whom you develop a relationship. This works with critics as well as fans!

Rather than trying to select from among literally hundreds of stories from around the globe, let me suggest a few meaningful habits I have developed over the years.

- Anyone can make an appointment to see me—even if I need to come early, stay late, or skip lunch.
- No one leaves my office without me praying for him.
- While in my office or in conversation, he has my full attention. I have become a disciplined listener.
- If he shares something before or after class, my hand goes on his shoulder, and I briefly seek God's mercy on his behalf.
- Sometimes I give extra credit if a student makes an appointment.
- I always correct those who apologize for taking my time by reminding them it is the Lord's time.

A professor's office can be a scary place, but candy on the coffee table, Kleenex always handy, and family pictures everywhere help students feel a bit safer. My fishing pictures alert them that I actually have a life outside of seminary. Because few people have an overabundance of those who genuinely care for them, simple gestures have a powerful impact. I honestly believe students who have been in my office for whom I have prayed give me better effort in their work.

9. We can motivate through the law of natural consequences. Of all the various tools, this is my least favorite. This most frequently comes up with deadlines. Every time I think I have heard every possible excuse, some creative student invents another reason why he cannot turn his work in on time—but should not be penalized.

I admit to leaning on the soft side when students come to me with their pleas. I cannot forget the merciless stress of my own student days. But sometimes I am not able (or willing) to untangle their negligence. One student turned in papers 1 and 2 but not 3 or 4. The syllabus specifically required papers 1 and 4. He objected to getting a *D* for the course. I explained that actually he should have failed the course because the syllabus specifically required papers 1 and 4. He replied, "I did not read the syllabus." His tone of voice and facial expression indicated he expected a favorable response. He did not get one. I wondered what he was doing while I explained the syllabus in painful detail on the first day of class and even emphasized the parts required to pass.

10. We can motivate through personal enthusiasm. No one wants to study with a teacher who does not love the material. However, anyone who has bumped around in academic circles knows all too well how quickly professors tire of the lowly introductory classes that cover all-too-familiar material. A scholar becomes a real teacher when he turns a love for the material into a love for those who are only beginning to learn the material.

Clearly, the best in the business was Dr. Howard Hendricks. His name appears more than once in this book. I studied under him, I taught with him, and I inherited his chair of Christian Education at Dallas Theological Seminary. In all those years, I never saw him on a bad day. He never gave anything less than his full energy to a lesson. But his true genius lay in his explosive delight when a student (any student) came forward with even the most meager insight. His exclamations lit up the room. Although he taught the same "Introduction to Bible Study Methods" for more than fifty years, he always reacted like a Super Bowl winner to a student's contribution. His interest, his enthusiasm focused like a laser beam on the student's learning rather than his own presentation. I watched it up close. He infected me with his viral enthusiasm for learning. I never recovered.

Conclusion

If Eugene Trester was right, and "Learning not teaching is at the heart of Christian education,"[41] then we ought to become experts in learning. How can we help our students succeed in their learning task? Their success rather than our own ought to focus our efforts. Sometimes I wonder whether we are fulfilling our Lord's expectations in his wonderful mandate to "make disciples." Do students leave our classrooms wanting to learn more? Or, did we merely inoculate them against the very subject we love? Have we really done everything we can to send them out as lifelong learners?

This significant piece of the professor's puzzle is often neglected in training teachers for higher education. Instead, teachers often rely on practices from previous generations who were not trained either. That may feel like a safe choice, but it may not be the best choice. Our responsibilities as Christians ought to motivate us to carefully examine what we create for students. The learning theory piece can guide us to make better plans for the students entrusted to our care and instruction.

---

[41] Gangel cites Trester ("Biblical Andragogy") in *The Christian Educator's Handbook on Teaching*, 160.

PLANNING SKILLS IN SYLLABUS DESIGN

"Begin with the end in mind."
Stephen Covey[1]

The invisible parts of teaching often surprise newcomers to teaching. Those who come to the profession through primary and secondary educational training expect the required planning and time-consuming assessments that bookend their courses. Both of these add substantial hours to the workload of course delivery. A teacher's failure to plan properly means students spend a semester wandering through material, unable to discern the significant from the trivial.

Young students who have not seen the underside of teaching sometimes question this planning piece of the puzzle. They invariably point to the Lord Jesus' style, which they perceive as more casual, informal,

---

[1] Steven R. Covey, *The Seven Habits of Highly Effective People* (New York: Simon & Schuster, 2013), 102.

and spontaneous. But Jesus' ministry was anything but casual, informal, or spontaneous. They have not thought carefully about Jesus' mission. In John 5, Jesus told his listeners that he only did what he saw his Father doing. In John 12, we learn that he only spoke what the Father told him. As we move deeper into New Testament theology, an eternal plan unfolds with attention given to minute and sometimes-painful detail (Acts 2:23; Romans 8; Ephesians 1). In fact, Jesus' life implemented a plan the Trinity agreed to in eternity past. Nothing about his life was left to chance. The God of the Bible plans everything, so if we are to be like him, we must also plan. But to this, we must always add, "If the Lord wills, we will live and do this or that" (James 4:15). Nevertheless, that does not relieve us from planning.

Perhaps the clearest example of Jesus carefully planning his teaching occurred on the road to Emmaus. Luke says, "Then beginning with Moses and all the Prophets, He interpreted for them the things concerning Himself in all the Scriptures" (Luke 24:27). Jesus' course on Christology must have been breathtaking. At least it created serious "heart burn" as the two reported later. Jesus' intentional selection of only those things pertaining to him exposes a clear purpose. His teaching had a direction; it had a beginning point; it had an ending point. He intended to connect himself with the entire Old Testament. If our teaching is to resemble that of Jesus, it must also have purpose and direction with a clear beginning and end.

Like Luke's account, a course syllabus reveals the grand scheme for a course of study.[2] The various elements indicate where the class is going (and perhaps why) and include what the class will be doing along the way. Creating a syllabus requires working interactively through a

---

[2] In reality, the syllabus also becomes a legal document binding on administration, faculty, and students. We typically prefer not to think of it in those terms.

series of steps. The final product becomes a highly interrelated whole. The course objectives refine the course description in terms of student learning.[3] The course schedule represents a reasonable progression through the subject, broken into manageable pieces but arranged to accomplish the course objectives. The course assignments and their assessments assure both the teacher and the student that course objectives were achieved.

I require students to create a course syllabus for an introductory level required course. That most certainly will be their assignment as new teachers. Good introductory courses ought to create a love for the area of study. Therefore, my students must ask themselves throughout the planning process, "What am I planning to help students love this material?" In their final submission, they need to indicate where they attempt to answer that question. In addition to the elements appearing in traditional syllabi, they must explain their rationale.

Beginning teachers often have a syllabus handed to them. Some are tolerable; others look like something from the twelfth century. But even a bad syllabus has room for creative elements to rescue you and your students from wilderness wanderings. We will discuss these ways in lesson planning. If you plan to design a syllabus from scratch, I recommend these five steps:

Step 1: Determine your course objectives.

Step 2: Create a course schedule.

Step 3: Design appropriate course requirements.

Step 4: Review and connect each session and assignment back to one or more objective.

Step 5: Write your course description.

---

[3] The field of education uses the terms "aims" and "objectives" interchangeably. Within this volume, I use aims when speaking of lessons and objectives when developing a syllabus.

Although these appear linear, the process should be interactive and fluid.

To illustrate the planning process in this chapter, I selected an outstanding example from one of my former students. Samples of Josh Vajda's work appear in each step in the planning process. His whole syllabus appears in appendix A and represents hours of development, editing, and refining. He graciously allowed me to use it.

Step 1: Determine Your Course Objectives

Initially, course objectives represent the broadest tentative ideas about what you hope to accomplish. As the planning process unfolds, these should be refined and edited for clarity and precision. Student needs— felt and real—as discussed in chapter 3, should be considered first when choosing course objectives. The more we know about our students and where they are headed in life, the more precise our course design can be in contributing to their development. Our second consideration should be where the course fits in the overall curriculum and mission of the school. Does this course build on other courses so certain knowledge or skills can be assumed? Does this course prepare for other courses so certain knowledge or skills must be included? Is this course largely independent of other courses, or does it introduce an entire area of study?

Some general guidelines govern the writing of course objectives. For a semester-long, three-credit course, the number of objectives should be around five and probably no more than seven. They always describe student activities in complete sentences. They should reflect what can realistically be accomplished inside the course, rather than larger life goals. When taken together, they should represent a variety of levels from the learning domain taxonomies. Good objectives easily lend themselves to assessment.

West Virginia University created an interactive "Bloom's Wheel." Their website guides you from the domain through the proper verb choice to appropriate student products.[4] This or something like it should be in front of you when writing your cognitive objectives. Simon Atkinson designed a similar "wheel" (though not interactive) for the affective domain.[5] The advantage of tools like these is their provision of both the verbs for the objectives and suggested student products for assessment.

Bloom's taxonomy has become "the gold standard" for creating both course objectives and lesson aims. His basic design breaks cognitive learning into six major categories and deals primarily with how students process information. The taxonomy represents movement from lower-order thinking to higher-order thinking. The categories are

1. Knowledge—requires only basic recall of information.
2. Comprehension—indicates an understanding of the information.
3. Application—demonstrates an ability to use the information.
4. Analysis—expresses ability to break information down into essential pieces or to examine underlying assumptions.
5. Synthesis—reflects skill in assembling information into meaningful combinations.
6. Evaluation—exhibits skill in discerning the value of various pieces of information.

Josh tackled a required "Christian Life and Thought" course at Cedarville University. Here are two of his objectives, along with his rationale. His verb choices appear in italics and clearly indicate what

---

[4] Accessed August 27, 2014, http://community.wvu.edu/~lsm018/Articulate%20Blooms%20Wheel/blooms_wheel.html.

[5] Accessed August 27, 2014, http://www.academia.edu/4289077/Taxonomy_Circles_Visualizing_the_possibilities_of_intended_learning_outcomes.

his students will be doing. The "Notes" that appear below and through-out appendix A reflect his rationale. I require the Notes section even though it is not a normal part of syllabus design. A syllabus with Notes, when presented as a whole to an academic dean, makes an impressive document, displaying an aspiring teacher's ability to think through the entire planning process. These two examples represent first the cognitive then the affective domain.

> *Objective:* The student will *develop* a biblical-theological framework for categorizing new information and assessing its trustworthiness.

> *Notes:* This objective relates to both application and learning how to learn. Students will be bombarded with new information for the rest of their lives. They must have the tools to help them know which sources are trustworthy and how new information relates to what they already believe, maintaining a Christian worldview for the rest of their lives.

> *Objective:* The student will *empathize* with those who view the world from outside the Christian faith and *explain* why such a view might be appealing.

> *Notes:* This objective relates to the human dimension and also contains a cognitive component. It is not enough to know the difference between right and wrong; students must be able to engage with others and understand where they are coming from either as believers or unbelievers. This involves attempting to see from another person's point of view and identifying ways that they have been deceived either about the world or Christianity. Above all students must learn to love others regardless of their differences, following Christ's own example.

It is expected that this empathy will naturally help students draw others to Christ.

As with anything written, objectives benefit from writing, rewriting, refining, and editing. Here we practice our word-crafting skills. Precise course objectives help students focus their attention for the semester-long journey. They also clarify assessment and guidelines for selecting course content in the next step.[6]

Step 2: Create a Course Schedule

Creating a course schedule involves a controlled collision when the calendar meets the content. So much fuzzy thinking surrounds this process. Teachers often complain, "There is just not enough time to cover the material." What exactly do the phrases "enough time" and "cover the material" really mean? How much time is enough?[7] Our information explosion creates an endless data supply. There is always more to explain and discuss about any given subject.

In the world of semesters, time is a fixed commodity. So, "covering the material" must fit inside the allotted time. Course objectives actually define what "covering the material" means. The course will not do everything, but it must do the things specified by the objectives.

Although fifteen weeks sounds like a lot of time, actual class time is around four eight-hour days.[8] Normally, class sessions break down into

---

[6] Accessed August 27, 2014; an additional concise and helpful resource by Lee D. Fink can be found at http://www.deefinkandassociates.com /GuidetoCourseDesignAug05.pdf.

[7] Donald Grey Barnhouse reportedly took ten years to preach through Romans. I wonder whether he felt that was truly enough time.

[8] Fifty-minute class hours multiplied by three days a week for fifteen weeks equals thirty-seven and a half hours. In the past, accreditation standards measured "seat time" or how many hours a student spent in class. Online courses have caused a huge revision in thinking. Some online, three-hour, graduate-level

meetings per week. A semester-long, three-credit course could have forty-five 50-minute meetings, thirty 75-minute meetings, or fifteen 150-minute meetings.[9] Even these meetings cannot be devoted exclusively to instruction. Tests, holidays, special events, snow days, instructor absences, and "housekeeping" all subtract from classroom meeting time.[10] Teachers ought to plan wisely and carefully use the actual number of minutes they have with students.

Another deceptive feature about a fifteen-week semester involves the student-learning curve. Note the following graphic. Let the straight black line in the figure below represent our carefully constructed syllabus with evenly distributed content from week one through week fifteen. The uneven lines represent three different students' learning curves. Note one student's early dip. Perhaps sickness, family crisis, or some other personal distraction pulled the student's focus away from the course.

Learning is not consistent over all 15 weeks

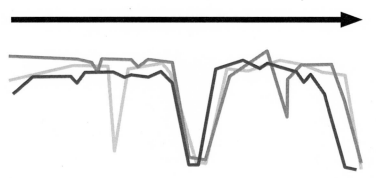

Week 1   **Week 15**

courses are done in only seven weeks. New definitions assign values to various student learning activities rather than counting minutes seated in a classroom.

[9] I prefer the latter for "time on task" reasons. I feel longer periods of time with more focused effort gives me better results than a lot of short pieces of time with smaller bits of information that get easily lost in the crush of busy student lives.

[10] This might include such things as explaining an assignment, reviewing deadlines, answering questions, going over the syllabus, etc.

Note how all three curves dip about midway through the semester. Days just preceding spring break or Thanksgiving often mark a divided focus or simple absence from the course. Our school finally gave up on the Wednesday before Thanksgiving. We now give students the whole week off. I wonder how their learning curve looks on the Friday before? These are simple realities that we should account for in our thinking and planning.

As the semester winds down, so does the learning. Just because a teacher gives information right to the last minute does not mean quality learning has taken place. Although we cannot account for every dip in the learning curve, we can plan more active learning around anticipated dips. Creative planning can soften the dips in those curves.

I have chosen not to reproduce Josh's whole schedule here. You should look at it in the appendix. In response to student learning curves, notice how he wisely planned a fun but practical activity for the March 3 session prior to spring break.

Worldview and Art
Notes: Watch a half-hour TV program and hold an informal class discussion about the worldview it presents. If a suitable show cannot be found, analyze commercials, YouTube clips, music videos, or some other short form(s) of entertainment. Make sure there is popcorn for the students.

Although I especially liked the popcorn idea (my father owned a popcorn business), educationally students will actually use what they learned up to that point. Josh also completes his heavy classwork well before the end of the semester but sustains interest and reinforces learning through student presentations. Although his classroom responsibility decreases, theirs increases—thus utilizing one of the keys to motivation with student participation.

Narrative Project Presentations
Notes: Emcee student presentations.

I found myself wanting to take his course!

Content selection needs as much careful attention as calendar planning. I often begin this process with a blank pad and a fist full of sticky notes. I brainstorm and on the blank pad jot down everything I can possibly think of related to the subject. Unfortunately, my mind does not always work in an organized linear fashion. In the midst of brainstorming, ideas about upcoming speaking engagements, family outings, or household projects pop up—the reasons for the sticky notes! Unless I write down the cluttering ideas, my mind refuses to release me to focus on content planning.

Now, I write small (an old accounting habit) and all over the page in order to get everything in front of me. Then, I begin a grading process. Each item receives a number: 1 represents "absolutely essential"; 2 represents "very important"; 3 represents "nice to know but not essential." Sounds simple, but loving what you teach makes deciding what to leave out as difficult as deciding what to include. I draw lines to connect naturally related items, which become units of study. Finally I arrange the items for logical sequencing.

After merging these content priorities into a trimmed-down but realistic course calendar, I look back at my course objectives. Each session must contribute to accomplishing at least one course objective. If not, I either change the session or adjust the objectives and remind myself that a syllabus should provide a *reasonable* guide for a semester-long journey.

Step 3: Design Appropriate Course Requirements

Course requirements provide the means by which students interact with the "stuff" of the course. Properly designed requirements represent learning strategies that allow students to demonstrate careful and thoughtful interaction with the material. Ultimately a value must be assigned to their demonstration. Requirements ought to strike a balance between busy work (work unrelated to any course objective) and overwhelming work (unrealistic work for student level or time allotted).

Traditional assignments such as reading, term papers, book reports, and tests form a stable core of options. But an endless variety of adaptations can make even standard assignments interesting. Many additional options offer creative alternatives as well.[11]

The purpose for reading changes as students move from secondary through undergraduate to graduate levels of schooling. At the secondary level, the textbook may provide the major source of information, while class sessions reinforce essential elements found in the text. At the undergraduate level, the text may provide one source of information while the class sessions provide an additional source of information. At the graduate level, multiple texts may provide both perspectives and essential information. Class sessions may never refer to those texts, but the student is expected to be familiar with the information they contain. I urge planners to choose textbooks wisely based on expected student abilities.

While book reports offer a familiar format, their online availability makes them a less reliable reporting device. Asking students to relate specific course objectives to their reports reduces the plagiarism risk considerably and reconnects the student with the goals of the course.

Term papers can be a great opportunity for students to interact with the ideas of others or formulate their own ideas. Too often, they suffer from last-minute "all nighters," and any real opportunity for learning is lost. To combat this, one friend requires the term paper to be submitted

---

[11] My daughter's third-grade class created an animated cartoon on a website available free to educators. The children created a script, chose the cartoon characters, selected appropriate voices, and the website did the rest. Repeated viewings of their own creation reinforced the learning.

in pieces for evaluation through the semester. The final grade represents a sum total for all the various pieces, but the process allows time for deeper consideration of the material.

The ever-present test is perhaps the most overworked and least understood of all the possible options. We will give careful detailed attention to this in chapter 7. There are many ways to adjust tests so they become genuine learning opportunities. In the end, students need to feel they had an opportunity to demonstrate what they learned, even if it did not match the professor's preferences.

The following represents Josh's choices for his course. You can read his explanation for each of these assignments in the full syllabus provided in the appendix.

Assignment	Due Date(s)	Percentage
Sire Readings	(Report by 5/8)	10%
Worldview Journal	2/8, 2/24, 4/7, 5/8	20%
Media Analysis Paper	3/29	15%
Interview Paper	2/22	15%
Exam 1	3/1	15%
Exam 2	4/12	15%
Narrative Project	4/26, 4/28	5%
Class Participation	Report by 5/8	5%
TOTAL		100%
EC: Group Exam 1	3/1	2%
EC: Group Exam 2	4/12	2%
EC: Grade the Prof	4/15	1%
EC: Biography Paper	5/8	1-5%
MAX TOTAL EXTRA CREDIT		+10%

Josh's design reflects many strong features. First, students have a variety of ways to demonstrate their learning. Second, students who may not excel on one particular assignment benefit from spreading the percentage values over a larger number of assignments. Last, his extra credit section allows students to regain some lost percentage points. This provision may appear gratuitous, but it keeps students working in the material for a longer period of time. Each of Josh's assignments will need a grading rubric as well. Though not part of his assignment, grading rubrics will come up in chapter 7.

Step 4: Review and Connect Each Session and Assignment Back to One or More Objective

Speaking of rubrics, here is the grading rubric for the syllabus assignment. My colleague, Dr. Mark Heinemann, designed this helpful tool to make grading more specific and to provide a checklist for final review before submission. I include it with his permission. Creating a rubric like this one takes a considerable amount of time in the planning phase but saves a lot of time in the grading. A high-quality rubric enables graders to be more evenhanded in their evaluations. Note these features as you read through it:

- Point values for each item are in the left column.
- Points awarded are assigned by the professor and put in the far right column.
- Some items have multiple issues such as "Objectives," which has four.
- Each issue specifies a sliding scale with desirable on the left and undesirable on the right.
- An equal number of points are available for the raw syllabus and the annotations.

Possible Points	Content and Format	Points Awarded
Sub-total = 4	***Choice of course***	**Sub-total =**
(4)	• Specific (college catalog page included) • Introductory level	
Sub-total = 44	***Content***	**Sub-total =**
(2)	1. Description of course purpose	
(8)	2. Objectives • student behavior ---------------- teacher behavior • at least two domains ---------------- just cognitive • objectives -------------------------------- methods • fit with purpose -------------don't fit with purpose	
(5)	3. Texts • up-to-date---------------------------------outdated • fit objectives ----------------------------- don't fit	
(12)	4. Requirements • reasonable ------------------------too light/heavy • creativity -------------------------------- uncreative • fit objectives --------------don't fit with objectives	
(6)	5. Policies (grading, attendance, late assignments, discrimination) • clear------------------------------------- unclear • reasonable ------------------------- unreasonable	
(8)	6. Schedule (week, dates, topics, due items) • complete ----------------------------- incomplete • clear------------------------------------- unclear • shows sufficient knowledge------------insufficient	
(3)	7. Other (project specifics, report forms, etc.) • clear------------------------------------- unclear	
Sub-total = 44	***Annotations***	**Sub-total =**
	For each of the 7 main syllabus sections listed in the previous section, explain your rationale for what you did and how you did it.	
(2)	1. Description of course purpose • clear rationale --------------------unclear rationale • sound rationale----------------- unsound rationale	
(8)	2. Objectives • clear rationale --------------------unclear rationale • sound rationale----------------- unsound rationale	

(5)	3. Texts • clear rationale --------------------unclear rationale • sound rationale---------------- unsound rationale	
(12)	4. Requirements • clear rationale --------------------unclear rationale • sound rationale---------------- unsound rationale	
(6)	5. Policies (grading, attendance, late assignments, discrimination) • clear rationale --------------------unclear rationale • sound rationale---------------- unsound rationale	
(8)	6. Schedule (week, dates, topics, due items) • clear rationale --------------------unclear rationale • sound rationale---------------- unsound rationale	
(3)	7. Other (project specifics, report forms, etc.) • clear rationale --------------------unclear rationale • sound rationale---------------- unsound rationale	
Up to 10 points off	***Exam question samples/project specifics—(points off if missing)***	**Sub-total =**
Sub-total = 8	***Formal (spelling, grammar, consistency)***	**Sub-total =**
(8)	• spell checked ------------------ not spell-checked • proof-read------------------------- not proof-read • consistent format ------------------- inconsistent	
Total = 100		**Total =**

Step 5: Write Your Course Description

Having thought through the syllabus multiple times, you are ready to write a brief course description. In three or four sentences, describe what a student might expect to experience. In reality, a catalog description may already exist. I ask students to work with an existing course description as a bit of a reality check. This requirement alerts them that a catalog description leaves a great deal of latitude for creativity. I do require their course selection to be introductory level and required for the general student body. I am convinced that introductory courses should capture the imaginations of students and head them in the direction of lifelong learning. Too many students endure introductory courses as another hoop of fire in their academic experience.

Planning for Online Courses

Online courses have both similar and dissimilar features with class-room-based courses. Both have course objectives, content delivery, interactions with and among students, assessment of student work, and fixed course length. Much of the planning in these areas remains the same. Online courses require substantially more preplanning in *how* content delivery and student interactions occur. While they may eliminate faculty time in a classroom, they add faculty time on the computer. Students in standard lecture-driven courses usually have little or no interaction with classmates and may or may not ask even one question during the course of a semester. Quality design features in online education substantially increase the conversations among students and between student and teacher.

Decisions on how to deliver content and create student interactions cannot be made until you know the capabilities of the platform approved by your institution. That platform will reflect a philosophy of education that is context specific. I am currently trying to learn the capabilities and limitations of the third online platform approved by our seminary. Platform designers constantly tweak their designs to keep up with changing hardware capabilities. I consider platforms a moving target.

Weaning yourself from the lecture format may be the most difficult task you face. Remember, student learning may not be tied to lectures at all. While students may or may not be helped by a lecture, in the final analysis, they take information and make sense out of it for themselves as they learn it. Some features of online education still feel odd. Online curriculum designers now suggest a self-generated video of the professor giving a brief personal introduction and welcoming students to the course. Who knew you could take a live video of your face for public consumption while working on your computer? Are students really ready for this full-face encounter? I digress.

More than likely, the institution you work for will have an online course format already in place. Your job will be to make sure the same course objectives in your classroom course are adequately achieved in the online environment. Quality must not be sacrificed on the altar of online education. For those wishing more specific but brief help in thinking through your options, I offer the following three resources:

1. Katrina A. Meyer, *Quality in Distance Education* (Hoboken, NJ: Jossey-Bass, 2002).
2. Donald E. Hanna, Michelle Glowacki-Dudka, and Simone Conçeicão-Runlee, *147 Practical Tips for Teaching Online Groups: Essentials of Web-Based Education* (Madison, WI: Atwood, 2000).
3. Mark A. Maddix, James R. Estep, Mary E. Lowe, eds., *Best Practices of Online Education: A Guide for Christian Higher Education* (Charlotte, NC: Information Age, 2012).

Keeping up with this field may feel like making the jump to light speed while still on the hull of the starship *Enterprise*. It moved; you didn't; now you hang in space. Don't forget: many educational basics remain the same while the gadgets, interfaces, and focus of your personal presence change.

Conclusion

Stephen Covey may not have had a syllabus in mind, but he summarized our process well when he said "Begin with the end in mind."[12] Though a course is taught forward, it is planned backward. By starting

---

[12] Covey, *The Seven Habits of Highly Effective People*, 102.

with student learning objectives, we build everything inside the course to facilitate those ends. Each step in the syllabus plan interconnects with every other step until we have a finished product. But the acid test comes when we teach the course. Did the students actually achieve the stated objectives? We may have started our plan with the end in mind, but was the end achieved when students completed the course?

After I teach a course, I solicit student evaluation. Their experience of the course probably varies from the course I planned. Their insights help me modify assignments/grading rubrics, clarify objectives, or rearrange the schedule. The constant redesign keeps the course fresh and attuned to student needs. When this piece of the puzzle receives constant attention, courses improve with each offering. I keep a working copy handy with "notes to self" adjustments for the next semester. Each time I teach, I move closer to the end I had in mind.

MASTERING CONTENT

"As knowledge increases, grief increases."
Ecclesiastes 1:18

I n just a few days, Mike, we will award you the master of theology degree. The problem is you may believe it." Those words culminated four years of strenuous academic effort on my part. For some of my classmates, the years barely challenged their intellectual capacity. In contrast, I now felt educated beyond my intelligence and said so to my friends. I had no awareness of God's future plans. No one would have accused me of mastering the content; I barely survived it. In fact, years later I asked one of my most respected teachers if, in his worst nightmare, he ever dreamed I would return to teach. Dr. Campbell took three very slow steps before answering. Because of his enormous diplomatic skill he responded, "You know how to ask hard questions, don't you?"

I share this story because many, if not most, of you who read this volume will be somewhere in the midst of your academic journey. You have found an appealing subject area. Others have indicated you show promise in this area. You hope that, with further studies, you might gain a firm grasp of the subject you enjoy and obtain a teaching position because of how much you know about your subject. Although becoming proficient in your subject certainly forms the foundation for a teaching position, other factors play a more significant role in your landing your dream job. So, this chapter is partly about mastering your content and partly about caveats related to content mastery.

Content Mastery

Comprehensive exams loom toward the end of doctoral programs. But simply because of time constraints, they rarely represent a thoroughgoing assessment of someone's knowledge. Instead, they generally sample a candidate's knowledge and assume the rest is in place. The process can be excruciating. The written portion represents standard fare because most course work requires written documents. Having been both a candidate and an examiner of the oral portions, I felt they mostly provided an opportunity to see whether the candidate could speak intelligently. This is typically the one time when spoken thoughts about a given subject spill into broad daylight. So, while comprehensive exams represent an important part of doctoral evaluations, they often leave a candidate with the nagging suspicion that his knowledge was not thoroughly examined. If that question tugs at your mind, here are some ways to evaluate your own mastery of content.

Higher-Ordered Thinking

Learning domains represented the first learning theory discussed in chapter 3. In that chapter, learning theories were examined from the point of view of a professor needing to know how students learn. This is especially important because, more than likely, the students will learn in different ways than any individual teacher learns. But learning theories can also be used for the teacher's personal assessment. Within the learning domains, the cognitive domain represents just such a help. The list of levels represented in the cognitive domain also appeared in chapter 3, but for the purposes of this chapter, I turned the list upside down.[1]

- Evaluation (discernment about value)
- Synthesis (reassembly)
- Analysis (breaking down into parts)
- Application (use)
- Comprehension (understanding)
- Knowledge (recall)

By turning the list upside down, you can see that Bloom thought simple recall was a lower order of thinking than the ability to evaluate the worth of information. This is also a good way to think about your own learning. My sense of many doctoral programs is that they equip students well up through analysis. In fact, most research analyzes something. Or, as the joke goes, the student learns more and more about less and less. In my opinion, the dissertation's literature review may be the only thing that saves students from complete myopia.

In order to evaluate your own movement toward higher-order thinking within your content area, you will need to answer three questions: (1) How well can I synthesize my content area? (2) Can I distinguish between essential and excessive information for entry-level students? (3) Can I trace how any given detail relates back to the whole?

Synthesis is not always a welcome challenge. Boiling things down to their essence requires rigorous thinking. Believing forty-five minutes to be the bare minimum, some of my classmates chafed at having

---

[1] Don Clark, accessed August 29, 2014, http://www.nwlink.com/~ donclark/hrd/bloom.html.

to preach twenty-minute sermons. Somewhat exasperated, the professor proposed a hypothetical situation. "It is Easter season. A local radio station calls and offers you a fifteen-second slot for free. You can say anything you wish about Easter." One student responded, "That is impossible." To which the professor responded, "So, you don't have anything to say about Jesus Christ in fifteen seconds?" Point made. The silence was deafening.

Synthesis takes a lot of time because somehow we must account for all the available data and do so briefly. The early church faced similar challenges. It needed to synthesize the essential teachings of Christianity for the oral societies. It formulated creeds that Christians memorized and recited. The syntheses have served the church well for centuries. Having served on faculty committees formulating mere policy statements, I have often wondered how they did so well. I cannot imagine how many countless hours they needed to state and restate each phrase. Of course someone would then cross-check to make sure the phrase represented the text accurately. Analysis is easier because we limit our field of inquiry and bear down on the details.

You may exercise your synthetic skills through a hypothetical exercise similar to the one given by my homiletics professor. First, choose a course you have taught or intend to teach. Or, if you are feeling particularly courageous, choose your major content area. Second, assume you had one of the following time limits to describe your course or content area:

- Five minutes
- Twenty minutes
- Seventy-five minutes
- Three hours
- Ten hours

Notice that all of these represent less time than you would normally have for a course. As you work through this forced-choice exercise, write down what you would say in the first two. Then try to say them out loud in the time limit. Ask yourself, Are these really the essential things? Would other teachers of this material agree with this list of essentials? Now, do the same thing for all the courses you are likely to teach or courses you took in your discipline.

Working on synthesis actually involves the final level of higher-order thinking, evaluating. At this level, we should be able to distinguish between essential and trivial. Some of my teachers did not appear to know the difference. True, something that appears trivial at the moment may prove to be the key to a wonderful new insight, but for the moment it must be set to one side or classified as an area for further research. This level calls for distinguishing between fact and opinion, identifying assumptions and presuppositions, validating supporting evidence, and tracing out logical inconsistencies. Sometimes, these can be discovered by defending an opposing point of view.

The second question requires the ability to decide between essential and excessive in the specific context. Data overload characterizes a great deal of schooling. The answers to this question may have little to do with how you were taught this subject. Because your God-given aptitude may make acquiring your subject easier for you, think about the most difficult subject you had to learn. Remember how much "non-essential information" came with the essential parts. Many teachers do not think through their material well enough to know the difference. They often tire of teaching introductory courses because they dislike covering familiar material semester after semester. They have gone so far into the forest that they cannot return to the edge and admire the trees with those approaching the forest for the first time. Be sure you can distinguish between the "nice to know" and "essential to know."

The third question deals with the ability to stay oriented. Moving easily back and forth between the big picture and the details demonstrates content mastery. In his excellent book on communication,

Donald K. Smith suggests material should be so familiar to the teacher that it can be taught out of sequence.[2]

The Gospel writers did precisely these things as they brought together their experiences with the Savior. They sorted through everything, gave us only what we really needed to know, and kept the big picture of his life and ministry before us. Otherwise, "not even the world itself could contain the books that would be written" (John 21:25).

Mastery Learning

The learning theory called mastery learning provides some helpful insight into content mastery as well. In schooling's approach to education, time is most often a constant and competence a variable. In other words, schools typically work on a fixed semester or trimester basis. Those designations have a fixed number of weeks to teach some portion of a subject. In that fixed amount of time, student achievement varies considerably. Some do well and some do poorly. In many cases, students pass the tests and complete the assignments only to forget the bulk of the course. Their residual competence in that subject may be embarrassingly low.

Years ago, some educational researchers asked quite a simple question, "Why?"[3] Why is time the constant and competence the variable? What if competence was the constant and time was the variable? While similar to time on task as a learning theory, mastery learning does not try to fit within the school-year model. Instead, mastery learning focuses on genuine competence regardless of how long the process takes.

---

[2] Donald K. Smith, *Creating Understanding: A Handbook for Christian Communication Across Cultural Landscapes* (Grand Rapids:Zondervan, 1992), 99.

[3] Vahid Motamedi has a helpful summary of the theory and its history in "Mastery Learning: An Effective Teaching Strategy," accessed August 29, 2014, http://www.nyu.edu/classes/keefer/waoe/motamediv.htm.

While your teaching may be limited to the school year, your learning is not. As a beginning teacher, your understanding of the subject may be more than your students', but you may still feel like you have not really mastered the content. As you consider content mastery, lay out for yourself what you really think a master of your content should know. Then, use that as a goal to set before yourself. Time is now the variable that works on your side. You do not face the constraints of the semester or trimester system. Keep moving forward toward your goal, realizing that mastery learning allows more time than normal school years. When you enter teaching, think ahead ten years and decide what you should know at that time. Do the same for twenty years, thirty years, and forty years. The best teachers are not those who have mastered the content but those who *are mastering* the content. And never forget what it feels like to be a beginner!

Teaching

Lastly, content mastery comes with the teaching. Sooner or later every teacher comes to the realization, "I always learn more when I teach." Moving from student to teacher requires both an emotional and cognitive jump. Even the first time teaching through material gives you a stronger grasp and better recall. Subsequent times through the same material increase your sense of competence. We all know repetition is a key to learning. Repetition works for teachers as well as it works for students.

The power of teaching to increase learning also explains why I often ask students to teach. Even if the material is minimal and the time is brief, they are less likely to forget what they have articulated in front of others. Although I cannot remember anything else about the class, I still remember portions of a really pathetic speech I gave in a business communications course more than fifty years ago. I also remember having to read my dissertation word for word out loud to my major professor at Oklahoma University. He never corrected me. The process forced me to function like a self-correcting word processor as I stumbled over one error after another. By all means, consider your teaching role as a continuation of your learning curve toward mastery of your content.

When you teach, can you eliminate the clutter that confuses those who begin their intellectual journey into your subject? Way too often the academic environment promotes "more." In other words the thinking goes, "If one book is good, two are better. If one paper is good, two are better." I argue "more" is not "better." More is only more. You will endear yourself to students if you really help them master what they really need to know.

Content Mastery Caveats

Most of us have an aversion to being wrong. In fact, that aversion drives us to either avoid or control situations where we might be challenged. As teachers, one way to control classroom challenges to our knowledge is to know so much that no one has the nerve to question our assertions. Another way, of course, is to intimidate any student who dares to ask a question. Because this volume seeks to present the role of the teacher from a Christian perspective, I have assembled five caveats to keep before us as our knowledge and content mastery becomes closer to reality.

1. Content Mastery Is More about a Direction than a Destination

Jesus called his followers "disciples" or students. If we retain the spirit of his label, we may never be content masters but always content students. As a new Christian I started watching the lives of older believers quite carefully. While some believers just got old and cranky, others seemed to collect unusual amounts of wisdom and sound judgment that they wrap in an aromatic humility. They did not seem to have any need to impress people with their vast store of information. They answered simple questions with direct answers. Although I have a long list of those I admired and learned from, here are a few names you might recognize.

- Dr. John Mitchell (founder of Multnomah School of the Bible) genuinely wanted my outline for John's Gospel. He was disappointed to learn that my outline was actually his outline that he had given in lectures at Dallas Seminary while I was a student.
- Dr. Carl F. H. Henry (former editor of *Christianity Today*) listened carefully and patiently as I explained my theological position, which was quite different from his. I did not persuade him to change nor did he persuade me. But he treated my view with genuine respect. He did not cut me short, though he was very familiar with my position.
- Dr. Vernon Grounds (former president of Denver Seminary) was as interested in my son's batting average in Little League as my ministry exploits or discussions of current theological issues facing the church. He probed my son with dozens of baseball questions.
- Dr. Billy Graham told our group of counselors at the Oklahoma City Crusade that *we* would be leading people to Christ that night. *He* was just going to get them to come to the stadium floor where *we* would have an opportunity to carefully explain the gospel to them. *He* would be praying for us while *we* met with them. He emphasized that he was not going to lead anybody to Christ that night but would delight in any and all whom we might lead to know the Savior.
- I would love to have visited at length with A. Wetherall Johnson, Lottie Moon, and Amy Carmichael as their biographies indicate they were women of great wisdom and passion for God.

Those I have met and those I would like to have met seemed to be on a journey toward God. That journey included academic growth as part of loving God with their minds and did not diminish as they became more proficient and skillful. They animated the term "disciple" by their very lives. I have asked God's Spirit to develop in me what I saw in them. I want to be his student until he takes me home.

2. Content Mastery May Be More of a Danger than a Blessing

The Information Age has pushed the boundaries of knowledge way beyond human capacity while creating a seemingly insatiable desire for more. Even entry-level teaching demands so much more knowledge than a generation ago. One article in *Forbes* traces an abbreviated history of our age through journal articles dating back to the 1940s.[4] Here are several quotes from the article summaries:

- "He [Derek Price] concludes that the number of new journals has grown exponentially rather than linearly, doubling every fifteen years and increasing by a factor of ten during every half-century."
- "The 1975 census already finds that information supply is increasing much faster than information consumption."
- "The imperative [for scientists] to save all the bits forces us into an impossible situation: The rate and volume of information flow overwhelm our networks, storage devices and retrieval systems, as well as the human capacity for comprehension."
- "Very powerful computers are a blessing to many fields of inquiry. They are also a curse; fast computations spew out massive amounts of data. Where megabyte data sets were once considered large, we now find data sets from individual simulations in the 300GB range. But understanding the data resulting from high-end computations is a significant endeavor. As more than one scientist

---

[4] Gil Press, accessed August 29, 2014, http://www.forbes.com/sites/gilpress/2013/05/09/a-very-short-history-of-big-data.

has put it, it is just plain difficult to look at all the numbers. And as Richard W. Hamming, mathematician and pioneer computer scientist, pointed out, the purpose of computing is insight, not numbers."

This amazing trend is unlikely to end as the capacity for retaining information grows. The Christian perspective on knowledge comes with Paul's warning label: "Knowledge inflates with pride, but love builds up. If anyone thinks he knows anything, he does not yet know it as he ought to know it."[5] And we know that God imposed a handicap on the apostle in order to restrain pride's development (2 Cor 12:7). The growth of knowledge remains a constant danger unless simultaneously accompanied by a growth in love. Whatever the world does with the vast amount of accumulated information, we must always keep it in perspective.

Solomon puts a little different twist on the same problem. He sets out to learn as much about everything as possible. Although God granted his prayer for wisdom, Solomon introduces the summary of his findings with these words, "For with much wisdom is much sorrow; as knowledge increases, grief increases."[6] Perhaps there is some truth in the old saying, "Ignorance is bliss." In any case, increasing your knowledge has a downside to it. If you believe Paul and Solomon are correct, then proceed with caution.

3. Content Mastery Probably Reflects More of Your Spiritual Gift than Your Spirituality

The simple distinction between the gifts of the Spirit and the fruit of the Spirit has haunted the church down through the centuries. Christians assume their charming, well-educated, articulate pastor is

---

[5] 1 Cor 8:1–2
[6] Eccl 1:18

also spiritual. The litany of such pastors who have disappointed their congregations with their unethical or immoral behavior testifies otherwise. Indicators of spirituality are found in the Spirit's fruit, including self-control.

Students often look at their professors with similar rose-colored glasses. Knowledge and teaching are, after all, spiritual gifts. They certainly need grooming to be most effective. In the final analysis, the Holy Spirit dispenses the gifts as it pleases him. We can take no credit for them because we did not choose them or earn them. While they are ours to use, God intended our gifts to build up, not impress others. On the other hand, the fruit of the Spirit demonstrates our submission to his moment-by-moment work in our lives. Even a momentary deviation erupts in impatience, unkindness, unfaithfulness, or loss of self-control. Our giftedness does not guarantee our spirituality. Our hearts must wage war with those who admire our gifts without really knowing the condition of our spirit. All too quickly, we ourselves may begin to trust the gifts to get us through, rather than the Spirit to stabilize our character.

If by us exercising our gifts of knowledge and teaching, our students accomplish great things for God, then our gifts have been used properly. *Mr. Holland's Opus* paints a graphic picture of this idea. While using our gifts to make a name for ourselves can be quite tempting, our gifts were intended to build the body of Christ. The actual results of our teaching gifts must be born out in the lives of our students. Only when the fruit of the Spirit accompanies the gift does it accomplish everything God intended.

4. Content Mastery Is More about God's Grace than about Your Ability

Have you ever bumped into verses in the Bible that even a seminary education failed to prepare you for? Here are two that caught me by surprise the first time I encountered them.

- *1 Corinthians 4:7.* Paul began in chapter 3 to deal with various alliances within the church. Some claimed to be followers of Apollos and others followers of Paul. He continued his discussion through chapter 4, which concludes with his sending Timothy to dissolve the spiritual competition among the groups. Tucked quietly in the middle of verse 7, Paul raised a most pungent question: "What do you have that you didn't receive?" That question deserves a verse all by itself or maybe even a chapter.

  My father believed the American image of a "self-made man." "I brought myself up by my own boot straps," he said many times. That statement was blasphemy for him and for anyone who shares that view. Whatever we have was given to us, whether that be basic intelligence, good health, educational opportunities, degrees, or teaching posts. We may not lay hold of anything and call it "mine." Whatever advantages we may have come from the generous hand of a loving God.

- *Luke 17:10.* The disciples asked Jesus to increase their faith. After he told them of the mustard seed, he explained their position as slaves with jobs to do. "In the same way, when you have done all that you were commanded, you should say, 'We are good-for-nothing slaves; we've only done our duty.'" By application, those words fit us too. At first blush they may rub the wrong way. Who wants to think of himself as a "good-for-nothing slave"? After some reflection, we may ask ourselves the more distressing question: "Did we really do everything he commanded?" How wonderful if any of us could truthfully say, "Yes!" And, if we only did what he commanded, what credit do we deserve? It takes great faith to live a life based on that truth.

So, we only have what we have been given and we only do what we were commanded. What can we attribute to our own abilities apart from God's instruction and grace?

5. Content Mastery Is More about What You Do with What You Know than Merely What You Know

Elitist educational systems, standardized intelligence tests, and competitive grading fit perfectly in a competitive society where nothing matters except winning. Although Christians need to function within that society, they need not embrace those values. We know from the teaching of Jesus that we were not entrusted with the same amount of "talents." At this time there is nothing we can do about that. He offers no competition to acquire more "talents." However, Jesus emphasized the proper use of both "talents" (Matthew 25) and position (Luke 12).

I have often longed for what I observed in others, such as a photographic memory, multilingual capacity, or James Earl Jones's speaking voice. At such times, the Spirit seems to bring to mind the words of Jesus: "Much will be required of everyone who has been given much. And even more will be expected of the one who has been entrusted with more" (Luke 12:48). Then I either meet or read about someone with world-class abilities who poured himself out in some remote place as a servant of the great King, and I am reminded of my role as a servant.

In America, no one grows up aspiring to be a servant. In fact, finding a living role model for that position is almost impossible in our society. I journeyed to Sri Lanka before meeting someone I thought qualified. Dionys watched the facilities of the Colombo Theological Seminary while serving the faculty and staff in humble roles. He made sure resident guests had proper meals delivered to their rooms. Without asking, he always knew whether I would eat in or dine out. He watched people prepare their coffee or tea only once. The next time, their cups were prepared precisely as they liked them. When guests returned to the school, no matter how late, they found Dionys waiting at the door. He did not have a high education, nor did he speak English. His humble spirit, sweet smile, and caring service preached convicting sermons. The school took great pains to honor him at their graduation exercises when he retired. I cannot wait to see how the Lord rewards him.

Dionys's service stirred in me thoughts of what loving God with all my heart, mind, and strength might look like. I may be wrong, but it seemed like he used everything God gave him for the benefit of others. He caused me to question whether I had maximized what God has entrusted to me so far. I consider Dionys one of my great teachers. His lessons still haunt my reflections. Content mastery may be more about what we do with what we know than merely what we know.

Conclusion

Sometimes students get the idea based on competitive grading that content mastery assures a job opportunity. They have done well when compared with their peers. Perhaps they have even accumulated the best grades in their classes and received academic awards. They expect a job offer will result. While good grades and grasp of content do matter, other factors often play a larger role in getting a teaching job. Auburn University published a study of junior faculty among theological schools.[7] They reported that an applicant's "being known in some way" contributed greatly to their hiring. When schools looked to fill positions, senior faculty expressed concern about the new hire "fitting in." Relationships and perceived attitudes greatly affected hiring practices. In their words, "connections count."

Content mastery may ultimately be the will-o'-the-wisp in academic pursuits. How is it possible for anyone to feel they have mastered

---

[7] Barbara G. Wheeler and Mark N. Wilhelm, *Tending Talents: The Second in a Series from a Study of Theological School Faculty* (Auburn, GA: Auburn Theological Seminary, 1997). Their study also highlighted some interesting differences between theological faculty and university faculty.

their content during an information explosion? Yet, I still hear similar terms in faculty conversations. Mastering the content, controlling the material, or even covering the material indicate a fixed amount of information. The reality of information accumulating so quickly and stored in such vast amounts has yet to sink in. All of us may have to resort more often to the phrase, "As far as I know now." This piece of the puzzle may be expanding too rapidly to fit easily in its designated place.

MANAGING SKILLS:
THE CLASSROOM EXPERIENCE

"But everything must be done decently and in order."
1 Corinthians 14:40

An escape from incarceration, a governor's pardon, and a commuted sentence all describe my high school graduation experience. I never quite acclimated myself to institutional living and often wondered what the difference was between a work/release convict and me. He went to jail every night while I went every day. Summer represented a sacred time undisturbed by mind-numbing routine. I consider myself a survivor rather than a beneficiary of schooling as an institution. Fortunately, I picked up enough basic skills to advance to the next level without a hiccup. Forgive me. I do not consider my sense of high school or my reflections anywhere near normative. I do think many manmade schooling structures and practices make administration easier without regard for those enduring the process. My granddaughter's "love" for school that presses her to get there early stands in stark contrast to my experience.

Some researchers have taken the time to study schooling experiences in depth. *Life in Classrooms* by Philip Jackson presents his firsthand observations of children's classroom activities.[1] The preface to the reprinted edition chronicles his journey as a researcher into one of the most common modern-day experiences. He confesses his difficulty in learning to see what had become so familiar as to be invisible. The classroom experience goes unquestioned as normative. Yet everything including architecture, furniture, decorations, and policies represent artificial constructs. I especially appreciated his concern that educators awaken to students' experiential realities. If classrooms were more humane and stimulating, life in them could be greatly improved.

A Christian professor, Cliff Schimmels, wanted to research the high school classroom experience in much the same way Jackson had done. He was refused access as a researcher so decided to enroll as a student. He published his findings in *I Was a High School Drop In*.[2] How easily we forget the emotions and stresses peculiar to those days until someone asks, "Who would like to be a teenager again?" and gets no volunteers. Schimmels's powerful and empathetic dealing with schooling realities should sharpen the sensibilities of anyone who oversees the creation of classroom experiences.

I have hope that you will take the time to read those volumes for yourself. Each is highly recommended reading if you accept responsibility for those spending hours of their lives in your classroom. But in

---

[1] Philip Jackson, *Life in Classrooms* (New York: Holt, Rinehart, and Winston, 1969).

[2] Cliff Schimmels, *I Was a High School Drop In* (Grand Rapids: Revell, 1986).

case you don't act on my suggestion, this chapter seeks to do for you what field research did for those gentlemen. Just reflecting on the title of the first volume makes me ask, "Is there *any* life in my classroom? How would students rank the *quality* of life in this room? Would those present consider me or themselves to be really *living?*" Those questions and others like them drive me to work hard at making my classes a stimulant to life rather than a narcotic.

I have chosen a management model to approach our discussion of individual lessons. The chapter on planning skills looked through the syllabus lens at the semester-long picture. The chapter on instructing skills will explore a variety of presentation options. This chapter examines areas that require attention in each and every lesson. Each one needs careful management to nurture learning and living in classrooms. Here are six components that will occupy our attention through the rest of the chapter.

1. Atmosphere: Is this classroom a safe place?
2. Space: Does the room decoration and configuration create anticipation?
3. Time: Have I carefully considered both calendar and clock?
4. Content: Does the content plan fit the time allotted?
5. Participation: When, where, and how will the students interact with the lesson?
6. Motivation: How motivated are the students to learn the material at hand?

Atmosphere and space are independent variables, meaning teachers can manage one without necessarily managing the other. Time, content, and participation are interdependent variables because a change in one invariably requires a change in the other two. Managing the first five well affects the sixth, motivation.

Atmosphere

Creating atmosphere begins immediately as the first student walks into the room. What greets students' eyes and ears and who greets them as persons sets the tone. Everyone knows we only get one chance to make a good first impression. My goal is to have a seating arrangement that promotes conversation, something bright and colorful on the screen prompting something fun to share about themselves with other students, appropriate music playing in the background, and a big smile on my face. If I come late and then spend three or four minutes setting up, I just sent a message. Sometimes this is unavoidable, as scheduling requirements may book two responsibilities too close together in places too far apart. In that case, I always greet the students first with an apology because they are paying for my time. Then I announce a brief exercise for them while I set up. Or, perhaps another class occupies the room, and my students and I basically arrive together. Again, I spend a little time greeting and conversing with them in the hall and while we get settled. I am consistently communicating that I am glad to see them and looking forward to time with them. If I am not eager to get there and be with them, why would they be eager to be with me?

At the beginning of each semester's first hour, I welcome students and introduce myself. How we introduce ourselves indicates clearly how approachable we are and how "warm" or "chilly" the class will seem. In the early days, I often suggested various titles that had been given to me over the years. My Boy Scouts called me "Noah" because it rained every time we went camping! On the other hand, one secretary at church named me the "Chubby Cherub." With a big smile I forbid the students to use that, and I threatened to put "frowny faces" on their papers if they did. With the advent of grandchildren, I became "Grandpa Mike" with a glowing story of my love for them. Because some of my lectures appear online, I actually get e-mail addressed to "Grandpa Mike" from young people as far away as mainland China. Introductions may vary given the age of the students and the teacher's personal life stage. How will you communicate that you are a safe person and this is a safe class?[3]

Students recognize their disadvantage when dealing with teachers. There is no level playing field. Often, the most stressful conversations center on grades, late papers, or absences above the handbook limit. I have never found an easy way around these. But, if I have created a welcoming atmosphere, students lay aside their fear of approaching me. And, as much as I hate to admit it, at times I have miscalculated a grade. Overall, I try to engage empathy as I listen, and if I err, err on the side of generosity. Generosity was a Christian virtue the last time I checked.

Of course, students worry about whether they can accomplish the tasks set before them in the syllabus. So, some discussion of course requirements always occupies a portion of the first meeting. But before we look at requirements, I have them look at the course objectives. Then we compare them to the requirements that help them accomplish the objectives. I want them to believe that the requirements actually have a purpose beyond busy work or even a grade. Between the classroom sessions and their outside effort, we should arrive at a happy destination by the end of the semester.

While various assignments make up most of their grade, "class participation" always accounts for 10 percent. I use this as an excuse to talk about my expectations for interactions in class. Everyone in this class must be treated with dignity and respect. At times I will ask students to participate in smaller groups where I expect everyone to listen carefully enough to be able to represent one another's opinions faithfully. Disagreeing is acceptable (even with me), but being disagreeable is *not*. I emphasize, "So, if I sense someone is repeatedly acting like a 'donkey,' I will not award the 10 percent for class participation." The class

---

[3] Make no mistake, papers that do not meet course criterion receive lower grades or sometimes are returned to revise. You will see what I mean and how this works in grading when you come to chap. 7.

participation requirement provides me an opportunity to discuss class-room behavior with someone who has had a bad day.

On the positive side, I try to create anticipation for the weeks ahead. Surprises, special guests, unanswered questions, and similar "don't miss this day" comments animate our discussion of the course schedule. All of these help maintain motivation as the weeks wear on and communi-cate in what ways this course will *not* be "business as usual." Instead, I am anticipating the fun of guiding them through these experiences and hoping they anticipate them as well.

All of these are done during the first class meeting to create atmo-sphere. Maintaining that atmosphere is easier when the assigned room does not have a class in it ahead of mine. Most of the time, schedul-ers honor my request. When they do, I always have music playing and an introductory assignment on the board or screen that immediately requires conversation with classmates. The music allows students to chat without having their voices sound like they sit in an echo cham-ber. The guided conversation or other activity helps bring their minds from [you name it] and refocus toward the subject at hand. Graduate students arrive during a window of time, and class begins when I pull them away from the activity.

In the good ole days, a school bell signaled the beginning of class. The best teachers busted out of the starting gate like Kentucky Derby thoroughbreds the moment it sounded. If a teacher was late, he missed out on delivering some really good stuff. If your school still uses bells, I highly recommend starting with a bang rather than a whimper! Once again, this communicates enthusiasm for the material and a desire not to waste the students' time.

I confess my difficulty with remembering names. I have to work really hard at calling students by their names, but the rewards justify the effort. Students sense when they are being treated as human beings or, better yet, as family members. My goal is to reduce the intimidation factor while increasing real learning. Inquiring about various activities or relationships unrelated to class helps anchor their names in my mind and sends the message that I care about them as persons as well as students.

A warm classroom atmosphere builds with bits and pieces and must be maintained throughout the semester. Just because you sit in a room with people does not mean you are a class. You become a class on a journey together through guided conversations and joint learning activities. You know the class has gelled when students hang around at the end of the semester, taking pictures and exchanging phone numbers.

Space

Classrooms teach too! Most often they reflect the industrial revolution's preoccupation with mass production. Architects draw lines on paper based on assumptions about presentation models of teaching. They calculate room capacity based on standardized allotments, which typically err on the stingy side. After all, how much room does a person need to sit and listen? None of my doctoral courses in education ever touched on room configuration. Nor did we ever meet in a room thoughtfully prepared for graduate interaction. Throughout my academic training, rooms were assigned places for students to sit, listen, and write notes (or doodle in my case). I assumed fixed seating, massive podiums, and dirty blackboards had some connection to learning. Room arrangement was just not my problem!

It never occurred to me that rooms could actually be designed to promote student learning rather than teacher talking. My first exposure to creative educational space allocation came through ICL and *Sunday School Standards*.[4] In the 1970s, Lowell Brown and Gospel Light

---

[4] Lowell Brown, *Sunday School Standards* (Ventura, CA: Gospel Light, 1986). I still use his book although I prefer the revised edition, which offers a handy synthetic chart not available in the first edition.

teamed up to offer Sunday school training seminars around the country. His book provided objective quality measurements to improve learning in Sunday school. Gospel Light designed their curriculum to reflect the active learning model used in the training. His book showed several possible room configurations other than rows facing a front wall. The seminar demonstrated how the configurations promoted student learning. Their design assumed volunteer students who vote with their feet. As the seminars moved from church to church, the leaders were faced with various classroom settings. They showed how to reconfigure the space to reflect the learning activities planned for the hour. They paid attention to podiums that created barriers between students and teachers.[5] Black or whiteboards were scrupulously cleaned and dressed with a few carefully chosen, artfully printed phrases. Strategically placed posters reinforced central lesson ideas. Handouts were thoughtfully placed on student chairs or tables. Students arrived to a room sending a different message, a message that created anticipation.

I have since learned to pay attention to focal points and traffic flow. Where is the natural focal point of the room? Are the chairs oriented for proper sight lines? Remember, well-meaning custodians, whose main concern is vacuuming, set up most rooms. On the facing page is an actual classroom designed by a licensed architect and set up by some well-meaning person without regard for focal points or traffic flow.

Note the following problems:

- Students in the section on the left face a blank wall.
-

---

[5] In my fifty years as a churchman, I have observed that many (most) adult Sunday school teachers model a downsized sermon. While I applaud their willingness to serve, their lack of training as either preachers or educators has limited the effectiveness of adult education in the churches. I have also observed they are the most resistive group to training as they presumably know how to teach having been exposed to much schooling.

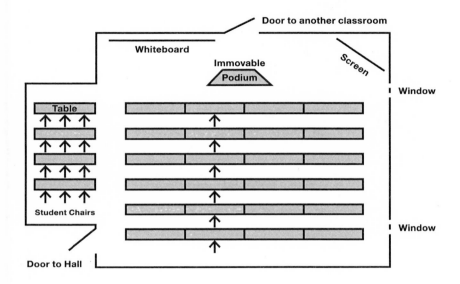

- The podium is mounted permanently into the floor, which prevents any realignment.
- The door to the next classroom robs wall space for visuals.
- The room works great when chairs are flush against tables, but when filled with students it becomes congested as student bodies take up space and prevent access to seats closer to the windows.
- Students seated on the right side of rows have no egress without disturbing an entire row. This assumes students do not need to take care of unexpected personal hygiene issues.
- The supposed aisle on the right near the window is practically useless because of the seats blocking the back row.

To make this room more student friendly, utilizing the natural focal point and easing congestion, the following adjustments could be made:

- Unbolt the podium from the floor, and make the podium movable.
- Reorient the room to the more natural focal point between the windows.

- Rearrange the tables to provide shorter rows and more aisles.
- Eight seats are lost, from the previous model, but the space is over-crowded anyway in my opinion.
- Often, ten to twelve square feet per adult is considered adequate and works if sitting and listening is planned. For table projects, discussion groups, and a myriad of other learning activities, I prefer twenty to twenty-five square feet per person.[6]
- This room still reflects a presentation model of learning. A collaborative model requires students seated around tables and allows for fewer seats.
- In reality, students almost never sit in the front rows unless the room is at capacity.

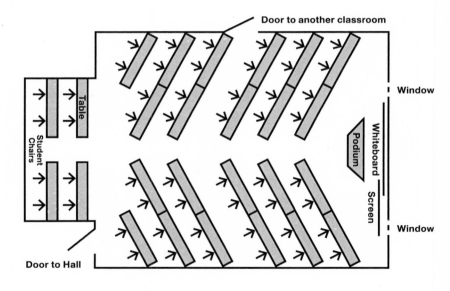

---

[6] The ten-to-twelve-foot allocation is based on the number of chairs that will fit in the room. The only realistic way to evaluate a room's capacity is to fill it with appropriate furniture configurations, equipment, and students until everyone feels crowded, then subtract until the room feels comfortable. Divide the square feet inside the room by the number of adults. This will provide a much more realistic allocation than the numbers architects assign.

Under severe space limitations, I have used standing conversations or allowed students to find spaces outside the classroom. This latter option works if the discussion takes an extended period of time. In any case, whatever we do to improve the classroom space will communicate our desire to help students enjoy their learning experience.

Time, Content, and Participation

"Time is money," as the saying goes. Around the world, starting and ending times range from precise to fuzzy. When time is measured precisely, a great deal more planning needs to be done. No matter how time is measured, no unlimited amounts exist. Teachers must manage both the calendar and the clock because everyone I know appreciates a respectful use of their time.

Managing the Calendar

Academic calendars generally use either the quarter or semester system. If a course is offered during a quarter, it usually runs for ten weeks plus a week for testing. For our purposes, we will assume a fifteen-week semester system as we work with the calendar. Obviously, a course planned for a semester would need to be downsized if offered in a quarter. Downsizing requires the realignment and subsequent decrease in course objectives, assignments, and meeting times.

The chapter on planning skills looked in more detail at how a fifteen-week semester breaks down. The big calendar management concern comes when the schedule breaks down for some reason. Even under the best of circumstances, when my choice of content looks like a perfect fit for the time limit, something unexpected happens. Although an endless array of possible interruptions can occur, let me suggest they fall into one of three categories.

1. *The administration cancels classes* (snow day, special event, building equipment failure, etc.). This can be particularly annoying if you have already included only the "bare essentials" in your course plan. Now, what can you possibly cut out? This is obviously a disaster (in your mind but maybe not in the student's). Remember God's words to Joshua: "Above all, be very strong and courageous" . . . and cut. Please don't try to make a fifteen-week course fit into fourteen or punish students with additional work to "make up ground." This is an excellent opportunity to remember that whatever "cover the material" means, it must bow the knee to actual time allotted. Time rules!

2. *Students want more time on a particular concern than you allocated.* Once in a while, students will simply not allow you to move on. Let me say that a different way. If you move on, you will not be taking them with you. They have unanswered questions, need more clarification, or only want more time to process stimulating thoughts. I make sure the whole class wants more time by calling for a vote and letting them know they have destroyed my lesson plans. They rarely feel pity for me or trade my fabulous future lessons for their present concerns. This is an excellent opportunity to remind myself that I am teaching real students moving at their own pace. Content should be adjusted to their needs.

3. *Two sections of the same class proceed at different speeds through the semester.* My first section left the classroom buzzing about the lesson on Acts 2. They took way more time than I had allocated. I had to delete some amazing material. The second section could not have cared less, which left me scrambling to find that "amazing material" I had deleted. I have since learned to plan for both the success and failure of each lesson. I am emotionally prepared to add or delete sections and/or whole lessons. This is an excellent time to note that just because something worked well with one group does not guarantee it will work well with

the next one. Like individual students, individual classes have their own unique personalities. One professor concluded his class an hour early by saying, "Let's stop here for today, and I will let you out a little early." No student ever complains about getting out a little early. He did not tell them he had run out of material, which is both a teacher and a preacher's worst fear.

Managing the Clock

The clock has never been my friend, either as a student or a professor. As a student, classes were always too long. As a professor, there is never enough time. Once again, time is generally a fixed ingredient in schooling. If I plan to talk the whole time with a question or two sprinkled in for color, then clock management is only a matter of restraining myself. Just remember to stop when students start closing their books or laptops, which always signals they're finished for the day. But, if we intend to do anything else, we need a lesson plan.

A lesson plan helps align the lesson's *purpose* (lesson aim) with the selected *content*, the *time* allocated, and the expected *participation* of the students. Each one affects the other three in one way or another. The purpose drives the selection of content. The content begins with some sort of introduction to the material, develops in the body of the lesson, and concludes at the end of the time. Students may become active participants in any or all of the three basic parts. A lesson plan should also include space for personal evaluation and any needed equipment or supplies. A basic model might look something like this:

Time	Lesson Aim: (purpose)	Student Participation	Equipment/ Supplies
	Begin		
	Develop		
	Conclude		
Evaluate			

Broken down, the components all work together in the following ways:

Lesson Aim (Purpose)

Everything in a lesson must contribute to accomplishing the aim. In essence it provides a compass to direct each portion of the lesson. By the end of the session, the student should be able to articulate the main features of the lesson because they are all tied to one central aim. Here is an initial set of questions to provoke your thoughts about purpose.

- What notions will you challenge?
- What opinions will you consider?
- What character will you evaluate?
- What material will you generalize?
- What question will you answer?

- What problem will you raise or solve?
- What concept will you explain?
- What ideas will you explore together?
- What propositions will you compare?
- What facts will you assemble?

Once you have a general notion, your purpose needs to be translated into a proper lesson aim stated in terms of the student. After all, the lesson is more about what you want the student to learn than what you plan to say. Once again, Bloom's taxonomy provides a guide to processing cognitive information. The taxonomy, along with appropriate verbs, can be found in an interactive format online.[7] For extended treatment of lesson aims, two volumes have survived the test of time.[8] I prefer LeRoy Ford's treatment because he goes beyond cognitive lesson aims and works with the affective domain, which concerns Christian educators a great deal.

A well-written cognitive aim:

- Begins with "The student will . . ."
- Contains an active verb selected from one specific level in the cognitive domain:
  — Knowledge
  — Comprehension
  — Application
  — Analysis
  — Synthesis
  — Evaluation

---

[7] "Bloom's Taxonomy Circle Design," accessed August 29, 2014, http://community.wvu.edu/~lsm018/Articulate%20Blooms%20Wheel/blooms_wheel.html.

[8] Norman Gronlund, *How to Write and Use Instructional Objectives* (Englewood Cliffs, NJ: Prentice Hall, 1995). LeRoy Ford, *Design for Teaching and Training* (Eugene, OR: Wipf and Stock, 2002).

- Describes clearly how the student will handle the information.
- Can be accomplished during the class hour.[9]
- Uses precise terminology rather than Christian "jargon."[10]

Here are samples of cognitive lesson aims based on Acts 4 and 5:

- The student will (TSW) describe the responses of the Christians in Acts 4.
- TSW compare and contrast the opposition he encounters with that encountered by the Christians in Acts 4.
- TSW analyze his response to opposition and compare it with that of the Christians in Acts 4.
- TSW identify two threats to the church found in Acts 5 and describe the church's response to each threat.
- TSW create at least two steps he will take to guard against the types of attacks on the church found in Acts 5.
- Based on Acts 5, TSW decide which of the two types of spiritual attacks present the greatest danger to his faith.

Of course, Christian teachers are not simply interested in cognition. We also want changes in student values and attitudes represented by the affective domain.

Well-written, affective aims may be the second part of a two-part lesson or combined with a cognitive aim to form one aim for one lesson. They always deal with a value or attitude at a specific level in the affective domain. When dealing with Scripture, the value or attitude should be reflected in the instructions or experiences represented. The combined aim uses the cognitive information to address the particular

---

[9] Some lesson aims look more like great life goals or semester-long course objectives. A lesson aim is small enough to be accomplished within the time allotted.

[10] *Disciple, Christlike*, and *mature* are Bible words but not precise enough for an individual lesson aim.

attitude or value. The value or attitude may be processed at any one of the five levels expressed by the affective domain:

1.   *Receiving* awakens an awareness of the attitude or value. Before conversion I was not aware that reading the Bible is an important value, and I had not personally read any of it.

2.   *Responding* calls forth an internal commitment to do something about the value. A few months after attending a Bible church, I decided I needed to read the Bible for myself. My effort was intermittent at best because I was unfamiliar with how to navigate the material.

3.   *Valuing* moves the attitude from casual response to significance. As time went by, Bible reading became a more regular practice.

4.   *Organizing* represents a reordering of attitudes and values based on the newly discovered attitude or value. Entering seminary required making space in my daily routine for Bible reading and/or reflecting.

5.   *Characterizing* means interweaving the value so tightly within that it characterizes the person. Today, one week away from my seventieth birthday, I don't need anyone to remind me to read my Bible. I love it and use it professionally and personally. I have since learned that while I am reading it, it is reading me and provoking more sensitivity toward God.

When we are teaching the Bible, each lesson aim should have both a cognitive and an affective element. Here is a sample cognitive lesson aim with several affective domain options to select from:

TSW examine Jesus' teaching on forgiveness in Matthew 18:21–35 and . . .

- Describe why deep hurts create struggles to forgive.
- Discuss immediate and future consequences for not forgiving.
- Suggest motives that promote regular forgiving.

- Discern personal barriers to forgiveness.
- Compare personal reactions to Jesus' proposal of unlimited forgiveness.

If you want a really scary way to test your aim, wait until the end of your lesson. Then hand out three-by-five cards and ask students to anonymously write down one sentence describing the lesson's point. Even if their reflections demonstrate the lesson was fuzzy, the fact that you solicited their help to improve your teaching will endear you to them. No one gets better without candid evaluation.

Begin, Develop, and Conclude

These three basic sections of any lesson obviously come in a bundle. Jack Presseau developed the most helpful initial guide to managing them I have found.[11] I have adapted and summarized his approach with his permission. The intent of his design model is not to be comprehensive but to be brief enough to understand how the parts work together and creative enough to be immediately applicable. We can expand his basic model in multiple directions. I am especially fond of his approach because he always works from the student's perspective. The following chart represents the three basic sections of a lesson with three separate approaches. The words on the left side of each square indicate the general approach needed to address the student's need or the way to handle the information involved. The second chart suggests specific methods suitable for each general approach. Some of the methods will be familiar, but for sake of completeness, a brief description of each method follows the chart.

---

[11] Jack Presseau, *Techniques: Creative Design for Teachers of Youth and Adults* (Atlanta: John Knox Press, 1992).

	Approach 1	Approach 2	Approach 3
Begin	REVIEW — The student has interest & knowledge	DISCOVERY — The student has interest but -0- knowledge	MOTIVATION — The student has -0- interest & -0- knowledge
Develop	PRESENTATION — The student needs information	ELABORATION — The information needs attention or consideration	GENERALIZATION — The information needs synthesizing
Conclude	APPLICATION — The information needs immediate use	SUMMARIZATION — The information is extremely large or complicated	CELEBRATION — The information deserves affirming or strengthening

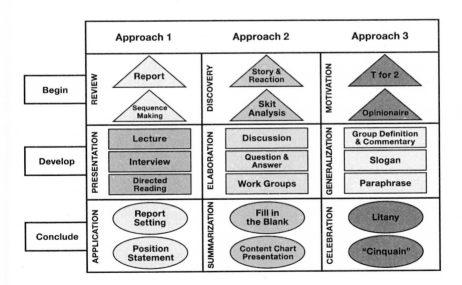

Beginning Activities

- Report—a basic summary of previous material
- Sequence Making—an outline, chart, or graphic representation
- Story and Reaction—students react to a particular question concerning a story[12]
- Skit Analysis—a brief drama by students that raises a concern dealt with in the lesson
- T for 2—two students briefly discuss their views on a question or comment
- Opinionnaire—an extended questionnaire raising issues dealt with in the lesson

Developing Activities

- Lecture—hopefully done well (see chap. 8, "Instructing Skills")
- Interviews—can be done with an individual or a panel
- Directed Reading—must be short enough to leave time for clarification or elaboration
- Discussion—must be focused on something specific for measured amounts of time
- Question and Answer—particularly helpful when everyone is really prepared
- Work Groups—a project that causes students to reprocess information taught
- Group Definition and Commentary—a reformulation of information by students
- Slogan—an abbreviated synthesis helpful for recall
- Paraphrase—a longer synthesis in contemporary language

---

[12] Stories can be presented in oral, recorded, or written format from a wide range of sources.

Concluding Activities

- Goal Setting—an intention of action hopefully reported on later
- Position Statement—an expression of group belief
- Fill in the Blank—an outline missing key words
- Content Chart Presentation—a graphic representation of material
- Litany—a planned expression of praise to God
- "Cinquain"—a five-line poem synthesizing material

Presseau's model demonstrates how students can participate in each of the three basic sections of a lesson. In actual practice, I find students appreciate every opportunity to participate. I use creative methods to both actively involve students in learning and to sustain their motivation throughout a semester. Therefore I tend to scatter a variety of methods through the sections, never using the same thing twice—with the exception of the lecture. This creates a bit of anticipation because whatever happens will not look like what happened at our last meeting. Even a PowerPoint lecture seems different with activities woven in before, during, and/or after it. So, every lesson plan includes some form of *student participation* but never quite in the same place or in the same way. Hopefully, students arrive expecting the unexpected.

Thinking through the details and preparing students to participate are major keys to success. If the learning activities are conducted poorly, they have about the same effect as a poorly done lecture. Research in education consistently points in the direction of active rather than passive learning. For more sophisticated approaches to lesson planning, I direct students to L. Dee Fink's *Creating Significant Learning Experiences* and Wilbert J. McKeachie's *Teaching Tips.*[13]

---

[13] L. Dee Fink, *Creating Significant Learning Experiences* (San Francisco: Jossey-Bass, 2003). Wilbert J. McKeachie, *Teaching Tips: Strategies, Research, and Theory for College and University Teachers*, 11th ed. (Boston: Houghton Mifflin Company, 2002).

Now the tricky part. How much time will each of these activities take? Here is what I have learned:

- More students per group means I must allocate more time. Four is my preferred size because it is too small to feel invisible and big enough to provide variety of insight. How long do I expect each student to share? If each talks three minutes, that is twelve minutes without time for shuffling chairs.

- Rearranging chairs and moving students into groups always takes more time than I planned. This is one reason I prefer seating arrangements in natural groupings when students arrive.

- Framing the project or crafting the question often takes a significant amount of time as this guides thinking. Thoughtful answers require more time as well.

- Student reporting is a bit unpredictable. I may get a relatively straightforward response or something totally unexpected.

I asked one group of German students to summarize a particular point by writing one new stanza for *Amazing Grace.* They wrote eight stanzas and performed them with instruments secured from their dorm rooms. Their enthusiastic response destroyed my lesson plan but created a tsunami of motivation we rode through the remainder of the course. One group of Mexican pastors working on a mural summary of the Old Testament would not quit working to demonstrate their efforts. I asked politely, "Are you about finished?" They responded, "We'll tell you when we're finished!"

Managing time on a lesson plan requires real thinking, but managing time during a lesson is an art learned only through the crucible of experience. There is no way to learn time management without doing it. Start slow, start small, but start! Doing little, purposeful activities at first will help you get an idea about time. If you have never done anything like this, sprinkle a variety of activities over the semester or quarter, then adjust, add to, or delete until you achieve a blend of teacher presentation and student processing of information.

Equipment/Supplies

There is nothing mystical about this section. In essence, this is a note to self and reflects the supplies or equipment needed for the lesson. Like Santa Claus, make your list and check it twice. Having a great activity planned but no supplies on hand makes you look really pitiful. Computer, projector, cords, remote, masking tape, markers, paper clips, staples, board cleaner, sticky notes, three-by-five cards, or whatever you need, obtain it. Don't take anything for granted. I was once assigned a room with my requested overhead projector only to discover there was no screen or extension cord. Nice!

Evaluate

At the end of every lesson, write down the things that worked and the things that need improving. As some activity unfolds, I see more clearly how to make it work more smoothly. Sometimes I discard an activity even though students loved it because it failed to reinforce the learning. Scrapping something that students loved is quite painful. This is where I remind myself that I am an educator, not an entertainer.

The lesson plan that follows represents an actual lesson plan for graduate students. It is one of a cluster of lessons about Jesus as a teacher. Almost everyone admits Jesus was a great teacher. Many study Jesus' teaching, but few analyze his behavior as teacher. Remember, he is no mere mortal; nothing escapes his attention. This lesson is designed to help students think about his role as a teacher and was the foundation for this chapter.

Lesson Aim (purpose):
The student will examine how Jesus managed one of the major components of teaching and evaluate the significance of the learning for long-term memory.

Time		Student Participation	Equipment/ Supplies
10 min.	**Begin** "What one quality do you find essential for a teacher?"	Students will discuss this question as they enter the room and for the first several minutes.	Whiteboard, overhead, or PPT with question on it.
2 min.	There are many essential qualities for teachers; one is to manage at least six components. In this lesson you will explore Jesus' management of those components.		
22 min. *Develop* 36 36 min.	The six components every teacher must manage are: 1. Motivation 2. Time 3. Space 4. Atmosphere 5. Content 6. Participation Look carefully at your assigned passage; work as a group; you have about 20 minutes to complete your task. (I will alert them when half the time is gone.)	Students will work in groups. Each group will get a different assignment, assuming there are only six groups. I may need to double up if there are more or present one of the components myself if there are too few.	*Handout:* This handout specifies the task for each group. Each group gets only their task.
	Here the students will present their various assigned tasks. I have allocated 36 minutes. (6 groups x 5 minutes each + 1 minute comment from me to emphasize their points or add an additional comment.)		

7 min.	**Conclude**
	I want to thank all of you for your contributions. Now I want you to reflect on your experience.
	Which one of these components are you most likely to remember long term? Why?
	What does this experience suggest to us about long-term memory as related to classroom activities?
	Which do you think is more difficult: planning what you are going to say or planning what students are going to learn?
Evaluate	

Handout: Managing the Major Components of Teaching

1. Look at how Jesus managed motivation in Matthew 17:19. Think carefully about the disciple's question, "Why couldn't we drive it out?" Draw your own conclusions for teaching. Then, as a group, create a thirty-second TV ad for a new TV series featuring Jesus' management of motivation.

2. Look at how Jesus managed time in John 11:6 and 15. Think carefully about Jesus' decision to stay where he was for two days and his subsequent explanation. Draw your own conclusions for teaching. Then, as a group, create a three-picture, living snapshot with commentary capturing Jesus' management of time.

3. Look at how Jesus managed space in Luke 5:3. Think carefully about Jesus' decision to put out from shore in a boat before concluding his teaching. Draw your own conclusions for teaching. Then, as a group, write two verses to the tune of "Jesus Loves Me" that summarize Jesus' management of space.

4. Look at how Jesus managed atmosphere in John 13:12–13. Think carefully about how the mood in the room might have changed from

anticipating the Passover Feast to having Jesus wash your feet. Draw your own conclusions for teaching. Then, as a group, write a song to the tune of "Amazing Grace" that summarizes Jesus' management of atmosphere.

5. Look at how Jesus managed content in Luke 24:27. Think carefully about Jesus' decision to explain the entire Old Testament in one lesson. Draw your own conclusions for teaching. Then, as a group, write a poem to the pattern of "Jack and Jill Went Up the Hill" that summarizes Jesus' management of content.

> Jack and Jill went up the hill
> To fetch a pail of water.
> Jack fell down and broke his crown,
> And Jill came tumbling after.
> Up Jack got and home did trot
> As fast as he could caper;
> And went to bed and covered his head
> In vinegar and brown paper.

6. Look at how Jesus managed participation in Matthew 17:25. Think carefully about Jesus' decision to seek Simon's opinion. Draw your own conclusions for teaching. Then, as a group, write and present a CNN newsflash summarizing Jesus' management of participation.

Motivation

In the previous lesson, I ask students to look at how Jesus managed motivation in Matthew 17:19. Think carefully about the disciples' question, "Why couldn't we drive it out?" Draw your own conclusions for teaching. Of course, this is the scene that finds Jesus returning from the Mount of Transfiguration. While away, his disciples failed to alleviate a child's suffering, which must have embarrassed them. Jesus expresses exasperation at both his disciples and the people in general.

In the discussion of motivation in the chapter on learning theories, I discuss the law of natural consequences. That is precisely what Jesus uses in this instance. The disciples' question exposes their problem. Note my emphasis, "Why couldn't *we* drive it out?" The power to deal with them does not reside in us. Ultimately any power the disciples exercised was derived from God and God alone. This lesson was designed to provoke their trust in him and not in themselves. In my opinion, Jesus was not only a master teacher; he was a master motivator.[14] Was Jesus not motivating his disciples when he

- said, "You give them something to eat" (Matthew 14)?
- slept while a storm raged around them (Mark 4)?
- probed them with questions about his identity (Luke 9)?
- washed their feet (John 13)?

I suggest he was constantly motivating as he called people back to a right relationship with God. Motivation was at the center of his work, John the Baptist's work, and every prophet's before them!

The work of the Holy Spirit originally empowered and even now replicates the motivating ministry of the Savior. The Spirit convicts, guides, convinces, fills, teaches, and empowers those who align themselves with him. How Christian teachers excuse themselves from the responsibility of motivating students baffles me. I fear we have drunk too deeply from an older university model and not deeply enough from the Bible's well of repentance and obedience. Everyone involved in researching education knows that motivation will surface as a major issue somewhere along the way.

---

[14] Jesus motivated but did not manipulate. Motivation causes us to do what we now believe is the right thing to do. Manipulation causes us to do what we do not want to do but must do or suffer grave consequences.

Managing in Online Education

With the exception of space, the very same variables exist in online education. Look briefly at how to adjust these for the virtual environment.

Atmosphere: While a cheerful introduction by the teacher can set the tone, conversations among the students requires more maintenance. I know one professor who "lurks" in the dialogues, commending appropriate comments to reinforce his expectations. As with verbal communication, written communication also has tone. We can and should choose our words carefully as we disagree without becoming disagreeable. Maintaining an appropriately respectful balance between encouraging one another and questioning one another's thinking may need a bit of grooming. Respectful disagreement means not calling someone's character into question and making sure ideas remain on the table for discussion without taking differences personally.

Time: With asynchronous courses, students log into the various pieces at their convenience. So the clock does not retain its unrelenting control of the class. A great deal of online education depends on the conversations. The course designer must make sure to allow for adequate time to digest material, construct a thoughtful response, read the responses of other class members, and post final comments or questions. Online courses do not by definition take less time. Rockbridge Seminary, a totally online seminary, offers eight-week courses.[15] Students must log in five days each week. Professors can see how long the student remained on site. Of course, students can mentally check out of online courses as easily as they do classroom-based courses.

Content: Adjusting content to the online environment requires thinking differently. Reading other student papers or responses expands the definition of content. The opportunity to reflect and ask questions in writing takes learning to a higher level. Reading a book in

---

[15] Accessed August 30, 2014, http://www.rockbridge.edu.

preparation for a test requires different mental exercises than reading, recording your thoughts, and interacting with others' comments as you move chapter by chapter.

Participation: Online education may have an advantage in this category. Without student participation, the online classroom reverts to no more than a correspondence course. The pressure to record thoughts in writing demands more from students. I personally think online education requires more interactive thinking from both teachers and students.

Motivation: Students who prosper in online education tend to be internally motivated. As with classroom-based instruction, maintaining their motivation becomes quite important. When students underestimate the workload demands, they often drop the course. If this happens too often, the course demands should be evaluated. Sometimes the hardware/software interfaces become too much of a barrier. Easy access to technical support becomes an essential ingredient.

Conclusion

I do not think the apostle Paul had the discussions of this chapter in his mind when he wrote, "Let everything be done decently and in order." I don't think he envisioned choir robes, electric guitars, or church bulletins either. I do think his words apply to all of us who seek to manage educational experiences. As Christian teachers, we represent an orderly God full of wonderful surprises. As we manage or neglect the various components discussed in this chapter, we reflect or detract from his character. Just as sheep scatter when shepherds go astray, so students become disillusioned with learning when those responsible for their experience neglect their duties. By God's grace, when students think of their experiences with us, may the words of the apostle Paul come to their mind.

This piece of the professor's puzzle has many moving parts. When they work together, they make the time in the real or virtual classroom both stimulating and educational.

EVALUATING SKILLS:
ASSESSING STUDENTS, COURSES,
AND PROFESSORS

"No one should study merely in order to pass an examination."
Karl Barth[1]

A s I sit to write this chapter, Dallas Seminary prepares for an accreditation site visit. Every aspect of the academic and administrative process will undergo quite a serious evaluation. From an academic point of view, the examiners will look at several things. First, they want to be sure that students accomplish what publications advertise. Second, they expect to see processes in place that measure institutional effectiveness. And third, they look carefully at what procedures ensure ongoing evaluation and improvement.

---

[1] Karl Barth, *Evangelical Theology: An Introduction*, trans. Grover Foley (New York: Holt, Rinehart, and Winston, 1963), 172.

The point is, no one escapes evaluation. Sometimes evaluations are designed well, and sometimes the results are used well—or not. This chapter examines the design and use of evaluation tools aimed at students. Chapter 4, on planning skills, included a section on evaluating courses. Chapter 8, on instructing skills, will include a section on evaluating teachers. When designed and used correctly, students, courses, and professors can benefit from evaluations.

Assessing Students

The most frequently used tool for assessing student achievement is testing. For years, on the morning my class was to discuss testing, they confronted a total change of environment. As they entered the room, a sign on the door asked for silence, while the slide on the screen presented these instructions:

> *Please take your seat; begin at once to fill out the puzzle*
> *with the descriptive terms used in class;*
> *do this individually without help from other classmates*
> *or reference to your notes.*
> *Do not talk or disturb others during this exercise.*
> *This pop quiz will conclude promptly at 8:10 a.m.*

They had a copy of the puzzle in their notes and had seen it multiple times. I show the puzzle every time we enter a new subject area as a reorientation to everything under consideration. It functions as a road map during the semester. Plus, the first day we discuss the entire puzzle at length. Now, a blank puzzle confronts them that looks like this:

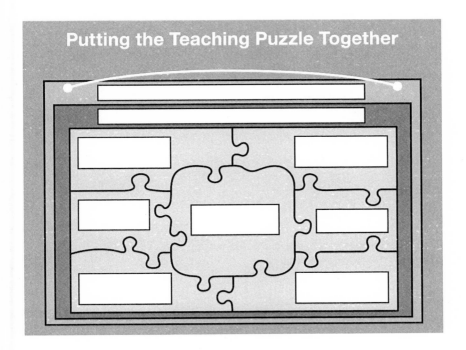

What makes this experience a bit more intense is my standing behind the podium (not my normal position in the room), staring smilelessly down at my notes—clearly avoiding eye contact (unlike my normal movement among the students, smiling and greeting them as they enter)—gesturing toward the slide should some brave soul venture a question as an attempt to clarify the instructions.

The students are generally stunned and confused. Some wonder whether I am angry with a classmate and taking it out on the class in general. (Would a Christian teacher ever do something like that?) Most students become exceedingly anxious in this experience. At least one says she has not forgiven me, although we have since become good friends. I suspect few will ever forget these mornings.

Actually, such mornings are quite difficult for me. I love students and can only hold a stoic noncaring face for a short period of time.

When my act breaks down, a huge sigh of relief breaks out in the class. Then I allow them to ventilate about the things they disliked. Their displeasure runs the typical spectrum of student complaints. Rarely does any student refer back to the syllabus, which says nothing about pop quizzes or a portion of their grade assigned to the quiz. They do as they are told and endure the experience because they know the arbitrary power resident in teachers. This provides an excellent opportunity to discuss what not to replicate in their teaching.

A forced-choice exercise follows the pop quiz. I ask students to group themselves in one of three spots in the room, according to their test preference. They must choose which kind of test they would prefer to take if they *had* to take a test. Students always respond they would rather not take any tests at all. "Had" is the operative word, so they choose between an oral exam, constructed response (essay) exam, or selected response (objective) exam. Invariably, students cluster around their "favorite." I have never had a class where one of the groups is not represented fairly well. I ask them to discuss among themselves why they prefer that kind of exam. Once they have had a moment or two, I ask each group to address the other two groups and explain their reasons. In the end, all of us come to a deeper appreciation of one another's perspective.

Each group believes the kind of test they chose gives them the best chance of demonstrating what they have learned. The point is clearly made as student groups listen to one another. Sometimes a student will object to another group's explanation, and I have to reinforce how important it is to listen carefully. Each group believes they are right. We then discuss transferring this object lesson into their role as teachers with students who have different preferences. Once the students have shared what they consider to be the advantages, they resume their seats, and I give a brief critique of each kind of test.

Oral exams have at least three disadvantages:

1. They tend to demand recall of isolated fragments. Often referred to as oral comprehensives, in reality they mainly look at portions selected by various judges. The selection is often arbitrary, and satisfactory answers are always in the subjective opinion of the examiners.

2. When the judges are not allowed to immediately confer, agreement among judges about scoring is low. Scores tend to converge only after judges discuss their responses.

3. Students are not the only ones who get weary during oral exams. Exam standards tend to soften as the hour, day, or days wear on. Examiners may also be distracted by personal agendas other than the exam and not be listening carefully.

But students who prefer this kind of an exam like the idea of physical presence, where they can ask for clarification and watch body language to see whether their answer is proceeding in a good direction.

Essay exams also have several limitations:

1. While they are easy to construct, they are difficult to evaluate except for the very good and very bad. Grade differentiation between a C+ and a B- is almost impossible without a highly defined and consistently applied grading rubric.

2. As with the oral exam, examiner congruence can be inconsistent, especially for the intermediate grades. Students complain about multiple graders for a single course varying greatly in their marks.

3. In reality, the essay exam needs to be scored by someone thoroughly familiar with the material. In my opinion, student graders who simply did well previously in the course do not qualify. Plus, students pick up on emphases (intentional or not) by the professor and try to include them in their answers. This is smart student behavior unrewarded by student graders.

4. Inadequate time for writing or penmanship can influence the grade significantly.[2] Inadequate time to evaluate or the time of day when evaluating can also influence the grade unintentionally. Only the very disciplined can avoid getting tired of reading the same thing over and over again.

5. Essay exams are notorious for having problems with reliability (does it measure accurately?), discreteness (does it measure without bias, i.e., penmanship, etc.?), efficiency (does it measure completely?), and congruence (does it measure consistently?).

But those students who prefer this kind of test like the idea of writing around an answer. Even if they do not know the precise answer, they hope to demonstrate they learned something. Even if they don't answer exactly what the professor asked, they gamble on getting partial credit. They also like the idea of having time to think about their answers as opposed to those who must answer directly and orally.

Objective tests also have limitations:

1. In spite of common practice, good test items are difficult to write well. Some researchers suggest only five to fifteen quality items can be written per eight-hour day.

2. Objective tests struggle to achieve a balanced evaluation between knowledge, understanding, and application. They tend to do rather well at evaluating knowledge with increasing difficulty in evaluating understanding and application.

But those students who prefer this kind of test stress how they like the concrete nature of the information base and find comfort in knowing

---

[2] My final exam in Church History consisted of two essay questions: (1) Trace church history from Acts 2 to the Middle Ages. (2) Trace church history from the Middle Ages to the present. There was a two-hour time limit and one blue book to write in.

that even when they don't know the answer, they might guess the correct answer.

If there is one fundamental assumption lurking in the back of a teacher's thinking, it might be, *Because I have taken so many tests, I know how to give one.* More harm has been inflicted on unsuspecting students through that one assumption than any other assumption I know in academics. Teachers also tend to administer tests based on personal preferences without considering student preferences. Although an enormous amount of accurate and helpful research has been done on testing, many teachers have never seen it or, worse, have consciously ignored it. But testing still occupies the position of Queen Mother in academics, so we must examine her in more detail.

Testing: Basic Test Design

Two basic questions drive test design, and each question has two basic answers. Question 1 asks, "What is the test measuring (or trying to measure)?" The two possible answers are (1) Achievement (summative evaluation) or (2) Progress (formative evaluation). If the test intends to measure achievement, then some predetermined standard must be established and published. A driving test provides a good example with both written and performance elements. Can you parallel park? Do you know the meaning of light signals? (Yellow does not mean speed up—except in Dallas!) If you successfully complete both parts, you pass the test and get a driver's license. The test does not measure or predict whether you will be a safe or courteous driver. It does measure whether you know certain key facts and whether you can start, maneuver, and park a car. Teachers and students need to know what a test is supposed to measure as well as what it does not measure.

If the answer to the question, "What is the test measuring?" is "Progress," then the test must measure how far the student has come since beginning the course of instruction. This kind of test seeks to understand whether and to what degree the course of instruction plus student effort has contributed to the student's development. The test presupposes a clear basis for the student's knowledge or ability at the beginning. Sometimes a pretest is used to create such a benchmark, or (and less reliably) receiving a passing grade from a previous course establishes the basis. The passing grade may or may not measure a student's long-term memory and ability to use the information from the prior course or guarantee a level of proficiency with the material.

Dallas Seminary attempts to measure student progress by administering the Test of Biblical and Theological Knowledge (TBTK) to entering students and graduating students. Without trying to defend the test itself, the goal of the test is worthy. The seminary wants to know whether students have improved during their studies of core Bible and theology courses. Interestingly enough, the test is not attached to any grade, nor is a "passing" grade required for graduation.

In order for any test to be a meaningful measure of student learning, it must have both validity and reliability. When test designers speak of validity, they want to discover whether the test actually measures what it is intended to measure or whether it inadvertently measures things it was not supposed to measure. For example, does the test measure what students know, or does it measure how quickly they can recall what they know? When designers speak of reliability, they want to know that the test measures the same thing consistently over time. For example, the scores on essay exams may be unreliable unless the grader(s) consistently uses a clearly defined grading rubric. The test itself may be unreliable if the students do not know the rubric ahead of time.

Major question 2 is "What are you measuring against?" Once again, the answer has two possibilities. The first possibility is what is called "norm referenced" testing. This test measures students against other students. This works reasonably well with standardized tests like ACT, SAT, or TOEFL. Individual test results are scored against thousands of

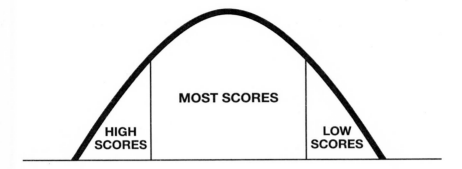

other scores. When plotted on a graph, these scores tend to form a bell curve with a small percentage of high scores and low scores at either end. The majority of scores will be somewhere in between. Norm referenced testing works best when an individual test can be compared with a large data base of scores.

Sometimes norm referenced testing is misapplied to small groups of students. My intermediate accounting professor (a recent Harvard PhD) gave a midterm exam. The highest score was a 57, awarded to my friend with a photographic memory who never received anything other than an *A* in his entire life. So, the professor "curved" the grades enough that a 57 was an *A*. In essence, he designed a lousy test and failed to teach us the concepts he expected us to know. But rather than admit he had created a terrible test (he probably never had a course on test design), he graciously agreed to curve the grades.

Another misapplication occurs when the bell curve is used to pre-determine grades. When a professor tells a class of thirty that only two will have the opportunity to get an *A*, he has misapplied the bell curve. The announcement comes even though he does not know the students, has not yet given any instruction, and has not yet administered any tests at all! This throws students into a competitive model of education that often becomes counterproductive by shifting the focus from learning to grading. I have been told that the grades I assign to every course ought to reflect a basic bell curve even though I never use any kind of standardized test. When I hear something like this, I know the speaker has not read any research on testing.

The second answer to the question "What are you measuring against?" is "criterion referenced" testing. In short, the student is tested against a predetermined set of information. Students must score at a high percentage in order to pass. For example, if the standard is 80 percent, then all the passing scores will be scattered between 80 percent and 100 percent. This style of testing moves students more toward proficiency and mastery. It does not account for long-term memory, which depends on repeated use of the material. And, the percentile considered passing is arbitrary and depends upon the critical nature of content mastery. No one wants to fly with a pilot who scored 80 percent on "landing planes" or an eye surgeon who cannot remember the names of the parts he is cutting out!

In summary, basic test design answers two questions, and each question has two answers:

Question 1: What are you measuring?
    Answer 1: Achievement
    Answer 2: Progress
    (Is the measure accurate [valid] and consistent [reliable]?)

Question 2: What are you measuring against?
    Answer 1: Norm referenced measurements
    Answer 2: Criterion referenced measurements

Each and every time you administer a test, you need to have very specific answers to these questions. The answers may also help you select the kind of test best suited as a measuring device. Most often, I suspect you will decide to measure achievement against a set of criterion with either a selected response (objective) test or a constructed response (essay) test. At this point it is good to remember that your test should be connected back to one or more of the stated objectives for the course.

Those objectives reflect some level of Bloom's taxonomy. For review purposes, that taxonomy is reproduced here:

1. Knowledge—requires only basic recall of information
2. Comprehension—indicates an understanding of the information
3. Application—demonstrates an ability to use the information
4. Analysis—expresses ability to break information down into essential pieces or examine underlying assumptions
5. Synthesis—reflects skill in assembling information into meaningful combinations
6. Evaluation—exhibits skill in discerning the value of various pieces of information

Depending on the course objectives, the exam should seek to measure whether students can function at one or more of these levels. Generally speaking, objective tests work relatively well at the knowledge or comprehension level. But if you wish to examine students at what we generally refer to as higher-order thinking, then an essay or some modification of it would better serve you and your students.

One way to help guide test design is to create a table of specifications. Some years ago, my course on teaching in higher education had a fifteen-week schedule. I created a sample table of specifications for that class to show how a final exam might be distributed across Bloom's taxonomy and the fifteen weeks of instruction. That table appears on page 168. Across the top of the table, the subject for the week is represented. Down the left-hand side of the table are the various levels in Bloom's taxonomy. The numbers at the bottom represent each week. The numbers throughout the table represent the points awarded to questions related to that material. Although I did not give a test over the whole course, I showed students how to make sure to spread questions out through the material and through the domains.[3] Notice how the questions tend to

---

[3] Dr. Kenn Gangel was the first one I ever saw use something like this. I adapted his model.

Table of Specifications

	Teaching Puzzle	Philosophy	Integration	Learning Theories	Cooperative Learning	Cognitive Domain	Affective Domain	Course Objectives	Course Assignments	Method Selection	Testing	Grading	Lecture Design	Improving Questions	Institutional Realities
Knowledge	5	5			5		5	5					5		
Comprehension		5	5	5				5			5	5	5		
Application										5					
Analysis				5		5							5		
Synthesis			5												5
Evaluation															5
	1	**2**	**3**	**4**	**5**	**6**	**7**	**8**	**9**	**10**	**11**	**12**	**13**	**14**	**15**

cluster around knowledge and comprehension. This represents a table for an objective test. If I really wanted a more even spread, I could create a combination essay/objective test. The key would be to create short enough essay questions to be answered in the time allotted.

Because this is only a brief chapter on testing and not a comprehensive text, I will make a limited number of key suggestions about constructing the various kinds of tests. Many excellent texts as well as innumerable websites provide precise guidelines for test construction.[4] By all means, start early in test construction, consult a good text or website (many constructed by universities), and work carefully on behalf

---

[4] Tom Kubiszyn and Gary Borich, *Educational Testing and Measurement: Classroom Application and Practice* (New York: John Wiley & Sons, 1999). The following site offers a tutorial on constructing various types of tests: "Test Writing Tutorial," https://sites.google.com/site/testwritingtutorial/multiple-choice-questions.

of the students. This is particularly important until the most significant rules are firmly entrenched in your thinking. Your motivation for thinking carefully about each test item will be much higher with an actual test in mind. I have benefitted greatly by reading really good sample test questions even if they are not in my field. Good questions stimulate better thinking on my part. Even though I do not administer tests, I need to understand how they work in order to provide accurate guidance for those who do use them. I hope you use additional resources, but in case you never pick up another text on teaching or evaluating, here are some of the most important things to remember when you create one of these tests.

True-False Tests

- ✓ Be sure the statement is absolutely true or false.
- ✓ Avoid specific determiners like "always" or "never."
- ✓ State the item positively and avoid negative statements.
- ✓ Include a larger number of false items.
- ✓ Provide a required explanation of their choice with partial credit for a wrong answer with a strong rationale.[5]

Matching[6]

- ✓ Make the directions clear and complete.
- ✓ Provide a longer list of alternative items than stimulus items.
- ✓ Provide marking spaces to the left of the stimulus items.

---

[5] For reasons I cannot explain, my mind always went to the one extremely unlikely but possible exception that caused the statement to appear false to me. Maybe you will have someone like that in your class. This will help you find them.

[6] Stimulus items appear on the left and are matched with alternative items on the right called distracters.

✓ Be sure the entire list appears on one page.

✓ Ten stimulus items work best with no more than fifteen maximum.

✓ Stimulus items should appear in alphabetical, chronological, or logical order.

Multiple Choice[7]

✓ Present the problem (stem) in a straightforward unambiguous form.

✓ The stem should include a verb and as much material as possible.

✓ The stem should be stated positively rather than negatively.

✓ Write one correct or clearly best answer and three or four distracters.

✓ Keep numerical alternatives (distracters) in logical order.

✓ Avoid grammatical, length, or specific determiner clues.

✓ Avoid the use of "all" or "none of these."

✓ Avoid redundant phrases in the distracter items.

✓ Provide a required explanation of their choice with partial credit for a wrong answer with a strong rationale.

Short Answer

✓ Form the question as precisely as possible.

✓ Prepare answer keys for each question.

✓ Provide guidelines for responding or scoring (i.e., one word, phrase, or sentence)

✓ The question should have only one right answer.

---

[7] The stem in a multiple choice item is always the opening statement.

✓ If in the form of a statement, delete the *key* word.

✓ Avoid lifting statements directly from the textbook.

Essay

✓ Several short essays are preferred over one long essay.

✓ All students must answer the same questions.

✓ Use Bloom's taxonomy to provide words like "compare," "contrast," "utilize," etc., to frame the question.

✓ Be sure the question relates specifically to one or more of the course objectives.

Ultimately, tests should inform both students and teachers about genuine levels of achievement. In the past, tests were used to force students to give attention to the subject. The negative motivation came through loud and clear. "Will this be on the test?" echoes through academic classrooms to this day. The test then becomes the benchmark for students' interest in the substance of a course. If something does not appear on the test, it is not worthy of students' time or interest. We now know that fear is not the best motivator for learning. There are ways to both reduce fear and increase learning. Three of the most common ways are to modify the test itself, stimulate better preparation, and utilize group testing options.

Modifying Tests

• Modify time requirements by allowing more time to take the test. Unless a professor is measuring speed, there is no need to rush students.

• Decrease the percentage of the grade affected by testing. Combine testing with other opportunities for students to demonstrate their learning.

• Provide copies of old test questions so students get some preview.

- Have students submit test questions, and guarantee one will be on the test.
- Create multiple attempts, as in testing for CPAs, attorneys, physicians, airline pilots, etc. This would be difficult to administer unless a large database of questions is available from which to draw a second test.
- Give partial credit for completing the instructional feature of the course and withhold final credit until a proficiency requirement is met.[8] This would allow students to be tested on their best day and avoid students taking multiple major exams on the same day. This would also provide real base standards for subjects with multiple levels of instruction.

Stimulating Preparation and Review

- Promote the use of study sheets.[9]
  — Developing a study sheet is an exercise in higher-order synthetic thinking.
  — Grade the study sheets, and count them for one-third of the test grades.
  — Allow one-third of the test to be taken with study sheets.
  — Grade the test without specifying which questions were missed and regrade after a rework using the study sheet.
- Give credit for group study, remembering that oral processing and group reinforcement enhance learning.
- Grade study sheets a week before the exam to provide time to upgrade the study sheet.

---

[8] For example, every student gets a *C* for completing the instructional portion but can only achieve a *B* or an *A* after completing the proficiency requirement.

[9] The development of study sheets and reworking of tests promotes "time on task," which is a valid learning theory.

- Score tests given during the semester in such a way that a high average exempts from the final test.

Group Testing Options

You may need a brief rationale for my thinking as this tends to run counterintuitive to so much of what we have been taught or experienced. "DO YOUR OWN WORK!" still rings in my ears. However, Christian academic institutions always tout "community" as a major component in education. I suggest that physical proximity does not necessarily translate into community. Few, if any, academic structures promote community. So, proximity has become a synonym for community. In fact, the pervasive nature of competitive grading promotes one of the highest forms of individualism. Whatever else students do at the fringes of academics matters little unless grades and community mix together. At this point, the "one another" Scripture passages ought to be shouting at us. Where does the Christian academy encourage students to embrace a genuine concern for others? Unless that encouragement finds itself securely attached to tests and grades, it will always remain a footnote to students and faculty alike. Cooperative learning through cooperative test taking provides an outstanding opportunity to promote community. I am embarrassed to admit that if you really want research in cooperative learning, you will need to look outside the Christian community. Consider some of the following options to promote both community and learning.

- Calculate each individual's score and give bonus points if the whole group performs above a predetermined level.
- Calculate each individual's final grade by adding the test score to the group average test grade. You will need to decide what percentage to award each part.

- Calculate each individual's final grade by the combined scores of all the members. If a group has four members, each would contribute 25 percent to the final score. Everyone receives the same grade in this scenario.
- Allow the group to take one exam and receive the same score.
- Allow each member of the group to take the exam separately, but grade only one of the group's exams randomly selected.
- Award two grades. The first grade is the actual test score awarded to the individual. The second score is a collaborative skills grade scored by members of the group based upon each individual's perceived contribution to the preparation process.

One benefit of rewarding cooperative effort in testing is for the stronger to help the weaker—a clearly Christian value. This also demonstrates care for what students consider to be the center of academics, namely grades. In addition, "There is considerable research demonstrating that cooperative learning produces higher achievement, more positive relationships among students, and healthier psychological adjustment than do competitive or individualistic experiences."[10]

While testing's main purpose is evaluating student achievement, it can also serve to evaluate teaching. If most of my students do poorly on something I supposedly taught, I automatically review and attempt to upgrade that portion of my course. Student performance does reflect on the teacher to some degree.

I was told my commencement address at a Korean seminary would not be necessary because the entire graduating class had failed their theology final and the required course for graduation. The academic dean taught the required theology course. Fortunately, the president and founder of the seminary was a pastor of immense diplomatic skill.

---

[10] David W. Johnson, Roger T. Johnson, and Karl A. Smith, *Active Learning: Cooperation in the College Classroom* (Edina, MN: Interaction, 1991), 1:25.

He called a meeting of the senior class and asked what had happened. The students reported that the dean had tested them over material he had not taught, nor was it in the textbook. The president's conversation with the dean went something like this:

President: "I understand the entire senior class failed your exam."

Dean: "Yes, that is true."

President: "Help me understand how that happened. You had them under your instruction for the whole semester?"

Dean: "Yes, I did."

President: "As academic dean, you are supposed to be the best teacher we have. How is it possible that they learn from you all semester but cannot pass the exam?"

Dean: "I don't know."

President: "If they had another chance, do you think it is possible they might pass a test over the material you taught them?"

Dean: "We can try and see."

Notice the president never directly confronted the dean. Losing face in an Asian culture is unacceptable. All the students passed the next exam, and my commencement message was . . . well, we are not evaluating that here are we?

Performance Evaluations

In addition to the more common forms of testing, sometimes we need to evaluate how well students can perform a particular task. Typing speed and accuracy is one such test. But sometimes, the task requires combining a complex set of skills such as those required in oral communication. In my introductory course on teaching, students are required to present a lesson suitable for a Sunday school class.[11] For many of them, this is their first time to offer instruction in front of anyone. Evaluating their work must be conducted carefully. Should they be measured against the standard of a seasoned professional or a beginner? In either case, how would you create a numerical value for such an evaluation? The evaluation design ought to specify where and how to improve.

The students get a copy of the evaluation form attached to their syllabus. From the beginning they know how their teaching effort will be scored. The categories and point scale are subjective and arbitrary but known ahead of time. The goal of the entire process is to motivate them to become better teachers. If the evaluation is too harsh, they may become discouraged and believe good teaching is unachievable for them. If the evaluation is unrealistically affirming, then they may feel no need to improve. I want them to believe that no matter how good they think they are or how long they have been teaching, they can always improve. Of course I expect them to become more knowledgeable about their subjects, but I want them to constantly improve in the teaching craft. That drive separates the average teacher from the master teachers.

On the facing page is a copy of the evaluation form I use. While students teach their classmates, I sit in the back with a copy of their lesson plans, writing down my observations as the class proceeds. Look over the form, and then consider the comments that follow.

---

[11] Almost every semester I have students who want to teach a class on "How not to Teach." The problem is, we all know what not to do. We have been exposed to way too much of that. I feel a huge amount of pressure to model all of the things I believe make up good teaching. Master teachers weave their methods seamlessly through their material. They become invisible to the students. I often stop and ask students to evaluate what they just experienced because they did not see why or how something worked.

EVALUATION FORM FOR TEACHING SESSIONS

	Maximum Points	Points Given
1. The Lesson Plan was submitted on time	5	_____
2. The lesson aim was clear	40	_____
3. The lesson stayed within the allotted time	5	_____
4. The lesson showed creativity & originality	5	_____
5. The lesson flowed smoothly with clear transitions linking the lesson together	5	_____
6. The lesson material was presented understandably	5	_____
7. The audio visuals were used correctly	5	_____
8. The lesson was insightful	5	_____
9. The teacher was enthusiastic	5	_____
10. The room arrangement was appropriate	5	_____
11. Each section of the lesson contributed clearly to the achievement of the lesson aim	5	_____
12. The lesson reflected the teaching of the passage accurately	5	_____
13. The lesson explained the passage or doctrine adequately	5	_____
Total	100	_____

Comments: _____

_____

_____

After the students finish their lessons, the class spends a few minutes debriefing using two basic categories for evaluation: things I really liked, and things I think might be improved. We always start with the positives because the student teachers invariably did some things right. Then we seek to help them improve. I always let the student teachers comment first on things they would improve. Everybody I know who seriously reflects on their teaching can think of things to improve the next time. Any strong concerns I might have wait for a later face-to-face interview.

If I give less than full credit, I always write in exactly what my concern centered around. Numbers 1, 2, and 10 relate to preparation. Obviously the lesson aim is heavily weighted because we spend a great deal of course time working on that. In my opinion, a strong lesson aim goes a long way toward establishing a solid lesson. You will notice that the only actual classroom presence item deals with enthusiasm. Were I to have another course, I would deal much more with the verbal and physical animation of a lesson. Although they might weight them differently, the students have a critique sheet for self-evaluation of their future lessons.

Evaluating Other Representations of Student Work

Term papers may be the second most popular form of student work to be evaluated. Term papers function almost exactly like essay exams with the exception of the time limit. They have similar limitations. Some suggest reading papers without reading names because all teachers gravitate to certain students without intending to favor one student over another. Grading rubrics also help make evaluations more even. Here is one I have used (the numbers across the top represent the number of papers submitted in a semester):

GRADING RUBRIC	1	2	3	4	5	Possible Points
Spelling						10
Punctuation						10
Clarity						20
Word Economy						20
Thoughtful						20
Researched						20
Total						100

- *Spelling and punctuation* do matter. In this scheme they only account for 20 percent. My business letter writing teacher awarded an *F* if even one of either appeared. We affectionately named her "Bloody Mary!" Teachers can vary the number and kind of items along with their weight. The weight given to each item depends on the grade level of the students and the nature of the course. I warn doctoral students that more than three spelling or grammatical errors causes me to stop reading and return their dissertation drafts. Dirty copy is unacceptable—even if it is a first draft.

- *Clarity* looks at the logic and flow of the paper. Does the writing make good sense? Does it read easily? As students move toward doctoral work, this becomes more critical. Doctoral candidates must not only do clean research; they must also write it up in a readable manner. Both are essential.

- *Word Economy* alerts students that I am not interested in "filler." I always worry a little when students ask for exact page limits. Everyone knows how to turn a five-page paper into a ten-page paper. I understand their concern and try to help them understand that more is not better; it is only more. When pressed, I sometimes set an outside limit.

- *Thoughtful* asks the student to engage the material with personal evaluative comments. I am trying to avoid a paper that essentially strings quotes together.

- *Researched* means what it says. I am not interested only in their opinion but their consideration of helpful thinking on the matter. I am always a bit surprised when a graduate student turns in a paper discussing the meaning and application of a Bible passage without having cited even one commentary.

Projects allow students to take more responsibility for their learning. Because projects tend to vary, specific guidelines and expectations will save countless questions by the students. Even then we may not get what we hope for. Not everything I have designed to engage student learning has worked. Semester after semester I failed to get graduate students to create a good test for my course. Yes, I gave them careful instructions along with handouts. I never received any more than pitiful recall questions about my outlines. I finally gave up and eliminated the project from the course. In retrospect, I could not weigh the project heavily enough for students to invest precious time learning how to construct a decent test. I suspect the imprint of poor tests may have also contributed to the demise of this project. Always use the product you receive to evaluate and improve your guidelines and expectations. In this case, I replaced this project with more emphasis on syllabus design and weighed it heavily enough to get the product I wanted.

Journals offer students an opportunity to reflect on what they are reading, hearing, or experiencing in the course. Not all course material lends itself to reflective thinking. When appropriate, reflecting can take learning to a much deeper level. At various times, I have asked students to reflect on the class lectures, other students' comments, or their reading. I do warn them not to reproduce my notes because I already have a copy, nor do I want to know what the author of a chapter says. I read the book. I still have students who must rework their journals. In one course I have them submit the journal several times to make sure they are truly interacting with the material. Emphasizing other students' comments often engages them more intently in those question-and-answer times. In each case I am actively pursuing their thoughts about these events. Students often report that reading my comments on their journals feels like sitting over a cup of coffee. I think I get as close to a personal conversation in these without them having to make an appointment.

Reading remains the bread and butter of education. Evaluation tools can vary widely. Of course testing remains one option. Book reports, critiques, and chapter summaries are valid alternatives. In one course, I ask students to list the ten most important things they learned from the text and a rationale for their choices. Of course, one of my least favorite students complained to the dean that my assignment was not academically rigorous. In fairness the assignment was not designed to measure "academic rigor," whatever that means. I did happily volunteer to create an academically rigorous exam for him if that would make him feel better. If it is critical that students read material before a class, have students write down at the beginning of class the three things that stood out in their memory of the chapter. Include it as part of their class participation grade.

Assigning Grades

Tests have served so long as a basis for assigning grades that we assume there is an organic connection. There is no organic connection. We like them because they render immediate numerical values, and Americans have an inordinate fascination with numbers. I have often wondered what an *A-* in Church History really means. No one can tell from that grade how many dates I can remember or whether I know the contributions of the most significant figures. But in case you are confused, my school translates letter grades into numerical scores. Therefore, my *A-* is worth exactly somewhere between 94 and 95 somethings. Or, it more likely means that at one time my work for the course was a little more valuable than someone awarded a *B+* and a little less than someone awarded an *A*. Almost everyone agrees that evaluating student work is easy, but assigning grades is my least favorite task.

Some years ago, the magazine *Time* reported on a popular Notre Dame English professor. He apparently attacked every assignment with a vigorous red pen but awarded an *A* to every paper. His electives were packed with students who learned how to write better from his merciless critique of their papers (but not their character). His dean complained one semester that he had awarded more *A*s than he had students. He suggested that the dean might know some needy students who could use them. I love that story!

Grades become a more critical issue when students apply for scholarships, grants, or the next academic program. GPA does matter in those cases. My application for the PhD program at Oklahoma University was summarily turned down over .05 of a point. I did not think I had been so careless as to overlook an obvious benchmark or miscalculate my GPA. I surprised the supervising graduate school dean by finding a discrepancy between the general catalog and the graduate school catalog. This created a clear legal problem for the school. I was admitted and the rest is history. Students are rightfully concerned when so much can rest on so little.

I have never been a real fan of European education, but a few years ago a friend of mine asked me to review the new European Union standards for accreditation. His school would need to come under their rules, and he could not understand their documents. He had been trained academically but not educationally. As I reviewed their documents, I was pleasantly surprised and even became mildly enthusiastic. According to the new standards, everything required of students must be given a value.[12] I believe they are headed in the right direction as they try to account for each and every requirement associated with the academic experience. This would press schools that require things like chapel or student appointments but give no academic credit for such experiences.

I also think that system fits nicely into the microexperience of a single course. We ought to be challenging students at every level but providing multiple devices to demonstrate their learning and assigning grades. In addition to grades, we must also alert students to deficiencies that will haunt them later on if not corrected. Here are a few alternatives to simple test scores representing the final grade.

---

[12] European Evangelical Accrediting Association, accessed August 31, 2014, http://eeaa.eu; see p. 3.2.4 in their *EEAA Manual*, 2006 ed.

- Accumulated scores: Here points are awarded for various required items based on both completion and quality. Just because a student completes an item does not mean he receives full credit. However, this does allow students a little more control of their final grades by monitoring their point accumulation as they move through the semester or deciding which assignments to tackle or leave alone.
- Menu scores: Here points are awarded from a menu of items. The menu can include choices from a variety of levels. The student must choose an entree (major paper or project), several vegetables (minor assignments), and a dessert (something fun). Again, scores on these may vary depending on quality.
- Contract grades: Here the student and the professor enter into an agreement about a final grade for work tendered. Once again, a quality standard must be met before the final grade can be awarded. Guiding a student through the construction of such a process requires answering five questions:

  1. What do I plan to learn?
  2. How do I plan to learn it?
  3. When will I finish learning it?
  4. How will I know I have finished learning it?
  5. How will I prove I have learned it?

I actually love these because the process requires students to take serious ownership of their own learning. I am always hopeful that this will launch them on their lifelong learning journey.

Evaluating in Online Education

Online education offers all the standard tools for evaluation. Projects, papers, journals, and even tests remain options. Rockbridge Seminary explains how their tests are monitored:

"In selected master's program courses, students are required to take a final exam using an online proctoring service that requires the student to use a computer with a web cam and microphone. Students schedule the proctored exam session and pay a modest proctoring fee directly with the proctoring service."[13] When the standard tools receive appropriate planning, they work as well in the online environment as they do in classroom settings.

The introduction of written student interactions offers a huge bonus in the online environment. While teachers often think they get great discussion in their classrooms, I have charted who speaks to whom in the classroom. Those charts reveal classroom verbalizers tend to dominate the discussions. More timid class members remain passive listeners. Those who dominate also tend to talk back and forth with the professor rather than with other students. The professor often feels like everyone participates because he constantly interacts. Online discussions offer the advantage of pulling even the most timid member into the conversation. I never get a real sense of a student's development until I "hear" him in a more casual encounter than a term paper. Evaluating student conversations gives me a better picture of how deeply or superficially students deal with the subject. Sometimes students give me unintended but extremely helpful insights.

Conclusion

On the opening page of this chapter, you have been reminded of Karl Barth's basic attitude toward testing. Although evangelicals have disdained his overall approach to theology, I am sympathetic toward his view of testing. Here is the entire quote:

---

[13] Rockbridge Seminary, accessed May 4, 2015, http://www.rockbridge .edu/learning-approach/academic-guidelines.

No one should study merely in order to pass an examination, to become a pastor or in order to gain an academic degree. When properly understood, an examination is a friendly conversation of older students of theology with younger ones, concerning certain themes in which they share a common interest. The purpose of this conversation is to give younger participants an opportunity to exhibit whether and to what extent they have exerted themselves, and to what extent they appear to give promise of doing so in the future.[14]

Barth's subject area was theology. However, I honestly believe we could restate his comment to fit any subject area. If we took the liberty to do such a thing, it would read, "When properly understood, an examination is a friendly conversation of older students with younger ones, concerning certain themes in which they share a common interest. The purpose of this conversation is to give younger participants an opportunity to exhibit whether and to what extent they have exerted themselves, and to what extent they appear to give promise of doing so in the future." That attitude should pervade our evaluation of students.

For many students, tests and grades furnish their primary source of personal evaluation. Our culture has emphasized these while excluding any kind of character evaluation. Of course, character development and assessment should normally come through the home. But the home in American society is in trouble and way too often does not provide the proper emphasis on character first and grades second. The church too should offer character development and assessment. But, in my opinion, the church has not structured itself to perform this vital function on a broad scale. Lacking other perspectives, students place too much value on grades, which results in test anxiety. I constantly remind students that the grade in a course does not reflect on their character.

---

[14] Barth, *Evangelical Theology*, 172.

As Christian teachers, we bear a grave responsibility in our evaluation of students. We must assess their work in our subject areas. The evaluation ought to be candid and realistic. But great teachers use their power in evaluation to go way beyond information. Great teachers always believe their students can do even better without making them feel inferior. They instill confidence to accept even greater challenges and reach the full potential God intends for them. They view the test, project, or paper as only a tiny pause in a long exciting journey. Sometimes they must believe it for the students because the students have been conditioned to believe they are not up to the challenge.

In my opinion, we probably spend too much time polishing our information base so as not to appear unscholarly and too little time crafting evaluation tools that allow students the best opportunity to demonstrate their learning. This piece of the puzzle can be painful for students if not handled gently by teachers.

INSTRUCTING SKILLS:
USING APPROPRIATE VARIETY

"The mind cannot absorb what the seat cannot endure."
Howard G. Hendricks[1]

T he entire student body is praying for you." The student's words surprised me just before I entered my most intimidating assignment
ever. The dead serious student had alerted me earlier to an issue students wanted me to discuss with their faculty. Half a dozen highly
trained German scholars waited on the other side of the door. With the
student's comment buzzing in my head, I opened the door. Questions
such as "Who were these scholars?" "What was the issue?" "What does
this have to do with a chapter on instruction?" may come to mind.

These scholars all taught at an excellent German seminary. This
wonderful collection of Christian men excelled in the German system

---

[1] I heard Dr. Hendricks, my mentor, say this many times.

of education. Some in that room before me had multiple PhDs in rigorous disciplines. But, to my knowledge, though highly trained in their disciplines, none had even one formal course on teaching.

By sheer force of modeling, the German system teaches the lecture method as the only method. I sensed German professors approach the lecture with the same intimidating precision German engineers approach problems. Students told me how the professors read their lectures word for word from the opening prayer until the closing bell. Then, marking a tiny *x* in pencil, announced, "We will pick up right here next time." Students were expected to write down and remember everything for their comprehensive exams, which might come two or three years later.

So, what was the entire student body praying I would discuss with their faculty? They wanted me to ask their professors to provide Xerox copies of the notes so they could better prepare for the exams. I wondered to myself, *In the age of Xerox, why would you not provide notes or at least detailed outlines—especially if this is exactly the information they must reproduce on the exams?*

Now, I was born and raised in Texas, and I don't blink before I shoot. In spite of the imposing presence of these dignified German scholars, I waited for the appropriate moment in the workshop, looked them squarely in the eyes, and asked, "So, why don't you provide a copy of your notes for your students?" Those gentle Christian men sat absolutely quiet for what seemed like quite a long time. You cannot imagine how much energy you spend keeping yourself from speaking into a deafening silence. I waited. Finally, one asked, "If we did that, what would we do?"

I thought to myself, *What a great question!* I'll share my answer to them toward the end of this chapter.

No book about teaching is complete without a chapter on instruction and especially a section on the lecture method. Notice I am distinguishing between these terms as I did in the philosophy chapter. While instruction is essential, in my opinion the lecture remains only one of its many options. We explored many more in chapter 6 on managing skills. So, is the lecture method the worst method? No, the worst method is the one a teacher uses all the time or the one he does poorly. No method works automatically. Each method requires a bit of expertise to make it work educationally.

For example, the lecture method itself contains two ever-present dangers. On the one hand, a lecturer may be quite entertaining but non-educational. One Old Testament professor of mine was so funny no one wanted to miss his lectures. We all needed laughter's emotional release. However, note taking became an exercise in futility. He scattered bits, pieces, quips, quotes, and other unrelated data throughout the hour. No one really knew where they went. He forgot where he was in his material, and we could not help him because we did not know either. He fell off the little teacher's podium laughing at himself. The performance made "Saturday Night Live" look serious. This was laughter therapy at its best. But if we wanted to pass his test, we had better memorize his book. If the lectures had not been funny, they would have been a total waste of time. We could have just paid our money, memorized the book, passed his test, and moved on.

The other danger involves impressing students without educating them. One professor bragged about spending a whole semester discussing the first three verses of Isaiah. Now that is truly impressive, but if the purpose of the course was to discuss the whole book, he failed miserably. His students now know a whole lot about a little piece of Isaiah. I would have asked for a refund, but most students simply suffered the teacher's choices for better or worse. Jesus avoided this trap when he said, "I still have many things to tell you, but you can't bear them now" (John 16:12). If anyone ever had more to say about anything, it had to be Jesus. One day he will impress everyone, but until that day, I think his words ought to guide the preparation of every lecture.

I consider the lecture to be the most overused and least understood teaching method. By "overused" I mean used even when other methods would work better. By "least understood" I do not mean least researched. The sheer volume of research on the lecture method resembles a black hole. ERIC, the major educational database, lists more than twelve thousand articles mentioning "lecture" in one way or another. With this much research, why are so many lectures barely mediocre? Why are we not better?

The roads leading to a teaching post do not always pass through the education department. As with those professors in Germany, a person can get a PhD and a teaching post but never take a course on teaching. The underlying assumption is, "If you know it, you can teach it." But we all know that knowing something and teaching it represent two entirely different competency levels.

Faculty workshops or webinars provide a bit of on-the-job training. But, in higher education, they are easily ignored in favor of tenure's pressure to publish. In most of the schools with which I am familiar, a professor cannot get tenured with great student evaluations but weak publishing. On the other hand, he can get tenured with average to poor student evaluations if he publishes exceptionally well. Where that is the case, publishing becomes a survival tactic demanding hours of work in addition to the usually heavy teaching, grading, and committee workload. Professors have limited numbers of discretionary hours to improve their lectures, so that task keeps getting pushed to the end of a very long "to do" list.

The "publish or perish" crush is not so heavy at the secondary level of teaching. More emphasis is placed on teacher certification for those entering without an education background. The certification process covers many of the same concerns mentioned in this text. Even there, little focused attention is given to the lecture method per se. In Oklahoma, one of the fifteen teacher certification standards speaks to communication in the classroom. It reads, "(6) The teacher develops a knowledge of and uses a variety of effective communication techniques to foster active inquiry, collaboration, and supportive interaction in the classroom."[2] This is as close as their standards get to addressing measurable criterion for lectures. Yet, I suspect lecture hours still dominate the average high school student's classroom experience. Where would an uncertified teacher turn to improve her lecturing skills?

Even though the lack of discretionary time or incentives to improve siphon off our motivation, I believe there is a more powerful reason why we don't get better. Us, you, me! Lecturing looks much like a golf swing with lots of moving parts, and they all belong to me. If I hit a bad shot and look around for someone to blame, well, you know the answer. And if I want to improve, I wonder which part to fix first and how many practice hours it will take—but the difference is motivation. Motivation drives me to pay an instructor and squeeze in the practice hours. Lectures have at least as many moving parts, and the question about motivation remains to be answered by you.

If lecturing lies in your future and occupies a substantial part of your teaching philosophy, you owe it to your Lord and your students to be as good as possible. Anybody can get better at speaking, and the remainder of this chapter is dedicated to helping you do exactly that. Improvement means working on one small thing at a time. In my (always humble) opinion, you have a better chance of permanently improving your lecture than permanently improving your golf swing.

When students voice their opinions about lectures, their responses cluster around two large concerns: clarity of presentation and quality of relationships.[3] When these two things consistently come together in

---

[2] "Full (Subject Matter) Competencies for Licensure and Certification," accessed September 1, 2014, http://ok.gov/sde/sites/ok.gov.sde/files/documents/files/Competencies.pdf.

[3] Brent A. Vulcano, "Extending the Generality of the Qualities and Behaviors Constituting Effective Teaching," *Teaching of Psychology* 34, no. 2 (2007).

a course, teaching moves beyond information dispensing toward genuine education. We actually know how to break lecturing down into manageable pieces subject to analysis and improvement.

Clarity of Presentation

Good lectures need clear structure and careful delivery. Either one makes a good lecture; both combined make a great lecture. But, the best lectures receive an occasional finely tuned enriched feature. One small chapter cannot possibly cover the vast amount of research on these areas. So, I selected things that you can improve with a reasonable amount of effort. You cannot do everything, you must do something, and you can improve if you work on one at a time. In order for you not to get lost, the following chart provides a clear road map for this section. The order of the items is also the order I believe you should follow in your improvement efforts.

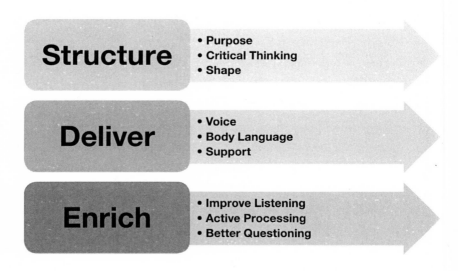

Structure
- Purpose
- Critical Thinking
- Shape

Deliver
- Voice
- Body Language
- Support

Enrich
- Improve Listening
- Active Processing
- Better Questioning

Structure

As with the syllabus, each and every lecture deserves a well-defined *purpose*. The apostle John and the physician Luke both revealed the purpose for their writings (e.g., John 20:30–31; Luke 1:1–4). We know each one selected material from the life and ministry of Jesus. While John intended to persuade his readers, Luke intended to reassure Theophilus. The only purpose for most of the lectures I heard was "more information!" "If a little information was good, more was better, and too much was just right," to quote Howard Hendricks.

If through a semester lectures vary in purpose, students sense the change of pace. If variety spices up life, it also spices the lectures of life. Here are only some of many possibilities for a clear purpose:

- *Motivate:* This is particularly important when the material must be mastered through practice outside of class.[4]
- *Challenge:* This comes in handy when students come with preconceived notions that need to be examined more carefully.
- *Question:* This is helpful when students hold certainties that may contain more ambiguities.
- *Clarify:* This is helpful when the material tends to be complicated.
- *Elaborate:* This is helpful when the material is so significant that it needs to be emphasized.[5]
- *Prove:* This is helpful when students need to accumulate information about why something is true.
- *Compare:* This is helpful when showing similarities between what students know and what they need to learn.
- *Contrast:* This is helpful when students need to distinguish between points of view.

---

[4] Motivational speakers get paid lots of money to motivate workers.

[5] Students often cannot distinguish between that which is significant and that which is trivial. Teachers really help students when they elaborate only on the significant features of the material they present.

The Christian message is not presented to us simply as facts to be intellectually assimilated. The New Testament calls for action, decisions, and changes. Those writers used each of the previous purposes. Look at the list once again, but this time look at the New Testament examples.

- *Motivation:* "Therefore, brothers, by the mercies of God, I urge you to present your bodies as a living sacrifice, holy and pleasing to God; this is your spiritual worship" (Rom 12:1).
- *Challenge:* "You have heard that it was said to our ancestors . . . but I tell you" (Matt 5:21).
- *Question:* "What do you think, Simon? Who do earthly kings collect tariffs or taxes from? From their sons or from strangers?" (Matt 17:25).
- *Clarify:* 1 "We do not want you to be uninformed, brothers, concerning those who are asleep" (1 Thess 4:13).
- *Elaborate:* "For I passed on to you as most important what I also received: that Christ died for our sins according to the Scriptures" (1 Cor 15:3).
- *Prove:* "After He had suffered, He also presented Himself alive to them by many convincing proofs, appearing to them during 40 days and speaking about the kingdom of God" (Acts 1:3).
- *Compare:* "To what should I compare this generation? It's like children sitting in the marketplaces who call out to each other" (Matt 11:16).
- *Contrast:* "This is the bread that came down from heaven; it is not like the manna your fathers ate—and they died. The one who eats this bread will live forever"(John 6:58).

Lectures should also utilize the guidelines for critical thinking.[6] One really helpful source to critical thinking has produced practical

---

[6] The Critical Thinking Community, accessed September 1, 2014, http://www.criticalthinking.org.

tools to teach and improve this area. I am particularly fond of the Critical Thinking Community's "Miniature Guide" series, as students (and myself) are able to get a helpful overview all at once and then build on the various pieces. None of my training included anything so clear and useful.

At the core of their approach to critical thinking lie eight elements of thought.

> All thinking is defined by the eight elements that make it up. Eight basic structures are present in all thinking: Whenever we think, we think for a purpose within a point of view based on assumptions leading to implications and consequences. We use concepts, ideas and theories to interpret data, facts, and experiences in order to answer questions, solve problems and resolve issues.[7]

Notice how each element provides an additional focal point for a good lecture. As you design your lecture, review the elements to see whether one of them would serve your purpose. In other words, would it be helpful to . . .

- Explore various points of view?
- Identify basic assumptions?
- Trace implications and consequences?
- Evaluate concepts, ideas, and theories?
- Interpret data, facts, and experiences?
- Accumulate data, facts, and experiences?
- Answer questions, solve problems, or resolve issues?

---

[7] "Online Model for Learning the Elements of Critical Thinking," accessed September 1, 2014, http://www.criticalthinking.org/ctmodel/logic-model1.htm#.

Lectures with a clear purpose that utilize critical thinking also ought to reflect a variety in shape. Even though lectures proceed in linear fashion with one word building on another, they actually can be pictured differently. Lectures do not need to look alike.[8] Below are a few possible shapes to consider. The first shape represents one possible way to visualize the shape of the Olivet Discourse. This was Jesus' lecture on the future kingdom, and I have chosen to break it down into three sections organized around his warning to "watch out." In this lecture, Jesus declared false teachers, the sudden nature of his judgment, and the ultimate true accounting for every wrong provide three quite different but strong reasons for his disciples to "watch out."

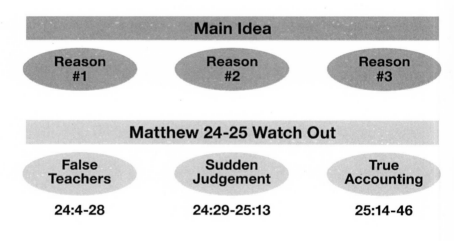

---

[8] These models utilize Haddon Robinson's approach. Good sermons and good lectures have many common features. I highly recommend Robinson's approach for proper outline form. I have reproduced this material in appendix C based on his classroom notes. Used with permission.

The second shape represents a possible way to visualize how three New Testament books explain one tiny verse in Habakkuk. Each book cites the same verse but emphasizes and elaborates on only one phrase within the verse. When taken together, Romans elaborates on justification (the righteous one), Galatians elaborates on sanctification (shall live), and Hebrews elaborates on faith (by faith). Likewise, a lecture could be devoted to explaining in detail each phrase in a small sentence.

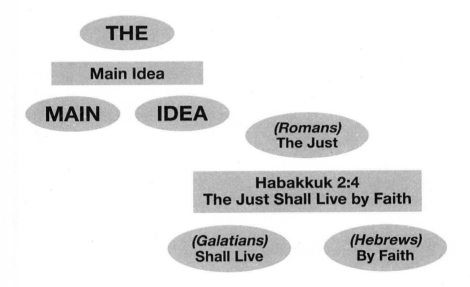

Although the third shape represents a much smaller portion of Scripture, it nevertheless provides another visual organization of material. Paul called on Timothy to "consider" or "reflect" on what he said in these three short verses. These were written for reflective consideration, not for skimming. Simply put, Timothy should suffer hardship like a soldier, athlete, and farmer. Each represents a different kind of hardship Timothy would face.

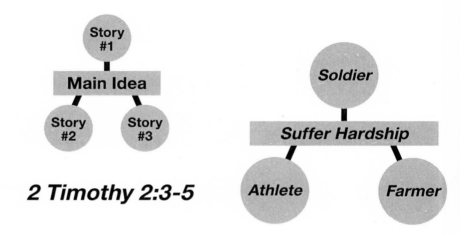

2 Timothy 2:3-5

If you help your students "see" the shape of your material, you will assist them in remembering what you say. These shapes represent only three samples of countless different arrangements.

Deliver

Surprise! As teachers, we are our lectures' audio-visual, and everything matters! Although this section will not deal with our appearance (personal grooming and clothing choices), it matters too. Most of us don't have the advantage of striking good looks or Neiman Marcus wardrobes, so we simply make the best of what we have to work with. Remember, students have to look at us. They do not have a choice. For their sake, don't let grooming and clothing choices interfere with the message.[9] We all struggle balancing between vanity and carelessness. Neither represents Christian values. This section does suggest some

---

[9] Shaving while lecturing, as was one professor's custom, is not a good idea. He no longer teaches at that institution.

recommendations for voice, body language, and lecture support that will improve your lectures greatly if you practice them.

Because most people avoid speech classes like the plague, few of us receive any proper training for our voices. I must admit, were they not required, I would have deleted the preaching courses from my training.[10] Although I did not emerge from them as the anointed cherub, I continued to review my notes and practice the principles until I managed an acceptable delivery to large audiences.[11] You can too. Improving your speaking voice is not rocket science, but it does take practice. Here are five elements related to voice and some simple ways to double check improvement:

1. *Volume:* Can the person sitting in the back hear you as well as the person in the front? Your conversational volume level must move up; the larger the room, the higher the volume. Until you're satisfied, have a student in the back of the room alert you when your volume drops too low. No matter how loudly you speak, your voice will not be damaged if you use your diaphragm. Anyone who teaches singing can help you learn this.

2. *Pitch:* Are you using your voice like the musical instrument God gave you? Every spoken word occurs on some musical note. Move your voice up and down the musical scale. Practice reading children's books with animation, using various voices. Imitate the sounds. In the early days, I suffered from adrenalin overload that caused my voice to range

---

[10] I am an accountant by trade. We prefer the safety of working alone with numbers and avoid public speaking whenever we can. You will have to ask God why he pushed me into the roles of pastor and professor—both of which require a lot of public speaking.

[11] You can decide for yourself if you listen to one of my chapel messages at http://www.dts.edu/media/play/what-i-ve-learned-about-love-lawson -michael-s/ (accessed Sept. 1, 2014). In fact, check and see if I actually practice the advice about delivery you are about to read.

too high. I remember devoting several messages to lowering my register while using the whole scale. Remember, you typically can work on only one thing at a time. When a student says, "I could listen to you a lot longer," what he means is, your voice variety made for easy listening.

3. *Speed:* Where will you find the balance between too fast and too slow? Listen to the best speakers you can. Imitate their speed. I always spoke too quickly until I started speaking through translators. That forced me to slow down for their sake, waiting for the translation. Good speakers vary their rate of delivery, letting some words or phrases hang in the air to give listeners time to fully embrace the meaning.

4. *Enunciation:* Can you recruit your teeth, lips, and tongue to help you speak more clearly? Speaking clearly requires clipping and punctuating each and every word. Leave spaces between words. Do not fill the spaces with "ah," "um," "uh," "you know," and so on. Use the spaces to assist your oral punctuation. Read short paragraphs into a recorder and exaggerate the sounds associated with each word, then scale back for public consumption.

5. *Projection:* Is your voice and presence fully representing your whole personality? If you are not tired when you finish speaking, you did not project any energy. This one is difficult to measure, but ask the students in the back of the room if they "feel" close to you. Hopefully, you are delivering your whole lecture through your whole presence to every person in the room. In some ways, it reflects the nonverbal body language clues we will discuss shortly.

If you choose to lecture and choose not to work on your voice, perhaps you should consider giving your students a discount. I remind you here of my lesson for Greek students: "Whatever you do . . ." You know the rest.

Body language represents another huge part of communication. These nonverbal parts of communication actually speak louder than our voices. When our nonverbal communication contradicts our verbal communication, students always believe the nonverbal. For example, if we possess a keen interest in the subject of our lectures but stare out the window as we deliver them, students will believe the subject is not important. Facial expressions, eye contact, gestures, and whole body movement combine with our voices to communicate our messages. In many ways, we are our messages.

Anyone who wants to improve his teaching skills owes a vote of thanks to Harry G. Murray at Seattle University, who developed the "Teacher Behaviors Inventory" (see p. 202). My first encounter with this little tool came through its 1988 publication in *The Teaching Professor*.[12] The entire inventory appears in appendix B, but I am reproducing the unit on enthusiasm here because it addresses many concerns in this section.[13] In the inventory, students simply rate the professor's behavior on a simple Likert scale. Note the point system:

1 = almost never   + = should do more
2 = rarely   − = should do less
3 = sometimes
4 = often
5 = almost always

Enthusiasm: use of nonverbal behavior to solicit student attention and interest

---

[12] *The Teaching Professor* is a publication of Magna Publications of Madison, WI. This little newsletter is must reading until the various pieces of the professor's puzzle become second nature. I have never failed to find something useful. I require my students to randomly select a past issue and read it in class. They too invariably find something they can use.

[13] "The Teacher Behaviors Inventory" could also be found online on May 4, 2015 at http://www.seattleu.edu/searchresults.aspx?cx=013219616 395457722490:ave_ey_xavm&cof=FORID:10&ie=UTF-8&q=teacher%20 behavior%20inventory.

1.	Speaks in a dramatic or expressive way	1	2	3	4	5	+	−
2.	Moves about while lecturing	1	2	3	4	5	+	−
3.	Gestures with hands or arms	1	2	3	4	5	+	−
4.	Exhibits facial gestures or expressions	1	2	3	4	5	+	−
5.	Avoids eye contact with students	1	2	3	4	5	+	−
6.	Walks up aisles beside students	1	2	3	4	5	+	−
7.	Gestures with head or body	1	2	3	4	5	+	−
8.	Tells jokes or humorous anecdotes	1	2	3	4	5	+	−
9.	Reads lecture verbatim from prepared notes or text	1	2	3	4	5	+	−
10.	Smiles or laughs while teaching	1	2	3	4	5	+	−
11.	Shows distracting mannerisms	1	2	3	4	5	+	−

When this inventory is used carefully, your student evaluations can become your greatest teachers. Note items 6, 9, and 11 prevent students from simply marking all 5s. And, just because an item is marked 5 does not mean it is favorable. Take item 2 for instance. You may move about while lecturing "almost always," but the students give you a "-," meaning you move about too much. Many preachers who move about the platform simply burn nervous energy. Their movements are not purposeful. Item 6 indicates purposeful movement away from the podium and toward the students to facilitate a bit of intimacy. This is especially important when students ask questions. Your body movements toward them indicate interest in what they have to say.

I highly recommend the entire inventory to you. The experts on your lecture style are those who have to endure it. At least once a semester, give your students an opportunity to grade your instructional behaviors. Use their counsel to improve.

In addition to voice and body language training, lectures improve greatly when they include appropriate support. Creative visuals, thoughtful handouts, and animated storytelling strengthen the infrastructure of any lecture. Remember, students seek clarity of presentation.

Visuals. Through hours of practice, I mastered the art of writing legibly on both the whiteboards and blackboards, not to mention their proper cleaning. I added the finer nuances of overhead projector use, such as aligning the visual and adjusting for keystone effect *before* turning it on. But, I freely admit the PowerPoint generation caught me by surprise. So, I asked a former classmate and trusted colleague, Don Regier, to help me with this section.[14] Here is what he said:

> Even the brightest professor can't compete with 5,000 lumens from a digital projector. Our eyes automatically gravitate to brightness, color, and motion. Use the attention-grabbing power of brightness, color, and motion to make your point.
>
> *Brightness:* Do your students know it's time for class to begin because the screen fills with lovely images of your computer desktop folders? You've just squandered an opportunity to grab students' attention! Whatever you leave on the screen loses potency and becomes "ho-hum."
>
> Arrive early. Set up ahead of class time. If your first slide isn't meaningful, begin with a black slide. Advance to the first image when appropriate. Otherwise, the eye adjusts to the brightness; your image loses its attraction and distracts from its message.

---

[14] Don is associate professor emeritus of Christian Education, adjunct professor in Media Arts and Worship, and director of Special Projects in Creative Services (part-time) at Dallas Theological Seminary. He has served Dallas since graduating in 1969. He suggests you follow Michael Hyatt's blog at michaelhyatt.com. Michael gives a lot of presentations and offers good advice. See a sample blog at http://michaelhyatt.com/029-7-rules-for-more-effective-slide-presentations-podcast.html.

As a general rule, use bright images and words against darker backgrounds. A white background draws attention to . . . the background.

Color: Bright, warm colors (yellow, orange, red) can direct attention to the relevant screen areas. Cool, dark colors (blue, green, purple) make good backgrounds.

Motion: If every line of text flies onto the screen, the effect loses punch. Could we have abused the power of this point so our students don't even bother to look up at the screen anymore? If so, our visual "support" just collapsed.

Remember: *you* are the presenter! Rather than competing with you, visual images should support your message. So there are times when you should use the magic *B* key to "blank" the screen and hold the class spellbound with your narration.

Evaluate your visual support to make sure it takes full advantage of brightness, color, and motion. Attract. Don't distract.

Handouts. Students greatly appreciate these summaries or elaborations of significant details. The key is knowing when to give them out. If the handout supplements your lecture, hand it out at the end of class, or students immediately begin looking through the handout instead of paying attention to you. If you plan to use the handout to guide students through some information, give them ample opportunity to read it first. Be quiet while they read—even though it is difficult. The electronic generation mostly prefers digital versions. I rarely upload them until I want the students to use them.

Storytelling. As with good sermons, good lectures require illustrations from time to time. The delivery of short stories is an art form in itself. I have listened to hours of the best storytellers I could find. Garrison Keillor, Ethel Barrett, and Jerry Clower rank among my favorites. I listen to the same story multiple times in order to pick up their delivery techniques. The deep pause, the repeated word, the whisper, and the change of pace are among their highly sophisticated tools. Their razor-sharp speaking skills reflect hours of practice. They make highly rehearsed discourses appear easy and spontaneous. They do this just to make people laugh. Can we afford to do less to educate our students?

In addition to listening, you can learn how to tell stories by reading Ethel Barrett's book.[15] My mentor, Dr. Howard Hendricks, told me on more than one occasion, "This is the best book on preaching I have read." Stories still offer the most powerful tool for driving points home. Jesus' stories provide classic examples. Remember that with every skill comes temptation. The temptation of good storytellers: entertaining without educating. The temptation of good scholars: impressing without educating.

Enrich

So far we have examined components of clear structure and careful delivery. Great lectures require both, but the best lectures include features that enrich the whole experience. Let me suggest three: improved listening, active processing, and better questioning.

If lecturing contains a fatal flaw, it certainly must be assuming everyone is listening. As talking is not teaching, listening is not learning. Schooling conditions adults to smile and nod politely even when not listening. Momentary distractions, emotional issues, or simple daydreaming may sabotage a teacher's lecture, but his mortal enemies have batteries and screens. Addiction to them leaves little time for thinking, let alone listening. Many students, then, are just fiddling. Because great teachers believe what they say is important, they find ways to draw

---

[15] Ethel Barrett, *Story-Telling: It's Easy* (Grand Rapids: Zondervan, 1965).

students into their lectures. When students practice good classroom listening skills, these also become useful life skills.

Many variations of the following techniques exist. Use these to stimulate your own modifications.

- Ask students to listen for elements of critical thinking like assumptions, facts, or points of view. Leave time for students to report so you can affirm their discoveries or clarify/add material they may have overlooked.

- Divide the class into fans and critics who listen then explain reasons for their favorable or critical conclusions. Your mother always thinks you're wonderful. Others? Not so much!

- Forbid note taking during twelve- to fifteen-minute portions followed by collaborative summarizing and reporting. Sudden alienation from their computer screens may cause minor withdrawal symptoms.

- Assign various roles to groups of students who listen with designated perspectives and report specific implications peculiar to that point of view. I have had students so embrace their roles that the whole group stood, taped a line in the floor, and announced, "Those who stand with the truth, join us on our side of the line!"

Students pay better attention when provided a task that turns them from passive to active listeners.

In addition to promoting better listening, the previous list also draws students into active processing. I never understood why Campus Crusade in the 1960s pressured a young convert to write out his testimony and say it out loud as often as possible. Now I know. The more often you orally confirm the experience, the more the reality settles in. It is one thing for you to say something; it is quite another for your students to say it. If you don't hear them say it, you won't really know whether they understand your meaning until the test or paper is due.

Chapter 6 provided many options for allowing students to actively process the course material. Even though your lesson may be given almost exclusively to lecture, opportunities to actively process material help students capture and retain its essential features.

The information explosion combined with immediate access through technology shifts the role of the teacher away from "the sage on the stage" to "the guide on the side." Rather than just giving information, we find ourselves not only showing students where to find accurate information but also how to analyze, evaluate, synthesize, and present information. In other words, the classroom experience can now focus on higher-order thinking. Of course we do that by wrestling with good questions.

Years ago Herman Harrell Horne wrote an exceptionally irritating little book.[16] Initially, its brevity excited me because it was assigned reading for a class. A quick glance at the table of contents increased my pleasure as chapters looked to be three to five pages each. But the book turned out tougher than I anticipated. Unlike propositional styles (as in this volume), Horne chose to generously wash his book in an interrogative style. He often piles question upon question that stick in your mind like needles and prevent you from hurrying through. Not until the chapter on Jesus' use of questions did I realize he had embraced one of the Savior's most powerful techniques. His annoying little book contains more food for thought per square question than any other book I have ever read, except the Bible.

Questions! Thorny, sticky, rash-producing ones never let the mind rest. What do you think about these samples from Jesus?

---

[16] Herman Harrell Horne, *The Teaching Techniques of Jesus* (Grand Rapids: Kregel, 1982). My original copy has since slipped away into someone else's library. The original volume, *Jesus the Master Teacher,* was first published in 1920 and faithfully reprinted since then. Any Christian book reprinted for almost one hundred years is worth a look.

- "What do you think . . . ?" (Matt 17:25)
- "What are you looking for?" (John 1:38)
- "Have I been among you all this time without your knowing Me . . . ?" (John 14:9)
- "Didn't you know that I had to be in My Father's house? (Luke 2:49)
- ". . . do you love Me?" (John 21:16)

Do these interrupt or irritate you? Did you skip over them quickly? Why? Did one make you pause only a moment? Which one? What thoughts ran through your mind during that pause?

Forgive me. I just wanted you to experience a little brain adrenalin from piling question upon question. Great questions provoke active thinking and enrich lectures. Improve your questions by thinking through their direction and purpose. Questions have a limited number of directions, and these designations are mine. Can you think of more than these five?

1. Questions you ask yourself are *Rhetorical*. You do not expect an answer as you plan to answer it yourself, or perhaps the answer is so obvious it does not require an answer.
2. You may call on a specific member of the class, in which case your question is *Direct*. You do expect an answer or, better yet, the student's opinion or thinking on the matter up to this point.
3. A *Reverse* question calls on the questioner to offer his best answer to his own question. Jesus used this with the rich young ruler.
4. Rather than answering a question directly, you may *Relay* the question to another specific member of the class.
5. When a student asks a really thought-provoking question, you may open it to the class with a *General* question like, "Who would like to propose an answer to that question?" Or, "Who will help us begin to answer that question?"

While questions have a limited number of directions, they have a wide variety of purposes. Is your question designed to . . .

- Accumulate facts?
- Define terms?
- Explain more clearly?
- Develop an answer more fully?
- Compare with something similar?
- Contrast with something different?
- Relate to other subjects?
- Return to the subject?
- Change the subject?
- Involve more class members?
- Clarify meanings?
- Extract expected answers?
- Bias responses?
- Stimulate application?
- Summarize findings?
- Arrive at conclusions?

What might be some other purposes you could add to this list?

Good discussions begin, expand, and then conclude. If you arm yourself with proper questions, you can guide your class through each of these significant movements. In the early days of teaching, I carried copies of these questions with me at all times. Opening questions changed from lesson to lesson but were always manuscripted with a clear purpose and were open ended.[17] Nothing sinks a discussion more quickly than a question like, "Who was Moses' brother?" A better

---

[17] I highly recommend *The Miniature Guide to the Art of Asking Essential Questions* by Linda Elder and Richard Paul. On September 1, 2014, I accessed their website, and you can purchase this guide at www.criticalthinking.org.

question might be, "In what ways did Moses' brother help and/or hinder his ministry?"

Expanding a discussion explores possible alternatives or opinions with questions such as . . .

- Why do you believe that?
- Is that all?
- Can you tell me/us more?
- Does everyone agree with that?
- What other passages of Scripture support that?
- Is that the most complete explanation we can give?
- Do all Christians agree with that?
- Have you heard other people give different answers?
- How would you explain that in light of . . . ?
- Would anyone like to add to that answer?
- Can you think of a real-life illustration (example)?
- Should we ask some others what they think?
- Why do some people disagree with that?
- John, how would you summarize what Bob is saying?
- How would you explain that to someone who is not a Christian?

Using questions like these can keep a discussion going as long as you wish. But if you fail to conclude your discussion successfully, students will complain, "We just pooled our ignorance."

You can conclude a discussion by offering questions that resemble one of these:

- What conclusions can we draw from our discussion?
- How would we summarize our thinking to this point?
- If we could summarize our thoughts into one, two, or three sentences, what would they be?
- If we based our opinion on only what we have explored here together, what would it be?

- Is it possible for us to summarize our thoughts?
- What would we conclude if this were the only passage available to us?
- What tentative conclusion might we draw, and what remaining questions do we have?
- What would you say are the most important points we have discovered today?
- If someone were to ask you what we discussed, how would you explain it in one or two sentences?

As with lectures, discussions have an Achilles' heel. Once the discussion opens up to the whole class, staying on track becomes a serious issue. Students know when a discussion loses its direction. In addition to opening, expanding, and concluding the discussion, a teacher must keep it focused around its purpose. When students offer comments that appear to lead down a different path or seem unconnected to anything said to that point, a follow up question is definitely in order. Try one of these:

- Can you help me understand how that relates to our discussion of . . . ?
- Would you mind repeating that and connecting it to our discussion of . . . ?

The class will appreciate a professor who keeps the discussion from wandering off into a foreign galaxy. But be prepared! I have had students make the most amazing connections. Sometimes I just stand there, stunned. On the other hand, I have had students say, "Oh, it doesn't have anything to do with our discussion. I just wanted to share that." I always express gratitude though I don't always know what really prompted the comment. Their admission allows me to redirect us back onto the question at hand.

Instruction in Online Education

Online education challenges the traditional role of teacher as information dispenser. The new role of educational designer feels uncomfortable and unfamiliar for many in my generation. In some ways, they feel exactly like the German professors who helped us open this chapter. They wonder what they will do if they don't lecture. Their classroom-based courses require approximately forty-five hours each semester. If they have been teaching for a while, the lectures bring a sense of security. They no longer wonder what they will do during the next class hour. Changing from an information dispenser to a guiding participant feels awkward. No lecture-seasoned professor wants to feel awkward. I say these things because I honestly believe the resistance to online education often occurs at the emotional level. The rational and legitimate concerns often veil deeper feelings of uncertainty and inadequacy in the new role.

If the real concern is information dispensing by a professor, technology provides adequate tools. Technology will continue to make these more seamless and trouble free. I suspect that by the time this book gets published, almost every reader will have experienced some kind of online course. In the asynchronous environment, professors can deliver information through streaming video of captured classroom lectures, narrated PowerPoint, audio podcasts, or transcribed lecture notes. For the motivated student, these offer some distinct advantages. Repeated viewing or listening is not available in the live classroom. Posting questions for clarification seems easier than raising your hand and interrupting the class. Being able to pause the video/podcast/PowerPoint makes immediate time for reflection.

Guiding participation opens new opportunities to stimulate learning previously occupied (at least in our own minds) by our scintillating lectures. The section in this chapter on questions could help make the transition in roles easier. Posing questions, stimulating more thinking, and evaluating responses offer some invigorating options only if we embrace learner-centered rather than lecture-centered education.

Conclusion

Now, are you ready to rejoin those wonderful German professors? I asked why they didn't give copies of their lecture notes to the students. They responded, "If we did that, what would we do?" I answered, "You could use the classroom hours to really discuss your ideas." They indicated this might have real possibilities even if they provided them in limited fashion. I wondered what wonderful discussions would have occurred if these scholars had been as skilled with discussion and questions as they were with research. I hoped they would provide their notes at least on a trial basis and thought, *One small step for professors; one giant leap for students!*

Dr. Hendricks's words still ring in my ears: "The mind cannot absorb what the seat cannot endure!" I try to remember his famous quote each and every time I teach or preach. My family often jokes, "You can speak longer than people can listen." It's funny and true! Just because I am talking does not mean students are learning. I can help them learn when I choose to lecture if I create a clear structure, make a careful delivery, and interject an occasional finely tuned enriched feature. This seemingly obvious piece of the puzzle needs a great deal more attention.

You may be wondering whether I have forgotten about the quality of relationships that students say contribute to their appreciation of lectures. Actually I reserved the next chapter for that extended discussion. Quality relationships clearly make Christian education truly Christian. Meet me there, will you?

CHAPTER 9

RELATING SKILLS: A PARTICULARLY CHRISTIAN IDEA

Those who love teaching help others love learning.[1]

The apostle John invited everyone into the upper room with Jesus. John elevated the significance of the evening by devoting roughly 20 percent of his Gospel to Jesus' discourse around the meal. Since this represents the Savior's final extended teaching for his disciples, we could reasonably assume he focused on essentials. John introduced the section by declaring that now Jesus fully displayed his love for the disciples by washing their feet. He even washed Judas's feet, though he would betray him later that evening. This unprecedented and unkingly behavior stunned his disciples and punctuated his later command to "love one another as I have loved you." Jesus concluded the dinner with a prayer request that the Father's love for him be replicated in them. Working

---

[1] Long ago, a student gave me a coffee cup bearing this anonymous inscription.

backward through the passage, note the connections and replications of
the divine love affair:

- John 17: Jesus prayed that the Father's love for him would reside
  in the disciples.
- John 15: Jesus commanded the disciples twice to love one another
  and added "as I have loved you" once. Loving one another demonstrated friendship with Jesus.
- John 13, 15: Jesus commanded the disciples three times to love one
  another "as I have loved you." Loving one another identified the
  disciples of Jesus.
- John 13: Washing the disciples' feet (including Judas's) was exhibit
  A of Jesus' love for them.

Working forward, Jesus displayed his love by assuming the role of a
common servant. He commanded them to love one another (which he
repeated five times), as he had loved them (which he repeated twice).
Jesus concluded the evening by asking the Father to duplicate his love
for him in his disciples. Jesus' expectations for them and for us could
not be laid out more clearly. The mandate to love one another should
govern relationships among Christians—whether they are supervisors,
subordinates, peers, or students. Failure to treat anyone with patient
kindness (Paul's first two defining terms in 1 Corinthians 13) reveals a
personal defect in relating to the Savior.

The centrality of interpersonal relationships was not lost on the
apostles.[2] Over and over again, the terms "one another" and "each other"

---

[2] Even among the apostles, there were differences that caused separation.
The issue between Paul and Peter dealt with a corruption of the gospel. The
issue between Paul and Barnabas dealt with a matter of policy about John
Mark, which Paul resolved later in his life.

appear in their written exhortations. For emphasis, here are the books and the number of times the words appear.[3]

Romans	6 times	2 Thessalonians	1 time
1 Corinthians	4 times	Titus	1 time
2 Corinthians	1 time	Hebrews	4 times
Galatians	3 times	James	3 times
Ephesians	5 times	1 Peter	6 times
Philippians	1 time	1 John	6 times
Colossians	4 times	2 John	1 time
1 Thessalonians	7 times	Total	52

When writing about "each other" or "one another," the New Testament authors keep their negatives simple:

- Don't grumble.
- Don't envy.
- Don't lie.
- Don't slander.
- Don't pass judgment.

This brief list sets the outer perimeter of acceptable behavior. None of us wants to deny the gospel, but behavior can deny the gospel as easily as words. The apostle Paul brought that actual charge against the apostle Peter when he broke fellowship with Gentiles in Antioch.[4]

Now, notice the delicious banquet of words the New Testament authors use to promote positive interpersonal relationships. Some of

---

[3] If you are curious, a simple electronic concordance quickly reveals the exact location of their frequent appearances.

[4] Gal 2:11–21.

these are repeated. All of them are connected to either "one another" or "each other" in the context.

Keep on loving	Bear with	Have fellowship	Live in harmony
Confess to	Encourage	Wait for	Offer hospitality
Pray for	Build up	Have equal concern	Be devoted to
Love deeply	Be kind	Submit to	Accept
Forgive	Live in peace	Teach and admonish	Serve
Agree with	Greet	Spur on to love	

When the Lord Jesus and the New Testament authors make the obligations so clear, I have always wondered why Christian history shows so many pockmarks of division and inability to work together. Granted, some cases represent real departure from the faith, but in many cases, the issues revolve around semantics or, worse, egos seeking preeminence. During a professional conference years ago, I visited with a denominational superintendent responsible to work with churches undergoing division. He had agonized with roughly a thousand churches as they moved through the painful days of separation. I asked how many churches split over genuine theological defections from the faith. He calmly answered, "Only one."

The Upper Room Discourse and the "one another" passages are no mystery to even casual readers of the New Testament. I bring them to this chapter because they somehow get lost in either the mundane routine or the emotion of disagreements. If our educational process authentically bears the Christian name, then our Lord's commands that the apostles reinforced must govern each and every relationship from the chief executive officer to the part-time custodian. We cannot forget this mandate, even when others do.

Relating in Every Direction

Of all the issues I bring before prospective teachers, the issue of inter-personal skills elicits the most yawns. Students do not feel the need for instruction on this topic, and if I ask them, they will tell me they don't want it. Many honestly believe that content mastery (chap. 5) is all they need to succeed. However, when surveyed after entering ministry, relating skills is the number-one area they wish they had had more of in their training. And, of course, teachers at every level call upon relating skills each and every day. In most cases, those relating skills actually become essential survival skills.

If you fail to use appropriate relating skills with your supervisors, you will lose your job. If you fail to use them with your peers, you will lose their respect. If you fail to use them with your subordinates, you will lose their help just when you need it. But, if you fail to use them with your students, an unkind impatient word may damage a child of God. I have watched professors destroy the confidence of more than one classmate. The remainder of this chapter will look at the nature of interpersonal relationships in general and the opportunities and dangers in relating to students.[5]

Interpersonal Relationships

Relationships can be analyzed quickly by looking at position and proximity. Whether the parties are equal or unequal in status reveals their positions in the relationship. Proximity describes how the parties feel about the strength of the relationship. In other words, one can be higher

---

[5] I highly recommend *Communication and Conflict Management in Churches and Christian Organizations* by Kenneth Gangel and Samuel Canine (Nashville: Broadman, 1992). They write specifically to Christian institutional relationships.

or lower in position while at the same time being near or far. For example, I worked at a snack bar during high school. I reported directly to a manager who supervised all of us. She reported directly to the owner, who also happened to be my father. While she was higher in position, I was closer in proximity to the owner, my father. He never contradicted her instructions for me, and he expected me to work as hard as everyone else. He also gave me instructions and shared insights about the business without her knowledge.

When looking at position, I distinguish between status and rank. Status is generally acknowledged by everyone, whereas rank might be an assigned position. They are determined in various ways. In Korea, age determines status. Even being born one day ahead of someone means he must show you respect. No one laughs about it. In institutions, titles often reveal rank but may not reveal status. Someone inside or outside an organization may hold high status but no official rank. A large donor, an esteemed alum, or a patriarch/matriarch may have such high status that their opinion overrules everyone else's.

In relationships with those who have higher status or rank, diplomacy and respect become valuable allies. I have repeatedly gone to Joseph, Daniel, Nehemiah, and Esther to teach me their survival skills. They reached the highest levels in ungodly governments without losing their integrity. I suspect they did not say everything they thought and at times chose to say nothing at all. Learning what not to say and when not to speak become fine arts in relating skills. We do not have to do everything someone with higher rank or status tells us as long as we are prepared to suffer the consequences. When in doubt, show respect and choose words carefully.

While using diplomacy and respect are not essential in relationships of equal status or rank, they don't hurt either. If you hear something good about a person, quickly pass it on, and, conversely, don't become a listening post for complaints. If you tend to be a competitive person, find an outlet outside your relationships at work. The disciples' ugly discussions about who was first ought not be replicated among those who possess the Holy Spirit. Paul's admonition in Romans echoes dozens and dozens of similar New Testament exhortations: "If possible, on your part, live at peace with everyone" (Rom 12:18). You cannot control what others do, but you can, with the Spirit's help, control what you say and do. Mouths often reveal immaturity in spite of advanced degrees.

How we treat those with lower rank or status marks our mediocrity or greatness. If we must clean our classrooms before we teach in them, our appreciation for a custodian will greatly increase. The same goes for mowing, painting, and repairing the facilities we work in and around daily. If we truly become the "servants of all" who Jesus invites us to be, we ought not to take for granted those who perform the routine duties around us. They are not invisible, and they have lives full of challenges much like ours. If we believe their lives have equal value before the Savior, then we ought to treat them with all the dignity and respect we wish for ourselves.

In terms of proximity, relationships slide up and down a continuum between close and distant. Close, strong relationships can survive more direct forms of communication, but they require ongoing maintenance in time, energy, and mutual encouragement. These relationships are tested under working conditions when individuals forget to maintain the quality of the relationship. Married couples make this classic mistake over and over again. During courtship, couples spend time, give energy, and focus on each other's strengths, thus nurturing the relationship's quality. After the wedding, suddenly the nature of the relationship takes a backseat to paying rent, washing clothes, cooking food, working long hours, and completing all the mundane necessary activities of life. They assume the relationship will remain close and strong while watching it erode daily before their very eyes. Their failure to work on the nature of the relationship sucks all the life out of it.

Everyone looks to Jonathan and David for an illustration of a close, strong relationship. Interestingly enough, their relationship exhibited both proximity and position. As the son of the king, Jonathan's rank and status was unquestioned. He had every right to inherit the kingdom. David, on the other hand, was the neglected son of an undistinguished family with neither rank nor status. Only within the military that flourished under his leadership did David have any real status or rank.

The most powerful commentary on their relationship came on David's darkest day when he was running from Saul. Jonathan found him afraid and exhausted in Horesh. There, the text says, Jonathan, "helped him find strength in God" (1 Sam 23:16 NIV). I would love to have heard the conversation between the prince and the fugitive. Had David neglected singing his own songs? Had God become smaller and Saul become larger in David's imagination? Had the memories of God's numerous and spectacular interventions on his behalf been clouded by his miserable immediate circumstances? One thing is for sure: we all need someone like Jonathan in our lives during similar dark days. But in my experience doing men's retreats, few men seem to develop close, strong relationships. I have not noticed them flourishing in academia either.

At the other end of the continuum are distant, weak relationships. Perhaps these never benefitted from any kind of nurture. These require major compensation when they undergo any kind of stress. As David and Jonathan illustrated classic close, strong relationships, Jacob and Esau illustrated distant, weak relationships. Could any two brothers be any more different or at odds with each other? Note the amount of time, energy, and planning Jacob gave to their meeting upon his return to the land. Even though their positions were equal, their proximity was distant and weak. Jacob was certainly no match for Esau in a fight but easily outmaneuvered Esau within the family structure.

All of this is rather academic until a conflict emerges, then everything comes into play. All the possibilities of position (rank and status) and proximity (strong and close) affect the nature and the outcome of the conflict. Those with the best relating skills will take into account both position and proximity before deciding on the best course of action. In essence, only four possibilities exist:

1. You can try to make it better.
2. You can decide to make it worse.
3. You can ignore it.
4. You can try to stabilize it.

But before you decide on one of these, try to do three things first.

1. *Listen* with your ears and your heart. Listen until you understand the emotion behind the words. Listen until you can paraphrase the concern. Genuine listening is so close to love most people cannot tell the difference.[6] The moment you become defensive, you lose your listening advantage. Try to discover what makes the issue so emotionally charged. James has sound counsel here as well with his admonition to be quick to hear and slow to speak.

2. *Explore* the issue with questions. Is that all? Are there other implications? How long has this been bothering you? Has this hurt anyone you know? How urgent do you feel this is? Will you be upset if this takes some time to figure out? What possible solutions do you see?

3. *Define* the problem carefully. Use words everybody can agree with. You cannot decide what action, if any, to take until you can accurately and precisely define the issue. Once you have a clear notion, write it down.

---

[6] I adapted this idea from a quote by David Augsburger I found in Smart Marriages, September 9, 2014, at http://www.smartmarriages.com /marriage.quotes.html.

Once you have listened, explored, and defined the problem, then make one of your four choices. Perhaps you will attempt to make the conflict better. If so, you already have gone a long way in that direction. Letting people verbalize at length about their concern often reduces the emotions that swelled up enough to surface their concern. Many options are available, ranging from apologies to seeking opinions from outside parties. I once helped a committee member write a minority report to the board even though I had voted with the committee against her point of view. My effort on her behalf resolved the interpersonal tension created by that vote.

Or, you may decide this issue represents only a small portion of a larger and more dangerous problem. In that case you may make the problem much worse before any resolution. Be sure the issue (there are some) is really worth your time and energy. Do not assume your point of view will prevail. Several pugnacious Sunday school teachers created enough conflicts that leadership had to decide whether they or I would remain. Although I survived, I would rather not have paid the huge emotional price on the conflict.

A third option is simply to do nothing. Be sure you know why you are doing nothing, and explain it to the offended party. Some things cannot be changed under the current circumstances or with the current personnel. If the issue continues to smolder in an unhealthy way, you may need to revisit your decision.

Finally, you may decide to stabilize the issue. In other words, you agree to disagree but, hopefully, in an agreeable manner. Differences of opinion ought to be able to coexist. If your institution has a confession of faith, then the differences must not violate that confession. Leave peacefully when you no longer adhere to their confession. I personally believe you ought to do the same thing when you can no longer support their policy decisions.

Jesus blesses the peacemakers in his Beatitudes. Peace from God, born by the Spirit, and promoted among God's family reverberates through Paul's letters as he used that one word forty-seven times. Relating skills matter for both personal health and corporate testimony.

Relating to Students

The relationship with students is under the absolute control of the teacher. So the first part of this chapter is devoted to finding ways to help rather than hurt students. A positive (read "patient, kind") relationship with them not only fulfills a Christian responsibility but also impacts their learning.

The student's perception of you, as a Christian teacher, is the platform from which you minister. Your behavior inside the classroom sets up the opportunity to minister outside the classroom. All of us make choices. I know one professor who kept inflexible appointment times, which eliminated students with schedule conflicts. Another instructed his secretary, "Get 'em in and get 'em out as quickly as possible. I am busy." She routinely interrupted the meetings when fifteen minutes were up. Another never looks up from his computer during student conversations. Is it any wonder students apologize for taking a teacher's time? We communicate constantly that what we are doing is so much more important than their obviously trivial concerns. If you choose to minister to students beyond your classroom presentation (although I am sure your presence is amazing), you must be intentional. Here are some suggestions that might help.

Classroom as a Platform

Some of these things I have read but cannot for the life of me remember where. Some of these things I have copied while watching others. And some of these I have stumbled upon as a pastor and brought over into my role as a professor.[7] Many of them are small things, but their cumulative effect can make a big difference. Everything is designed to promote student encounters.

- Introduce yourself carefully at the beginning of each semester. My credentials are as boring as my dissertation so I use some of these:
  - Family members (always described at their most lovable best, never with sarcasm—especially my wife, children, daughter-in-law, and grandchildren)
  - Hobby (fishing—especially black bass, which keeps me from committing "mayhem")
  - Favorite movies (*The Wizard of Oz*—there's no place like home!)
  - Favorite TV program (*Star Trek*—the original, not the knock-offs. Remember, Captain Kirk saved the universe weekly!)
  - Summer travel and ministry stories (especially ones that magnify the accomplishments of others)
  - Why I particularly enjoy teaching this course (because I get to meet *you*)
  - The hardest course I ever had and why (Business Letter Writing with "Bloody Mary"—I used every trick my marginally criminal mind could muster to escape her clutches.)
  - My eagerness to visit with them beyond the course material (because God has placed something wonderful in their hearts, and I want to hear about it)
  - Students are the reason I teach; they are never an interruption (I am not here for the buildings, though they are really nice; the library, which is well stocked; or even my colleagues, although

---

[7] In our modern world, we have made clear distinctions between those who pastor and those who teach. Jesus was simultaneously the Great Shepherd and the Master Teacher. Those who wish to be like him must be both.

I like all of them. And, yes, of course I am busy, but who wants to visit with someone who has absolutely nothing to do? I also learned from my Mexican friends that the person I am with is more important than the person I am getting ready to see.)

— Teaching is what I do, not who I am.

- Show personal interest in the students

  — Provide a "getting to know you" form to be filled out on the first day:

Name

Family:

   Spouse's Name

    Working?

   Children: Name   Nickname   Age

Degree/Major:

Goals after graduating:

Expected Graduation Date:

I am taking this course because . . .

One thing I'd like you to know about me is . . .

One thing I'd like to know about you is . . .

  — Use the next to the last question as a way to initiate conversations before or after class and to assist you in remembering their names.

  — Use the last question as a way to begin class sessions for a while. This alerts everyone that you are interested in letting students see your human side.

  — Ask to see pictures of family members, especially children.

- Let your office speak for you. My goal was to make my office a friendly place to visit. The office of a pastor or teacher carries an intimidation factor. Students frequently find it difficult to know how to begin a conversation. The following items on public display give them something to ask you about that does not have to sound profound. Notice how the first three relate directly back to the introduction.

  — Family pictures reaffirm a commitment to relationships beyond school.
  — Travel mementos add a bit of curiosity and something to ask about.
  — Hobby displays reinforce my life outside of the classroom.
  — Candy bowl—because chocolate heals just about everything.
  — Kleenex—because I have had students walk in, sit down, and start crying from sheer stress.
  — Chairs positioned for chatting casually—because sitting across a desk is extremely formal and creates a stiff atmosphere.

- Practice the art of conversation before addressing the purpose for the meeting. I often ask or say,

  — Are you sure you are OK?
  — Tell me about your family.
  — How did you get to our school?
  — How did you come to faith?
  — Were you raised in a Christian family?
  — Tell me about yourself.
  — What is your dream job/ministry?
  — Do you have any summer plans?
  — Are you planning something fun over Christmas?
  — I really enjoyed learning about [insert the item from the Getting to Know You form].

You don't have to use all of these; one or two will get the meeting started on a personal note.

- Welcome the student into your office by name.
    - No matter what is going on in your life, greet him with a smile.
    - Your face is a commentary on what he can expect to occur in the meeting.
    - Never, never, never let students out of your office without praying for them, even if it is only brief. Did I say "never"? I mean it!
    - Give him your full attention while he is with you.[8]

Only Pollyanna believes that all relationships with students will be wonderful and positive. Students are humans, too, and they bring all kinds of behavior into the classroom. Even here, patient kindness still governs our conversations and behaviors.

Common Classroom Problems

Whether you are being confronted or confronting others, real confrontations create emotional experiences difficult to replicate. Therefore, all of us have difficulty preparing and rehearsing properly for them. I have found that students are better prepared to meet those challenges if they have an opportunity to prethink possible responses. To assist them in their prethinking, I created the following exercise. What makes it powerful is the opportunity to discuss their options with peers. Although

---

[8] A friend used to work on Jack Nicklaus's personal airplane. He told me that Jack stopped for anyone who asked for an autograph and remained until everyone who asked got one. But when finished, he hurried off to the many responsibilities brought on by multiple business ventures mixed in with his many tournaments.

the exercise represents a postsecondary setting, some of the same issues could surface with somewhat younger students. See what you think.

> You have become a new faculty member at the Cranberry Theological Academy and are assigned the task of teaching the introductory course in your discipline. Your class of 50 represents a mixture of males and females ranging in age from 21 to 43. After the first few weeks, you notice a mixture of problems reoccurring in class. You decide to discuss these with another faculty member in your department and between the two of you determine a precise course of action.
>
> Problem #1. Two young male students who regularly sit in the back of the room appear to be playing computer games periodically during the class.
>
> Problem #2. One student from another country is chronically late to class.
>
> Problem #3. One female student appears to attend only one out of three sessions.
>
> Problem #4. One of the older students, while extremely respectful, always wants to share some story from his experience that relates to your point but takes a great deal of classroom time.
>
> Problem #5. One student who transferred into your school from another institution appears to have an IQ almost as large as his ego. He eagerly points out anything he thinks is a flaw in your logic or research. Sometimes he is right.
>
> Problem #6. You discover that a student who looks up and smiles at you frequently is secretly working on his language cards (for the language you are not teaching).
>
> Problem #7. The body language of a student strongly suggests that she is uninterested, unengaged, and could not care less about your class. She rarely takes notes, makes little eye contact, hardly laughs or smiles, and just leans back in the chair with folded arms.

Problem #8. A student frequently nods off in class. You observe him dozing almost every class period, but he occasionally contributes to class discussions and is very pleasant when you talk to him before and after class. In other words, he's really a nice guy!

Student pairs have thirty minutes to formulate their initial responses to one of the assigned problems. In the discussion that follows, I make sure to highlight some of the following principles:

- Try not to take student behavior personally, even if the student intends it to be personal. Remember, everyone has fans and critics. Wisdom suggests you should not believe either. You are probably not as great as your fans think nor as bad as your critics imagine. The actual truth probably lies somewhere between the two.

- Make sure the initial personal encounter is private. This might be as simple as taking an opportunity after class to move close to a student and quietly asking, "Are you OK?" or "You appear really [unhappy or disinterested or preoccupied or sleepy or . . .]. Remember, patient kindness may not be what they deserve, but it is what your Savior mandates. If no opportunity presents itself or the behavior seems to need more discussion, ask them to make an appointment. Many issues can be defused in private where you demonstrate genuine concern for the person as well as disapproval of behavior.

- Never assume bad motives.[9] This is a good policy in every relationship, including marriage and family. When framing a concern

_____

[9] One of my professors accused a classmate of lacking devotion to Jesus when he failed to do his homework assigned in the previous session. Actually, the two classes were Friday afternoon and Saturday morning. My classmate worked all night on the loading docks to pay his tuition and care for his family. He just did not get it done. That professor assumed bad motives and deeply damaged my classmate.

in terms of appearances, a student (or family members) has an opportunity to give an explanation. I am amazed at how many students lack proper training in manners and personal decorum.

- If needed, ask the student what a reasonable consequence might be. Another question might be what he expects from you if the behavior is repeated. This opens the door for the student to take ownership of the offense and personal responsibility for the consequence.

- Be sure you are familiar with the student handbook. Teachers are expected to manage certain issues but mandated to report some offences. If there was an apparent violation, you might ask, "Were you aware of the policy . . . ?" As your friendly police officer will remind you, "Ignorance of the law is no excuse!"

- If the issue is over the mandated nature of the course, remind him that mandated courses can be as hard on professors as they are on students. A single professor does not mandate required courses. Mandated courses generally start with a recommendation from a curriculum review committee and are approved by academic affairs then submitted to the president, who must have board confirmation. A lot of people have looked at this course and determined this needs to be in the curriculum—even people from the student's favorite department. Then to further disarm and perhaps even win a little favor, I will sometimes ask, "What could I do to make this more endurable?" I have even solicited their prayers because it is much more difficult to criticize someone you are praying for.

Be sure and focus on the students who really want to learn. The others may take up more time than they deserve. This is so hard to remember that as a department chair I had to encourage my teachers over and over again that some of their students really wanted to be in the classes and enjoyed their teaching. Melancholy personalities tend to believe only the negative; big egos tend to believe only the positive.

Legal Issues for Teachers

Some issues grow beyond the interpersonal to become legal problems. In a society that demands its rights, you will be wise to consider the legal implications of your profession. Each and every state has laws that govern education. In addition, the federal government also has extensive legislation that both limits and protects you. Legal confrontations are not limited to public institutions. Different laws may apply to private secondary schools, private colleges, and private graduate schools.

Columbia University lists seven areas where professors or schools may face legal issues emerging from their classrooms.[10] I encourage you not only to read the entire article but also to become familiar with the laws of your state. The list belongs to Columbia; the comments are mine.

1. *Academic Freedom in the Classroom*: The issue revolves around whether students can expect a content-neutral classroom. At this point, courts have sided with faculty rights to determine classroom content. The freedom to teach within a doctrinal framework is still protected. Students still respect carefully thought-through personal opinions as well. Treating opposing views with dignity and respect always creates a healthy academic setting.

2. *Accommodating Students with Disabilities*: Federal law requires you and your school (both public and private universities) to make reasonable adjustments to avoid discriminating against students with disabilities. Sometimes your effort to accommodate a student may end up benefiting all your students. A tactile model of learning theories I created for a blind student ended up being a better model for my sighted students.

---

[10] "Legal Issues in the Classroom," accessed September 9, 2014, http://www.columbia.edu/cu/tat/pdfs/legal.pdf.

3. *Grading*: Grading creates stress for everyone. Legal concerns arise about who is authorized to assign grades and who is authorized to change them. At times I have offered to collaborate with the student's department chair to reevaluate his work. No one has ever taken me up on that one.

4. *Intellectual Property*: The question about who owns your course material is becoming more difficult as universities put course information, including video of your lectures, online. This landscape changes so rapidly that you will need wisdom in dealing with the new realities.

5. *Letters of Recommendation*: Requests for letters of this kind automatically become an unwritten part of your job description. Being honest, candid, and cautious about your thoughts requires a high level of literary craftsmanship. Be careful what you put in writing in this age of accessible personal portfolios.

6. *Sexual Harassment*: What everyone thought was cute in college changes in the workplace. Women in particular are sensitized to unwanted comments and behavior. You will have nothing to worry about if you treat every woman like your mother, sister, or daughter.[11] The New Testament still gives the best advice in two words: "above reproach."

7. *Student Privacy*: Student information and grades must be kept confidential. Posting grades with student names is no longer acceptable. Access to your grade book must be carefully monitored. Restricting what a student sees about others' grades when reviewing his own is essential.

---

[11] Every Christian man working among women ought to read *Mixed Ministry: Working Together as Brothers and Sisters in an Oversexed Society* by Sue Edwards and Henry Rogers (Grand Rapids: Kregel, 2008).

None of these are laughing matters. Attorneys get paid a lot more than you do. Some take cases on the condition that they get a portion of the settlement, keeping the cost to file a suit minimal.

Relating in Online Education

I admit my personal preference for face-to-face relationships. I enjoy casual hallway encounters. I dread time on my computer. I love spontaneous coffee chats. I have not made friends with any technology I possess. I tune in to vocal tones and body language. I find every form of virtual electronic communication awkward. I find humans fascinating. I am only on Facebook because my son posts pictures of my grandchildren. Having said that, intensifying interpersonal relationships still motivates students.

In the online environment, various tools move from least personal to more personal.

- Comments on a student paper or presentation
- Questions or thoughts in the threaded conversations
- Casual chat-room interactions
- Personal e-mails
- Texting
- Phone calls
- Skype or FaceTime calls

As we all move more deeply into the online world, these tools will need to become as familiar as the physical interpersonal skills I enjoy. The next generation of teachers and professors will most likely have an intuitive sense about how and when to employ them. All relationships require effort. Intensifying those relationships always requires even more effort. A teacher's words, whether written or spoken, can make a powerful impact for good. Intensifying interpersonal relationships, whether virtual or physical, pays big dividends in the lives of those we hope to turn into lifelong learners.

Conclusion

With a few glaring exceptions, teachers throughout my schooling experience were adversarial. They relished their advantage over students. Some enjoyed playing games with trick questions on tests and explained later, "That will teach you to pay attention and read carefully." Others favored creating unreasonable assignments like memorizing the logarithm tables. They basked in their superior knowledge of the material and reminded us frequently of how little we knew. Because "sink or swim" seemed to dominate their educational philosophy, I sought help only under extreme circumstances. They rarely contradicted my worst fears. I literally have no happy memories of learning through grade school or high school. The only happy memories I have of college years have nothing to do with the educational process.[12] As I concluded my college career, walking across the stage at North Texas State University to receive my degree, I muttered to myself, "If I ever read another book it will be too soon!" What a tragic way to end sixteen years of my educational journey.

Fortunately, God had other plans. Imagine my chagrin when God literally dragged me into Dallas Seminary's four-year ThM program. Although I had many good instructors, early in that experience, one professor changed my approach to learning forever. Unlike the others, he got excited about what I was learning. No one in my sixteen years of schooling had ever been excited about what I was learning. He thought one or two things I said or wrote were really good and

---

[12] There I met and married the prettiest girl at North Texas State University. Her contribution to my life belongs in Broadway's neon lights, not in a footnote.

specifically pointed those out. More importantly, he believed I could do better and specified ways to improve. Unexpectedly, I found myself working harder on his assignments. I found myself wanting to live up to his high expectations of me. I even tried to do more than the assignment called for (an absolute first for me). My offerings to him were the offerings of a novice. That was precisely what he expected. Everybody starts as a novice, but that is not where they have to stay! The more excited he became about my work, the more energy and time I devoted, and the more excited I became about learning. He turned me from being an educational survivor into a lifelong learner.

Now, lest you get the wrong impression, I was not his favorite. I did not receive his department's graduation award or any other award for that matter (to no one's surprise). Other students got closer to him than I did. Because of his popularity, large numbers of students wanted his time, many speaking engagements sought his expertise, and of course he had a sweet family. I only got a tiny piece. But when he was with me, he gave me his full attention. When he read my paper, he truly read my paper. And, his excitement about my progress was undeniably genuine. By God's grace, I never forgot his lessons for me, and I inherited his enthusiasm for learners.

When I was a new professor at Dallas Seminary, a student brought me a coffee mug inscribed with these words: "Those who love teaching help others love learning." At last I had a simple summary of what Dr. Hendricks taught me. After we have inflicted our educational process on students, what did we actually accomplish? Did we give them only more information, or do they now really love learning? Have we maximized the advantage we have as educators for their benefit? This piece of the puzzle comes with a battery pack to energize students like no other piece really can.

INSTITUTIONAL REALITIES

"Memorandum to Michaelangelo: Tenure denied."[1]

Institutional realities sometimes appear like a sneak attack on the uninitiated. Teaching, the honored profession, hides many of its challenging features until one is inside. Some discover too late they are ill suited for what they perceived to be the academic lifestyle. In this chapter I peek at a few institutional inner workings and the challenges for those who teach in them. But before I do, perhaps it would be beneficial to make some comments about general differences in schools.

Speaking from an American perspective, the most obvious difference is between domestic (stateside) and international schools. Christian schools sponsored by mission agencies outside the United States offer the widest range of opportunities at every level. Numerous Christian schools have stepped out from under their mission umbrella or

---

[1] Selma Wasserman, "Memorandum to Michaelangelo: Tenure Denied," *Improving College and University Teaching* 32, no. 4 (Fall 1984): 186–87. Available at http://www.jstor.org/stable/27565644. Reprinted with permission.

have emerged under national leadership. In any case, these schools need teachers who can raise most, if not all, their financial support. When I mention the preponderance of opportunities in these settings to my students, they act as if I just recommended them for service in the gulags of Siberia. In private conversations they voice their preference for secure salaries offered by prominent stateside schools. Some of them are still waiting for those offers.

Far be it from me to encourage anyone to do anything the Lord is not leading him to do. But, I do often ask students to give international opportunities serious and prayerful consideration. If their only discomfort comes from the inconvenience of raising support, I point out at least one major advantage. The time spent raising support for an international teaching ministry may provide more job security in the long run. Schools change. Domestic schools change, and international schools change. If a person needs to change jobs internationally, he takes his salary with him. That is not a disadvantage, but it does require more work on the front end of a professional journey. In either case, make sure the Lord leads you.

Schools also differ on the basis of their public or private support. The lack of public funding requires a private institution to constantly persuade donors of their unique benefits and contributions. The smaller the school, the more likely teachers and professors will be recruited to help in this never-ending and critical task. Teachers who tend to think, *That's not my job*, may be surprised or quickly unemployed. Although public institutions have access to tax dollars, a teacher's value to the school increases with research grants and stipends. These also help with retention and tenure. In either case, some responsibility for funding may become an unexpected part of a teacher's job description.

A wide range of secondary, undergraduate, and graduate schools are among the private Christian institutions. For the purposes of this volume, the following list may provide a general overview:

- *Christian Secondary Schools:* These come in a variety of shapes and sizes. The Association of Christian Schools International is the largest association of these schools with a strong reputation and track record. It has a long list of both domestic and international schools.[2] Mission agencies also keep lists of recommended schools for the children of their missionaries.

- *Bible Institutes:* Historically, many of these were precursors to what now have become Bible colleges and Christian universities. Around the world, mission agencies use these to provide nonformal training for local pastors and church workers. In addition, numerous churches have begun to develop schools for those who wish more than Sunday school courses.

- *Bible Colleges:* Many Bible colleges have disappeared over the years. The strongest survived and remain a clear option for many students. Their existence depends upon a strong administration with a stable support base. A list of these schools is available through the Association of Biblical Higher Education.[3]

- *Christian Liberal Arts Colleges:* Some Christian schools believed liberal arts to be their mission from the beginning. In addition, some Bible colleges needed to broaden their focus to attract a viable number of students.

- *Christian Universities:* Although many denominations have sponsored these, few have remained evangelical. Over the years, a few Bible colleges continued to expand their offerings and have now become accredited universities with quite strong programs. The Council for Christian Colleges and Universities has a helpful list and website.[4]

---

[2] Association of Christian Schools International, accessed September 10, 2014, http://www.acsiglobal.org.

[3] Association for Biblical Higher Education, http://www.abhe.org /pages/NAV-Directory.html.

[4] Council for Christian Colleges and Universities, http://www.cccu.org.

- *Seminaries:* Many but not all of these are denominational schools. A complete listing is available through the Association for Theological Schools.[5]

The remainder of this chapter discusses the realities these institutions and their faculties face.

Institutional Issues

Funding

Private institutions fund their educational programs through student tuition and gifts from supporters. That's it! If either of those falter, somebody or some bill will not get paid. Once in a while, a school sponsors a special fund-raising effort, but those account for a tiny fraction of the overall income picture. Schools, like businesses, face increasing costs over which they have little control. Utilities and insurance head the list of invisible offenders. Businesses pass these costs on by gradually increasing their prices to the customer. When schools increase tuition too much, students tend to take fewer hours, and prospects may choose another school.

Appealing to donors is the other funding option, but donors prefer building projects over operating costs. Their dollars seem to evaporate when their gifts pay electricity bills or provide necessary insurance. Buildings provide tangible evidence that their dollars matter. One final way to cover the increased cost is to cut expenses in another area. So, as a faculty member, do you wonder why you went another year without a raise? You may need to write a thank you letter to the utility and insurance companies.

Downturns in the economy hurt both donors and students. Gifts to schools usually represent discretionary dollars, which can shrink

---

[5] Association of Theological Schools, http://www.ats.edu.

rapidly. When tuition money shrinks, families compensate by sending fewer children into private education, and students take fewer courses. Sometimes teachers must take a cut in pay or teach extra courses without extra remuneration. These expose unhappy realities.

Budgets offer another mystifying element for those without financial training. Schools play a guessing game trying to anticipate how much income they expect in the following year. Their guess may be educated, thoughtful, and conservative or not based on the quality of the leadership. Under any circumstances, this always remains a guess. Then, school leaders attempt to make sure their anticipated income covers their anticipated expenses. Any given department within a school is allocated a portion of those imaginary dollars to use. The numbers in a department budget do not represent money the school has in hand. Rather, the school is saying, "If we get X dollars in income this year, you will get Y dollars to spend." In reality a budget is only a hopeful forecast of what might happen, assuming a stable income stream and no unexpected expenses.

Budgets have an irrational side. If income appears to be shaky, administrators rightfully ask for spending restraints or impose spending freezes. Loyal departments follow the guidelines. But, when the budget review committee discovers unspent money in a budget, some leaders conclude no real need existed and propose a budget reduction for the following year. While a rational explanation for this remains elusive, the reality exists in institutions. So, sometimes departments spend money to protect against a budget reduction. I am only reporting, not recommending, this reality.

I offer one final note on finances. Look up the word *exigencies* as it occurs in every faculty handbook I know anything about. One definition says, "Financial exigency is understood as a state of financial affairs that requires urgent action." That means anyone can lose his job. Normally tenured faculty expect to get a contract every year and to be preferred over nontenured faculty in case of reductions. But the little word *exigencies* means the administration has the authority to reduce staff and/or faculty until the anticipated expenses match the anticipated income.

Enrollment

Students are the reason schools exist. Each and every school needs a steady stream of new students each year—sometimes each semester, depending on the dropout rate. In reality, these are the paying customers of the education that is offered. In secondary education, a simple nose count reveals whether enrollment and, therefore, income will be up or down. In higher education where students take varying numbers of hours, administrators prefer FTE (full-time equivalency) or billable hours to reveal the needed income from tuition. Without being crass, each student represents part of the finances needed to keep the doors open. Schools can sometimes find themselves in the embarrassingly precarious position of not wanting to dismiss a student because they need the tuition dollars.

The proliferation of schools and online offerings has made competition for students quite intense. Secondary schools must demonstrate how their education offers ready access to first-rate universities. Undergraduate schools must show access to either good jobs or graduate schools. A caring faculty becomes an important asset in the recruiting process. Parents want to sense that teachers have a genuine concern for the well-being of their children. Rigorous studies administered by gentle hands make an appealing combination.

Because enrollment forms such a critical component to a school's ongoing presence, faculty are often called upon to meet with prospects, speak at luncheons, host visitors, make phone calls, answer e-mails, and other duties that never appear in a job description. Faculty who help draw students to the school quickly increase their long-term value and prospects for continued employment.

Credentials

Faculty credentials do not tell everything about a school or even the most important things; however, they offer the easiest things to verify when checking whether a school can provide competent instruction. The search for better-trained faculty never ends nor does the press for faculty to continue their education and upgrade their credentials.

My parents were considered exceptional in their families because they both graduated from high school. I was first on either side to graduate from college. In my lifetime, the academic credentialing bar seems to have been raised multiple times. When I began at DTS in 1965, a number of faculty had the ThM as their terminal degree. They could not be hired today. Not only are doctorates required; faculty with double doctorates are not uncommon. While a bachelor's degree may be acceptable in secondary education, schools prefer a master's degree.

In pastoral work, a Bible college degree served many pastors well years ago. Today, most Western seminaries consider a master of divinity entry-level preparation for the pastorate. Indeed, the vast majority of pastors worldwide have less than a high-school education. In the West, as various professions increased their expectations, congregations began to expect their pastors to upgrade their credential and continue their education. In the early 1970s, seminaries began to add a doctor of ministry degree to their pastoral training tracks. These degrees are slowly being recognized as appropriate terminal degrees for teaching in practical ministry areas.

Wherever you end up teaching, you should expect to continue your education. Those may seem like sharp words for someone recently completing a PhD, but the realities are there. Gone are the days when you got a PhD, a teaching post, achieved tenure, and went on cruise control for twenty or thirty years. Honestly, I had a professor in the 1960s who was using the same notes he created in the 1940s.

Accreditation

If you are thinking that evaluation ceases when you finish your schooling, think again. If you enter the teaching profession, I predict an accreditation experience looms in your future. Accreditation affects a school's perception in the community, whether graduates are accepted in other schools, student funding, and donors' generosity. Few schools can afford to ignore the responsibility of reporting to an outside agency.

Accrediting agencies generally look at three large areas:

1. Basics: The examining committee will look at obvious things like facilities, budget, funding, programs, and credentialing. All of these are relatively straightforward.

2. Congruence: All schools put forth promotional pieces that make claims about various advantages of their school. The examining committee expects the school to bring forth evidence that the claims are valid. This cautions schools to avoid exaggerating what can reasonably be accomplished within the confines of the educational program being offered.

3. Improvement: In recent years, the US government has been pushing accreditation agencies to expect schools to improve. Here examiners look for plans to add value to the student's educational experience.

Because faculties deliver the advertised education of schools, they must participate heavily in the evaluation. The extra committee work and document writing add to a normally heavy work schedule. Generally speaking, faculty, staff, and administration are all stressed until the site visit is complete. The heaviest part of the process usually lasts a year, but planning for the process may begin two years or more before the actual site visit. Everyone is generally relieved when it is over. Some superficially wonder if it is worth the effort. Accreditation is a severe institutional reality.

Administration

On a good day, school administration is a tough assignment. In all likelihood, no matter what decision an administrator makes, someone will not like it. Students, faculty, staff, donors, parents, and alumni all have a vested interest in the decision. Sometimes the government or the local community can get tangled up in the process as well. And, in this society, the quite real possibility of litigation always lurks in the shadows like the Grim Reaper. When administrators do their job well, they empower teachers to excel.

The actual power structure of any organization may not always appear on the organizational chart. I watched a choir director run a very large church, but a series of senior pastors apparently thought they were in charge. Big mistake. I have seen a person run a church who did not bother to attend the board meetings. An unwritten code required checking with that person before any big decisions were made. Schools function similarly. Patriarchs, matriarchs, large donors, and even former prominent people can set the educational agenda. Take note of anyone on faculty or staff related to a large donor. "One man, one vote" is not always operational. Wisdom suggests we carefully observe how things actually work.

The priorities and emphases of any given administration can change as the administrators or board changes. The best institutions maintain a sense of stability with slow changes. Slow change is both good news and bad news. Young faculty with fresh ideas can chafe under a slow change process. Be sure of this, a change of administration almost always will bring new priorities and emphases.

One last word to the wise: don't make the mistake of treating secretaries and custodians like wallpaper. They often see, hear, and know more than almost anybody about how things work. When they are your friends because you treated them with respect and gratitude, they can put your name on a crowded calendar, provide special assistance for setup or cleanup, or in my case save your doctoral defense by providing an "unauthorized" form. Days will come when you need all the friends you can find; make them whenever and wherever you can.

Faculty Issues

All institutions tend to take on a life of their own. They grow; they decline; they develop unique personalities. No two schools are exactly alike. The following list represents some faculty realities everyone faces and some possible realities. In any case, they expose areas to explore in the interview process.

Workload

Much of a faculty member's workload remains invisible to the casual observer. When I described how difficult it was for me to do research, students thought I was only being lazy. Finally, I reduced my duties to writing because the generic job description for department chair-man did not reveal my actual responsibilities. The following actually represents my workload for the academic year 2000–2001. Note how grandchildren and fishing appear at the end of my job description. They remind students that life exists outside of institutions. Because I am on sabbatical at the moment, reviewing this makes me quite tired.

COURSE LOAD	PERIODICAL READING	WRITING PROJECTS	BUDGET REVIEW
Master's Level	*Teaching Professor*	5 articles for Russian journal	Graders
CE 102 History & Philosophy	*Bibliotheca Sacra*	15 sermons for Thomas Nelson	TAs
CE 103 Teaching Process	*The Journal of CE*	*Theology for Children*	Remodeling
CE 215 Teaching in Christian Higher Education	*Matrix* (not the movie)	Book reviews for *BibSac*	Equipment
WM 450 CE in Intercultural Contexts	*Current Thoughts and Trends*	Annual catalog revisions	Conferences
+ CE 205, 210, 220, 425, 435, or 715 as needed	ACSI publications		Student activities
(usually a total of 4-5 courses a year)	*Newsweek*		
Doctoral Level	*Distance Education Report*		
CE 11 Learning Theory	Other various journals		
CE 17 Strategic Resource Development			
CE 34 Creative Problem Solving			
(no more than 2 courses in winter or summer sessions only)			

SUPERVISION	COMMITTEES	CHAIR DEPARTMENT	STUDENT RELATIONS
4 full-time faculty 5 adjunct MA faculty adjunct DMin faculty Full-time staff: Receptionist Admin. assistant Interns: Picnics Welcoming meetings Fanfare Graders	D.Min. Distance Education Department Chairmen Women's Ministry Track (Ongoing evaluation) Institutional Effectiveness Fund-raising events	Review course syllabi Review all courses Check course bibliographies Oversee development of new courses & new tracks Spiritual development Faculty development Finalize biweekly agenda Develop department goals	Supervise placement Academic advising Four hours of student appointments weekly Drop-ins
DOCTORAL SUPERVISION	**SCHEDULING**	**OTHER DUTIES**	**OUTSIDE INTERESTS**
DMin Student degree programs 9 final projects 24 DMin CE students PhD cooperative agreement with UNT Student advising (4 hrs. min, weekly) 3 doctoral committees	Extension courses & professors Summer school & professors Evening courses Weekend courses Semester offerings & course loads Three-year course projections DMin in CE curriculum & sequence of course offerings	Meet prospects Greet visitors Visit with alumni Attend chapel (3 times weekly) Attend faculty meeting (weekly) Correspondence & references Phone consultations	International teaching (4-6 weeks a year) Teacher training conferences Preaching in churches Men's retreats PACE (professional organization) Church Partners (church consulting) Fishing Grandchildren

Sadly mistaken are those who think professors simply talk for a few hours each week and contemplate infinity the remainder of the time. "Michigan State University has instituted a faculty orientation for midcareer and started workshops to help associate professors develop leadership and managerial skills since so much of the job is about directing and serving on committees."[6] In that same article, a tenured associate professor complained of her eighty-hour work week running pretty much year-round. The demands on faculty are unlikely to diminish anytime soon. The article goes on to point out a great danger for all teachers but especially for those with doctorates.

> People who enter academe were frequently the highest-performing students all the way through school. Their top grades and test scores earned them places in prestigious graduate programs, which eventually put them among an elite group of people with doctoral degrees. Beating the odds and landing a tenure-track job in an increasingly competitive academic job market sets professors up to feel even more special. But the work that scholars end up doing once they join academe is not always quite as special as they imagined, says Ms. Trower. And by extension, she notes, neither are they.[7]

Certainly, we all are tempted to think more highly of ourselves than we ought to think. And, the temptation to feel good or bad about ourselves based on school performance is great because schooling plays such a dominant role in our lives during our most formative years. Christian teachers are wise to remember that everything we possess, including intellectual acumen, is a gift from God. We are mere stewards of what God has given, nothing more.

---

[6] "Why Are Associate Professors So Unhappy?", accessed September 10, 2014, http://chronicle.com/article/Why-Are-Associate-Professors/132071.
[7] Ibid.

The workload for faculty in secondary education is as demanding but in different ways. In secondary education, the teaching/grading is heavier because graders and teaching assistants are totally out of the budgetary question. Students tend to be less mature and more irresponsible. Parents get factored into the equation, especially when grades come into question. Expected attendance at student activities soaks up more personal time. Being evaluated by student performance on standardized tests adds stress. There are many more lesson plans and great effort expended in making the instruction clear. One group of high schools calculated teacher workloads as follows:

High school faculty are expected to be on site from 8:00 until 3:30 daily. . . . The full-time equivalency is 27.5 units. A unit is determined as follows:

- 5 units for a class that meets 5 periods a week for a year
- 1 unit for a class that meets one period a week for a year
- 2 units per 3-week main lesson block
- 2 units for class sponsor
- 1 unit per individual student advisee[8]

To get close to the equivalence, a high school teacher would teach four to five classes during the year plus enough additional responsibilities to get to 27.5. Four or five hours of teaching five days a week during the school year plus grading will keep a teacher quite busy. Up and down the academic scale, workload is an ongoing concern.

While students feel the pain of writing papers and taking tests, grading them can be even more painful. One teacher writes, "*The sheer drudgery and tedium.* When you're two-thirds of the way through 35 essays on why the Supreme Court's decision in the case of *McCulloch v. Maryland* is important for an understanding of the development of

---

[8] "Effective Practices: Human Resources," accessed September 10, 2014, http://www.whywaldorfworks.org/11_EffPractices/hr_11.asp.

American federalism, it takes a strong spirit not to want to poke your eyes out with a steak knife rather than read one more."[9] He later adds, whatever one does to resolve this issue, ". . . hide the steak knives."

In order to relieve stress from students, I often explain my procedures. I always grade with a smile on my face. If I find myself not smiling, I may need to remind myself that this is only a bad paper—not a bad student—and mark accordingly. I never grade while Oklahoma University is losing. I mark only a select number of papers at a time before breaking so I can come back fresh to the task. I begin with the assumption that the paper deserves a 100 and mark down according to a predisclosed rubric. Last but not least, I try to mark where the paper is really good as well as what went wrong. I have found that students are often as interested or, at times, more interested in the comments than in the final grade. One student wrote, "I felt like we were having a cup of coffee together as I read your comments."

Thorough grading requires a severe time commitment and is my personal gift to students whether they deserve it or not. If I intend to speak into their lives in other ways, I must first demonstrate my genuine interest in their work. Often, but not always, this reputation elevates students' efforts or elicits an apology when they cannot give me what they consider to be their best effort.

Professional Development

One part of the workload always relates to professional development. Most schools allocate certain work days to attend professional conferences. These can be helpful if for no other reason than they provide a change of pace. I find the interpersonal exchanges more helpful than

---

[9] John Tierney, accessed September 10, 2014, http://www.theatlantic.com/national/archive/2013/01/why-teachers-secretly-hate-grading-papers/266931.

either the headline speaker or the breakout workshops. But, choose wisely to associate with those who have a positive outlook on their God-given responsibilities. Gripe sessions never take anyone to a healthy destination.

Other parts of professional development are expected without regard to how much personal time they absorb. Electronics have made life and teaching so much more complicated. Software facelifts, e-mail systems, online platforms, electronic recordkeeping, hardware idiosyncrasies, and PowerPoint—to name only some—have all robbed me of precious time. Technology does not smile while demanding our subservience. We will keep up, and we will not get more time to do it. We will absorb it into our schedules somehow. Imagine a time prior to electricity and prior to the printing press when books were handwritten and hand copied. If a person wanted to learn something, he listened very carefully to what someone had to say, reflected on it, then tried it out. If it didn't work, he didn't hear it correctly, he didn't implement it correctly, or the person who taught it simply made something up.

On two different levels, I have been responsible to assist teachers with personal development. One group was highly motivated adult Sunday school teachers. On the one hand, they loved to study in preparation for their teaching. But, like many adult teachers, they assumed they knew how to teach. As we thought together about the following year, I asked them to find ways to improve their teaching skills along with their knowledge. They could read, listen to trainers, watch videos, or attend conferences. In the end, I asked them to add one or two items to their toolkit for teaching. When counseling professionals, I have taken the same approach. All of us should broaden our understanding of our subjects and sharpen our teaching skills. I often ask graduate students for such a plan. Having a thoughtful three- to five-year personal development plan to show in your first interview may help you land the position you seek. This is especially true if you demonstrate a genuine interest in being both a better scholar and better teacher.

Collegiality

You might think that highly educated people could not possibly be tacky and catty, but they can. If you doubt me, read the comments that follow the article I cited earlier from the Chronicle of Higher Education. The wonderful article by Robin Wilson describes the difficult professional transition from tenured associate professor to full professor. The first comment says, "I am baffled as to why these professors are referred to as 'Ms.' rather than 'Dr.' in this article." The following discussion reveals an abysmal display of discourtesy as one after another of the responders argues for calling them Dr., Professor, Ms., or their first name, rattling off like adolescents in a paint ball contest. To call the electronic diatribe trivial pursuit would be way too kind.

- Teachers can be biased.
- Teachers can be opinionated.
- Teachers can be politically self-serving.
- Teachers can make pronouncements about things they never studied.
- Teachers can be exceedingly human.

As I said to a professor I shall quote later, "I thought more highly of professors until I became one." On our worst days, we can be brilliant snobs and on our best days lovers of God and others (even others with whom we disagree).

On the other hand, those with whom you teach may become your close friends. Those who work alongside you in teaching understand the unspoken demands and challenges. Friendship and collegiality, though highly touted, is never automatic. All good relationships require sustained effort. They work best when we make room for others to move around our narrow expectations of them. Everyone enjoys trusted colleagues who allow you to ask difficult questions that go respectfully unanswered. How refreshing to wonder out loud about things that remain open to various points of view or hidden within the counsels of

God. Too often, Christians create answers where God remains silent. If Job's counselors had kept their speculations to themselves, they would have avoided God's harsh commentary and necessary atonement.

Students and faculty learn quickly who can and cannot be trusted with ambiguity. I once asked a trusted professor about his decision to switch his theological conviction from unlimited to limited atonement. We had enjoyed many thoughtful discussions about that subject as each side appeals to favorite texts for support. He was fully capable of defending either side but had long been known for his allegiance to unlimited atonement. I asked, "Did you just get tired of defending unlimited atonement and shift to defending limited atonement for a while to see what it feels like to be fully committed to a different point of view?" He quickly replied, "That may be as good an explanation as I have."

Two watchwords that promote collegiality are "dignity" and "respect." Practice them whether you are dealing with the top leader of the institution (who may have irritated you) or the lowliest employee (who may have disappointed you). Promote them in conversations that may be headed in a different direction. Step away from conversations that cannot be redirected. Being concerned for another person and his family beyond the "professional moment" builds solid ground on which strained relationships can stand together. Christians have a distinct edge if they allow the Spirit of God to use them in these relational settings.

Sabbaticals

One friend of mine used to say, "There are only three good reasons to teach: June, July, and August." I think that may still be true at the elementary and perhaps even at the secondary level. The thinking is that since teachers get three months off every year, they have no additional need for time off. In general, teachers in these grades have no access to sabbaticals. Those who teach in mission schools often get a furlough that quickly becomes cluttered with speaking assignments and raising support.

Recent trends in higher education continue to move toward a year-round experience with greater emphasis on summer and winter intersession courses, weekend courses at extensions, and online offerings throughout the year. When I began my teaching career, our school had no extensions, no online courses, no weekend offerings, and summer/winter intersession courses were offered at each professor's discretion. Now, all of those possibilities are written into our contracts as potential parts of our workload. Any one of these added to an ordinary workload shrinks the amount of time needed to reflect and evaluate courses or research and publish articles and books. As the workload increases, sabbaticals become an even more important piece of the professor's puzzle.

Creativity, research, and writing all take uninterrupted blocks of time. In my own experience, productive writing requires at least a four-hour block. I am not constantly punching computer keys during that time. Some days pushing the words through my fingers is painfully slow. At other times, pages stack up quickly, and my fingers can hardly keep up. In any case, I could never do reflective thinking or creative writing without extended summer breaks or sabbaticals. The fall/spring workloads are simply too hectic to squeeze in four-hour blocks on any regular basis.

Each school has its own particular set of criterion for granting tenure. Some are generous; some are stingy; all expect the sabbatical to increase the value of the professor to the school. Some require a signed book contract, while others allow time to restructure courses that have grown outdated. Sometimes the nature of the book being written is an issue. Be sure and read the faculty handbook carefully, and visit with your department chair or academic dean way ahead of time. I suggest you begin planning at least two years away from the approval deadline. The more work you can do and detail you can provide, the more likely your sabbatical request will be approved.

Sabbaticals are normally funded in one of two ways. The most common is for the faculty to fund the sabbatical. That means the school pays your salary, but your colleagues take up the slack left by your absence. These are often subjected to much more negotiating depending on how thin the faculty is spread over the courses being offered. Research grants offer a second means for funding a faculty sabbatical. These are almost always awarded because the institution is relieved of your salary, which becomes available to hire adjunct replacements.

Tenure

Those who aspire to teach often consider tenure the Holy Grail. In theory, tenure preserves academic freedom, protects against age (and salary) discrimination, and offers a secure work environment. As with anything worth having, it typically must be earned. How one earns it becomes the question. To say that it has been misused by administrators, abused by faculty, and wrongly awarded or withheld by colleagues describes its actual history.

You can skip this section if you prefer not to listen to a bit of personal cynicism. I have watched tenured faculty released and untenured faculty retained. I have seen faculty awarded tenure with no publications and withheld from faculty with publications. I have grieved with those whose tenure was denied for seemingly unscholarly publications or not enough publications though the quality and quantity were nowhere required or specified. From my experience, no level playing field exists. I wish my experience was unique, but as you will see I am not alone in my concerns.

I do not know of anything less rational or more political than the road to tenure. You will have to find your own way through the institution you serve, and it probably will not involve the yellow brick road. Years ago, I bumped into an intriguing article entitled "Memorandum to Michaelangelo: Tenure Denied."[10] Dr. Selma Wasserman claims to have discovered this rare document "inadvertently attached to some discarded sketches." I have included the entire article, which was republished several times:

Lorenzo de Medici University

MEMORANDUM

To: Sr. Michaelangelo Buonarroti

From: Sr. H. Condivi,
Chairman

Date: 18 August 1511

Faculty Tenure Committee

Dear Sr. Buonarroti:

The Tenure and Promotion Committee of the Faculty of Education deeply regrets that we are unable to recommend you for tenure.

We have given your case considerable thought and much discussion, and while we think that your work has great promise, we feel that it is insufficiently scholarly to merit tenure at this time. The committee wishes to point to its recognition of your outstanding teaching capabilities-in particular, your work with young artists in a mentor capacity, your ability to inspire others, and your thoughtful and sensitive instruction.

---

[10] Selma Wasserman, "Memorandum to Michaelangelo, Tenure Denied," *Improving College and University Teaching* 32, no. 4 (Fall 1984): 186–87. Available at http://www.jstor.org/stable/27565644. Reprinted with permission.

However, in the area of scholarship, your performance has been found wanting. I refer specifically to the following:

(a) In the Faculty of Education, it is not important that you, yourself, be engaged in artistic endeavors. It is far more important that you spend time writing about how others should become artists. This you have failed to do.

(b) Your work, Michaelangelo, is, I'm afraid, too clear, too unambiguous, and too straightforward. It is geared too much for the practitioner. Unfortunately, it is insufficiently obscure to be significant for academics.

(c) While you have given us *David,* which is truly a thing of beauty, you did not, unfortunately, complete a review of the literature on sculpting. This indicates a grave shortcoming in your ability to do a critical analysis of scholarly sculpting.

(d) Finally, sir, your output is inordinately slow. It has been over three years since you have begun work on the Sistine Chapel and it is far from complete. Others in this faculty have generated dozens of manuscripts each year. You are a slow worker, Mike, and it is production here that counts.

We all like and admire you as a colleague—even though you do dress rather oddly and very unlike what is suitable for an academic, and there is frequently a lot of paint in your hair. If you were to move quickly to incorporate these suggestions, the committee believes you have a good chance to earn your tenure at the next hearings. After all, this is only your first consideration.

Sr. H. Condivi

Sr. H. Condivi,

Chairman

Conclusion

I had a difficult time choosing which quote to use to summarize the chapter on page 239. Among those that tempted me were . . .

- "No, tell Billy G. I do not have his paper, and it was due yesterday."
- "Yes, the dean's office has scheduled me for two committees that meet at the same time."
- "Are you aware that Professor So-in-so has three small children at home?"
- "I am happy to review your paper. What if I decide I graded it too high?"
- "I'm sorry. I just cannot add another independent study to my load."
- "You were a student of mine how many years ago, and you still want a recommendation?"

I chose the Michaelangelo article title because it represents a painful reality. The sense of rejection by peers or being considered unworthy are bitter pills to swallow. For those who have tied too much of their identity to their jobs, it can prove devastating.

As Christians, I remind students, bruised faculty, and overworked administrators, "We work for the Great King." His opinion ultimately condemns or vindicates our service. Too many times, we in the Christian community hurt one another. This piece of the puzzle has some rough edges. You may have to work hard to keep it in place. No matter where you go to teach, the realities of the institution you serve will swirl around you. Keeping those realities and yourself in eternal perspective will enable you to maintain your equilibrium and sense of direction.

May God bless your every effort in the service of the Great King.

APPENDIX A

BEGE-1710 CHRISTIAN LIFE AND THOUGHT

SYLLABUS[1]

JOSHUA D. VAJDA

I. COURSE DESCRIPTION

"[BEGE-1710 is] a foundational course designed to introduce the student to a Christian worldview. Attention is first given to the definition, function, formation, and evaluation of worldview. Then Christian responses and applications will be developed from a survey of biblical theology with emphasis upon the teaching about the Creator, creation, redemption, and consummation."

(*Cedarville University Undergraduate Catalog 2010–11*, p. 199)

---

[1] Josh is an outstanding former student of mine. He graciously gave me permission to reprint his syllabus here.

Notes: This course is to teach students how to see the world as a Christian should and live accordingly. There are likely at least two kinds of students in this class: those who realize they have a lot to learn about Christianity and those who think they already know all they need to. In both camps some cleanup is necessary, but the latter group will need special attention right from the beginning. This class must generate interest in deeper study and a love for knowing God and understanding His creation. The description divides it into two parts: worldview and biblical theology.

Part 1: Worldview. "Worldview" is simply shorthand for the recognition that everyone sees the world from his or her own unique perspective. It is a way of talking about how we think about life so that we can more easily make that perspective as much like that of Christ as possible. (The goal is not to become objective; this is impossible for anyone but God.) One might as well talk of a personal theology or philosophy. Our beliefs about the world come from people such as our parents, church leaders, friends, teachers, and celebrities but also our personal experiences, nature, forms of entertainment, socioeconomic status, geography, etc. In short, students must first become aware of the views they hold, where they came from, and why they matter. Finally beliefs must be evaluated by some standard, in this case the historical understanding of a biblically based Christian faith, which will be discussed in the second half of the course. I believe this first half will prove to be more challenging in its topics and tasks than the latter. Students need to be convinced that this is a process worth undertaking.

Part 2: Biblical Theology. This part of the course is essentially about understanding the Christian metanarrative, the story the Bible tells about how everything in the world fits together, giving it all meaning and purpose. The central characters in this story are God and humanity, the stage is the created world (itself a character of sorts), and the plot is the act of creation, man's fall, redemption through Christ, and His return to restore all things for eternity. There is a great deal of freedom in this part of the course and lots of opportunities to help the students fall in love with God, His people, and the world. However, application must not be neglected here. The goal is to show the students where they fit in the story, the part they must play in the world, and how to play it well.

II. RATIONALE

You see the world differently from everyone else. There is a complex tapestry of ideas and experiences woven together to make you the person you are, to think what you do, and to live according to those beliefs. God designed you to be unique and has a special plan for you; however, there is still a right and wrong way to interpret life. How can you be sure that you see and feel and think and know the way a Christian should? This perspective is called a Christian worldview, and without it you and your loved ones are in danger of being deceived. In fact, some of the most dangerous ideas in our lives are the ones we do not recognize we hold. Worldview studies address how we make sense of what is often a confusing world, how we relate to others who believe differently than we do, how we can find our place in God's plan, and much more.

Notes: This course is foundational to both life and thought, as the class name indicates. As such the principles are so general it can be difficult to make them practical enough to be felt by students. The most tangible value is in what a Christian perspective accomplishes for the person who holds it. This class is required during the first two years of college, and students during this time typically struggle with cementing their own beliefs now that they and their friends are away from their parents. Many will be dealing for the first time with problems they have never dealt with before and systems of beliefs they have never encountered. They need to be assured that they are on the right track without becoming proud or overconfident. (The Christian metanarrative is assumed to be a component of a Christian worldview and therefore merits no explicit mention here.)

III. COURSE OBJECTIVES

Cognitive Objectives

A. The student will *identify* the essential elements of a distinctly Christian worldview.

Notes: This objective relates to foundational knowledge. Students must be able to distinguish basic Christian beliefs from those of other religions before they can begin assessing the beliefs they hold. It is imperative that they learn a standard by which they can judge belief systems. These are the essential theological doctrines of the Trinity, the incarnation, human depravity (sin), and Christ's return.

B. The student will *develop* a biblical-theological framework for categorizing new information and assessing its trustworthiness.

Notes: This objective relates to both application and learning how to learn. Students will be bombarded with new information for the rest of their lives. They must have the tools to help them know which sources are trustworthy and how new information relates to what they already believe, maintaining a Christian worldview for the rest of their lives.

C. The student will *describe* the Christian metanarrative in broad strokes and *explain* how a given person, subject, or object has meaning and purpose because of where it fits in God's story.

Notes: This objective relates to both foundational knowledge and integration. Christianity is not simply a collection of abstract truths, but it is God interacting with mankind through creation, judgment, redemption, and glorification. It is this interaction that gives everything meaning. God has a purpose for each student that they can better fulfill if they comprehend the big picture. This not only includes where they fit as people, but their passions and possessions as well.

Affective Objectives

D. The student will *value* a distinctively Christian worldview as a set of beliefs that are the truest, most beautiful, and of the highest character.

Notes: This objective relates to caring. The Greek philosophers sought after the True, the Good, and the Beautiful, but it is a search that the whole world knows well. The Christian religion paints a picture of reality that is completely true and unfolds a moral guide for successful living. Lives conducted according to God's creative design reflect the beauty of God himself. Students need not only understand this and internalize it but enjoy it! If Christianity were not true or the best or beautiful, it would not be worth believing. As students learn to value these aspects of Christianity, they will grow in their love for God.

E. The student will *empathize* with those who view the world from outside the Christian faith and *explain* why such a view might be appealing.

Notes: This objective relates to the human dimension and also contains a cognitive component. It is not enough to know the difference between right and wrong; students must be able to engage with others and understand where they are coming from either as believers or unbelievers. This involves attempting to see from another person's point of view and identifying ways that they have been deceived either about the world or Christianity. Above all students must learn to love others regardless of their differences, following Christ's own example. It is expected that this empathy will naturally help students draw others to Christ.

F. The student will *value* theological study as a means of pursuing a deeper relationship with God.

Notes: This objective relates to caring. The mind is an important part of who we are, and it must be sharpened for God's use just as much as the body, heart, and soul. Students must see that theology is not an attempt to master God but a way to discover the depth of His love for us and to respond in turn.

IV. COURSE TEXTBOOKS

A. Required

Sire, James W. *The Universe Next Door: A Basic Worldview Catalog*. 5th ed. Downers Grove: InterVarsity Press, 2009. (293 pp.)

Notes: This is the standard overview of different systems of belief, great for purposes of comparing and contrasting the Christian religion with other religions and philosophies. The most important aspect of this course is not so much teaching students what to think (i.e., giving them additional content to learn) but how to think in a Christian way. This reading should help make students aware of different views as well as meet a number of course objectives.

Any English Bible

Notes: Hard to form biblical theology without a Bible. Differences in translation can occasionally bring up issues worth talking about.

B. Suggested

Additional resources will be suggested in class via discussion and handouts.

Notes: My goal is to create and maintain a collection of annotated bibliographies. These will be easier to maintain by topic rather than course, as I add to them constantly and have each list available for multiple classes as needed.

V. COURSE REQUIREMENTS

A. Reading Assignments (10%)

The only textbook for this class is Sire's *The Universe Next Door*. This book is an excellent resource, but we will only read the chapters that are relevant to class discussion. Students will submit a reading report at the end of the semester listing the percentage of the chapter read before the class period.

Notes: The reading is important primarily for awareness of other worldviews. It is not crucial to understanding one's own worldview, thus the relatively low grade percentage assigned.

B. Written Assignments (50% Total, +5% EC)

A Note on Formatting: All paper assignments must be written double-spaced and utilize in-line text citation. Handouts will be supplied in class with specific guidelines.

1.   WORLDVIEW JOURNAL (20%)

Students will keep a journal of issues related to the class to be submitted for feedback periodically during the semester. You may want to comment on something that stood out in class, something in your own life related to your Christian worldview, a particular issue regarding the Christian metanarrative, etc. Anything goes so long as it is relevant to class; if you are concerned, feel free to contact me. Submissions must contain original thought and not merely repeat what was said in class. Entries that fail to do this will receive no credit. A minimum average of one entry per week is expected at each checkpoint and a minimum of two pages. Due in class on February 8, February 24, April 7, and May 8.

Notes: Keeping a journal is one of the most effective ways I know to force students to reflect and thus help them appreciate and value what they are learning. The check-in times are for feedback and to keep the journals moving along. Virtually anything can be related back to worldview, so the assignment is easy enough provided the student begins to see life in these terms—which will be a major part of the course. Page limits are guidelines for students rather than hard-and-fast rules for grading.

2. MEDIA ANALYSIS PAPER (15%)

Each student will write a four- to six-page essay analyzing the worldview of a media presentation of his or her choice. Television, film, music, news, and theater are all examples of acceptable media. Students are encouraged to interact with the media in a group, but papers must be written individually. Due in class on March 29.

Notes: The media exposes people to alternative worldviews perhaps more than any other sphere of life, and it is often done at a nonverbal level. It is important for students to be able to see through the message and the medium to the statements the creator is making—which may themselves be communicated subconsciously. Page limits are guidelines for students rather than hard-and-fast rules for grading.

3. INTERVIEW PAPER (15%)

Students will interact with a nonbeliever, either through personal interview, published biography, or a collection of creative work (news articles for a journalist, speeches for a political figure, songs for a songwriter, etc.) as approved by the professor. Students will then write a paper explaining elements of that person's worldview and why those beliefs seem right to the interviewee. This paper must be at least four pages long; there is no upper length limit. Due in class on February 22.

Notes: This paper is designed to help students empathize with people who live by non-Christian worldviews. The goal is not to shake their own faith—although there should be freedom in class to express doubts and deal with them in a healthy way. Rather Christians often approach non-Christians with fear, anger, or pride instead of love as Christ commanded. Page limits are guidelines for students rather than hard-and-fast rules for grading.

4. **EXTRA CREDIT: BIOGRAPHY PAPER (+5%)**

This is an optional extra credit assignment. Students who decide to write this paper will research a famous person whose specific belief or experience made a pronounced impact on his or her life. This paper is worth up to 5% extra credit, and points will be awarded based on (a) the uniqueness of the experience or the subtlety of the belief or idea addressed, (b) the magnitude of the effect felt in the person's life, and (c) a clear, persuasive argument for the connection between the two. You should be able to accomplish this in a four- to six-page paper. May be submitted at any point during the semester, but no later than May 8.

Notes: This assignment encourages students to investigate the power of beliefs, ideas, and experiences on the way a person lives. Students will hopefully walk away with a greater appreciation for the importance of their own beliefs, ideas, and experiences upon the way they live and view the world. Page limits are guidelines for students rather than hard-and-fast rules for grading.

C. **Tests and Exams (35% Total, +4% EC)**

1. **EXAM 1 (15%, +2% EC)**

Exam 1 will be given the week before Spring Break (on March 1) and may be taken in groups for 2% extra credit. The focus of this exam is to show that you can discern beliefs arising from various worldviews and begin to apply Christian thought to problems.

Students may choose to retake the incorrect portions of this exam anytime before exam 2 (April 12) for a higher grade.

Notes: This exam will include multiple choice, short answer, matching, and short essay questions. They will all attempt to demonstrate whether students understand basic worldview issues and can identify which beliefs arise from which worldviews. The test should take an average of 20-30 minutes individually, although in groups this may take longer. Testing time will be limited to the 75-minute class period. My job as a teacher is to make sure they know what will be on the exam (i.e., how to prepare) and to focus the questions on crucial issues.

To retake the incorrect portions, students will be provided a blank exam in which they can answer only the questions they wish to revise. They may bring a list of question numbers to focus on with them. This may only be done individually and *not* in groups.

2. EXAM 2 (15%, +2% EC)

Exam 2 will be given during week 12 of class (April 12) and will cover issues relating to Christian worldview distinctives and biblical theology. The final may be taken in groups for 2% extra credit.

Students may choose to retake the incorrect portions of this exam during finals week for a higher grade.

Notes: This exam will be administered three weeks early to allow time for the exams to be graded and returned before finals week so that students may retake the incorrect portions if they so choose. It will include the same types of questions as exam 1 and be administered in the same format. It will attempt to demonstrate whether students understand the core tenants of the Christian worldview and where they are found in the Bible.

To retake the incorrect portions of the final, students will be provided a blank final in which they can answer only the questions they wish to revise. They may bring a list of question numbers to focus on with them. This may only be done individually and *not* in groups.

D. Narrative Project (5%)

During the last portion of the semester, students will form groups to creatively demonstrate how a specific subject of study relates the biblical metanarrative. This project can be as simple or complex as the group desires, but every project will be presented in class on April 28. I will be glad to help you choose a subject if need be. Details of the project should be finalized and submitted the class period before presentations (April 26).

Notes: The goal of this project is to get students thinking creatively about the big picture. It is intended to be an inspiring time where students can have fun taking a break from studying and working together. The grade is primarily earned by simply accomplishing the project and presenting it in class; no further restrictions are needed. At the end of the presentations, I will connect the creativity demonstrated in class to that of the Father working with mankind.

E. Class Participation (5%)

Class interaction is an important part of learning, especially when dealing with a person's worldview. Students who do not participate in class may be docked up to 5% of their final grade at the professor's discretion.

Notes: Students will be forced to engage in class, so this should not be an issue. However, it will hopefully encourage them to engage willingly. It also gives me the freedom to push students who need extra motivation.

F. Extra Credit: Grade the Prof (+1% EC)

In an effort to meet your needs as a student and teach the class better, I would love your honest feedback. While I would greatly enjoy meeting with you at any point during the semester to discuss class or get to know you better, I have designed this assignment to give you an extra opportunity to say what is on your mind and earn some bonus points for it. Your response may be delivered anonymously if you prefer, although I hope you will feel comfortable enough to discuss sensitive matters with me in person. Assessments will be accepted anytime from exam 1 until the first class after Spring Break (March 1–15).

Notes: Fairly self-explanatory. Anonymous credit will be given by checking the student's name off in the grade book at the time of accepting the assessment.

VI. COURSE POLICIES

A. Letter/Numerical Grade Scale

A	95-100	A-	90-94	B+	87-89
B	83-86	B-	80-82	C+	77-79
C	73-76	C-	70-72	D+	67-69
D	63-66	D-	60-62	E	0-59

Notes: This system is based off of a standard grading scale used in many undergraduate institutions. Students will be graded graciously and given opportunities to improve their grades through extra credit work.

B. Late Assignments

Late assignments will lose a half a letter grade for each day they are late. Exceptions will only be made for *unforeseen* and *unavoidable* emergencies at the discretion of the professor.

Notes: This standard is intended to be a stern warning. Students who are consistently late will feel more of its force than a student who perhaps misses only one assignment by one day. I have no intention of punishing students, but beginning students in particular will likely need boundaries to help them establish good study habits.

C. Weighing of Course Requirements for Grading

Assignment	Due Date(s)	Percentage
Sire Readings	(Report by 5/8)	10%
Worldview Journal	2/8, 2/24, 4/7, 5/8	20%
Media Analysis Paper	3/29	15%
Interview Paper	2/22	15%
Exam 1	3/1	15%
Exam 2	4/12	15%
Narrative Project	4/26, 4/28	5%
Class Participation	Report by 5/8	5%
TOTAL		100%

EC: Group Exam 1	3/1	2%
EC: Group Exam 2	4/12	2%
EC: Grade the Prof	4/15	1%
EC: Biography Paper	5/8	1-5%
MAX TOTAL EC		+10%

D. Attendance

Class attendance is essential to learning, especially in courses such as this one. However, it is the student's responsibility to get his or her money's worth out of the class. See university policies for official attendance requirements.

Notes: I believe college students should be treated as adults and responsible for taking initiative in class. This unfortunately can end up giving the student enough rope with which to hang himself. I will engage with the students to encourage class attendance in every way I can, but otherwise they are on their own.

E. Discrimination

CU does not discriminate on the basis of disability, age, gender, color, ethnicity, or weight in either admission or employment. For more information, see the university's full statement on discrimination and diversity or contact Student Services. Special accommodations can be made in advance for students with disabilities.

Notes: My desire is for all students to get as much out of class as possible and to help them personally in any way that I can, especially with regard to those who are often left behind.

VII. COURSE SCHEDULE

Week	Date	Topic	Assignments
1	Jan 25	Course Introduction & Syllabus Notes: Begin building relationships with students and setting the tone for the semester. Let them know what to expect and alleviate fears as much as possible. Cover no content! Demonstrate love in all things.	
	Jan 27	The Marketplace of Ideas Notes: Define "worldview" and discuss the relationship of worldviews to each other. Show how it is impossible to be truly objective or secular in one's views.	
2	Feb 1	The True, the Good, and the Beautiful Notes: Relate the goal of a worldview to that of philosophy: to guide you to a proper understanding of what is superlatively True, Good, and Beautiful.	Read Sire Chapter 1
	Feb 3	Worldview Formation Notes: Have students briefly discuss in pairs some of the factors that have most influenced the way they view the world. Collect student answers in classroom discussion. Guide class discussion so that the following groups are identified: revelation, experience, authority figures, and internal reasoning. Discuss how they relate to one another and why we trust them—for better or worse.	

3	Feb 8	Naturalism Notes: Our first worldview discussion is on one of the biggest in America, purported to be what intellectually honest people believe. Discuss Sire reading.	Read Sire Chapter 4 Journal 1 Due
	Feb 10	Faith and Reason Notes: Set up the conflict between Christianity and science. Explain the historic Christian view of faith seeking understanding.	
4	Feb 15	Faith and Reason (cont.) Notes: Continue clearing up misconceptions about the relationship between faith and reason. Demonstrate how reason is a powerful tool if subjected first to faith in God and His Word.	
	Feb 17	New Age Spirituality Notes: The other large non-Christian worldview in America. Summarize with a content chart.	Read Sire Chapter 8
5	Feb 22	In-Class Exercise: Case Studies Notes: Divide the class into work groups and give them worldview case studies to analyze and discuss. In the remaining minutes have them explain their findings to the class.	Interview Paper Due
	Feb 24	Exam 1 Review Session Notes: Explain what will be on the exam in terms of types of questions and content. Answer questions about material covered in class thus far.	Journal 2 Due

6	Mar 1	**Exam 1** Notes: See rationale under "exam 1" in course requirements.	Exam 1
	Mar 3	Worldview and Art Notes: Watch a half hour TV program and hold an informal class discussion about the worldview it presents. If a suitable show cannot be found, analyze commercials, YouTube clips, music videos, or some other short form(s) of entertainment. Make sure there is popcorn for the students.	
7	Mar 8 Mar 10	**Spring Break: No Class**	
8	Mar 15	Christian Distinctives: The Supernatural Notes: Contrast with the lesson on Naturalism.	Read Sire Chapter 2 EC Grade the Prof Due
	Mar 17	Christian Distinctives: The Trinity Notes: Explain what makes the Trinity one of the most unique and difficult doctrines in history. Have students wrestle with this in class discussion. It is not expected that students master this at this time.	
9	Mar 22	Christian Distinctives: The Incarnation Notes: Explain what makes the Incarnation of Christ one of the most unique and difficult doctrines in history. Have students wrestle with this in class discussion. It is not expected that students master this at this time.	
	Mar 24	Christian Distinctives: The Return of Christ Notes: Inspire students with hope about the return of Christ. Shades of the meta-narrative discussions to come. Conclude this section with a litany.	

10	Mar 29	Key Doctrines: Inerrancy Notes: Have students discuss what they have been taught about inerrancy and survey the general views, putting the doctrine in perspective.	Media Analysis Paper Due
	Mar 31	Key Doctrines: Human Depravity Notes: Have students discuss what they have been taught about human depravity and survey the general views, putting the doctrine in perspective.	
11	Apr 5	Key Doctrines: Salvation by Grace Notes: Have students discuss what they have been taught about faith versus works and survey the general views, putting the doctrine in perspective.	
	Apr 7	Exam 2 Review Session Notes: Explain what will be on the exam in terms of types of questions and content. Answer questions about material covered in class thus far. Use part of class to play the name game: have students try to describe a figure or doctrine that will be on the exam by asking other students yes or no questions.	Journal 3 Due
12	Apr 12	**Exam 2** Notes: See rationale under "exam 2" in course requirements.	Exam 2
	Apr 14	The Christian Metanarrative in Scripture Notes: Demonstrate God's plan unfolding in Scripture	

13	Apr 19	The Christian Metanarrative in Scripture (cont.) Notes: Demonstrate God's plan unfolding in Scripture	
	Apr 21	The Christian Metanarrative in Culture Notes: Demonstrate the presence of redemption themes in otherwise secular culture.	
14	Apr 26	The Christian Metanarrative and You Notes: Discuss how students individually relate to God's story.	Narrative Project Due
	Apr 28	Narrative Project Presentations Notes: Emcee student presentations.	
15	TBD	**Finals Week** Notes: Allow students to retake exam 2 during this time if they so choose. Paper assignments may be turned in at the office anytime this week.	Journal 4 Due Attendance Sheet Due Reading Report Due EC Biography Paper Due

TEACHER BEHAVIORS INVENTORY[1]

Editor's Note: Very often evaluation instruments do not describe effective instruction concretely. They focus on what effective instructors are like— enthusiastic, friendly, accessible—as opposed to what those who teach do. The distinction is an important one because if you are interested in improving your performance in the classroom, it is much more helpful to identify what you are doing than what you should be.

This Teacher Behaviors Inventory makes an important contribution in this area. Its developer, Harry Murray, reviewed research that attempts to identify some of the components of effective instruction. He then hypothesized what teaching behaviors might be associated with those components. In subsequent research he found that a number of the behaviors did correlate significantly with student ratings of overall instructor effectiveness.

This instrument is not copyrighted and may be reproduced for any valid research or instructional development purpose.

---

[1] This inventory, developed by Harry G. Murray, appeared in the October 1988 issue of *The Teaching Professor*, a newsletter of Magna Publications. The "Editor's Note" appeared in that publication. Used with permission.

Instructions to Student

In this inventory you are asked to assess your instructor's specific classroom behaviors. Your instructor has requested this information for purposes of instructional analysis and improvement. Please try to be both thoughtful and candid in your responses so as to maximize the value of feedback.

Your judgments should reflect that type of teaching you think is best for this particular course and your particular learning style. Try to assess each behavior independently rather than letting your overall impression of the instructor determine each individual rating.

Each section of the inventory begins with a definition of the category of teaching to be assessed in that section. For each specific teaching behavior, please indicate your judgment as to whether your instructor should increase, decrease, or make no change in the frequency with which he/she exhibits the behavior in question. Please use the following rating scale in making your judgments:

1 = almost never
2 = rarely
3 = sometimes
4 = often
5 = almost always

Clarity: method used to explain or clarify concepts and principles

Gives several examples of each concept	1	2	3	4	5
Uses concrete, everyday examples to explain concepts and principles	1	2	3	4	5
Fails to define new or unfamiliar terms	1	2	3	4	5
Repeats difficult ideas several times	1	2	3	4	5

Stresses most important points by pausing, speaking slowly, raising voice, and so on	1	2	3	4	5
Uses graphs or diagrams to facilitate explanation	1	2	3	4	5
Points out practical applications of concepts	1	2	3	4	5
Answers students' questions thoroughly	1	2	3	4	5
Suggests ways of memorizing complicated ideas	1	2	3	4	5
Writes key terms on blackboard or overhead screen	1	2	3	4	5
Explains subject matter in familiar colloquial language	1	2	3	4	5

Enthusiasm: use of nonverbal behavior to solicit student attention and interest

Speaks in a dramatic or expressive way	1	2	3	4	5
Moves about while lecturing	1	2	3	4	5
Gestures with hands or arms	1	2	3	4	5
Exhibits facial gestures or expressions	1	2	3	4	5
Avoids eye contact with students	1	2	3	4	5
Walks up aisles beside students	1	2	3	4	5
Gestures with head or body	1	2	3	4	5
Tells jokes or humorous anecdotes	1	2	3	4	5
Reads lecture verbatim from prepared notes or text	1	2	3	4	5
Smiles or laughs while teaching	1	2	3	4	5
Shows distracting mannerisms	1	2	3	4	5

Interaction: techniques used to foster students' class participation

Encourages students' questions and comments during lectures	1	2	3	4	5
Criticizes students when they make errors	1	2	3	4	5
Praises students for good ideas	1	2	3	4	5
Asks questions of individual students	1	2	3	4	5
Incorporates students' ideas into lecture	1	2	3	4	5
Presents challenging, thought-provoking ideas	1	2	3	4	5
Uses a variety of media and activities in class	1	2	3	4	5
Asks rhetorical questions	1	2	3	4	5

Organization: ways of organizing or structuring subject matter

Uses headings and subheadings to organize lectures	1	2	3	4	5
Puts outline of lecture on blackboard or overhead screen	1	2	3	4	5
Clearly indicates transition from one topic to the next	1	2	3	4	5
Gives preliminary overview of lecture at beginning of class	1	2	3	4	5
Explains how each topic fits into the course as a whole	1	2	3	4	5
Begins class with a review of topics covered last time	1	2	3	4	5
Periodically summarizes points previously made	1	2	3	4	5

Pacing: rate of information presentation, efficient use of time

Dwells excessively on obvious points	1	2	3	4	5
Digresses from major theme of lecture	1	2	3	4	5
Covers very little material in class sessions	1	2	3	4	5
Asks if students understand before proceeding to next topic	1	2	3	4	5
Sticks to the point in answering students' questions	1	2	3	4	5

Disclosure: explicitness concerning course requirements and grading criteria

Advises students as to how to prepare for tests or exams	1	2	3	4	5
Provides sample exam questions	1	2	3	4	5
Tells students exactly what is expected of them on tests, essays or assignments	1	2	3	4	5
States objectives of each lecture	1	2	3	4	5
Reminds students of test dates or assignment deadlines	1	2	3	4	5
States objectives of course as a whole	1	2	3	4	5

Speech: characteristics of voice relevant to classroom teaching

Stutters, mumbles or slurs words	1	2	3	4	5
Speaks at appropriate volume	1	2	3	4	5
Speaks clearly	1	2	3	4	5
Speaks at appropriate pace	1	2	3	4	5
Says "um" or "ah"	1	2	3	4	5
Voice lacks proper modulation (speaks in monotone)	1	2	3	4	5

Rapport: quality of interpersonal relations between teacher and students

Addresses individual students by name	1	2	3	4	5
Announces availability for consultation outside of class	1	2	3	4	5
Offers to help students with problems	1	2	3	4	5
Shows tolerance of other points of view	1	2	3	4	5
Talks with students before or after class	1	2	3	4	5

APPENDIX C

PROPER OUTLINE FORM[1]

1. Each of the points in the outline should be a grammatically complete sentence.
2. Each of the points should be a statement—not a question.
3. The major idea appears in the outline in the place where its statement naturally occurs in the message.
4. Transitions between the points are put in parentheses.
5. Roman numbers are used for the main points—not for "Introduction" or "Conclusion."

Example of Outline Form

Introduction
1. Most people want to understand what the teacher says.
2. Most teachers want to be understood.
3. Understanding comes through proper outlining.

---

[1] I have reproduced this material based on Haddon Robinson's classroom notes. Used with permission.

Main Idea: We must outline to be understood.

    I.   Outlining helps the speaker to develop his ideas intelligently.

        A.   The process of outlining helps the speaker clarify his thinking.

            1.   Outlining helps us to see what we are saying.

            2.   Illustration:

                Jim Smith had only a hazy notion of what he wanted to say until he wrote a series of carefully worded sentences outlining his idea. (Furthermore)

        B.   The process of outlining calls the speaker's attention to gaps in the logical structure of his speech.

            1.   Tom Smart failed to see how little evidence he had to prove his main idea until he put his points down on paper.

        (Not only does a good outline help the speaker, but)

    II.   Outlining helps the listener remember what is said.

        A.   Experiments conducted by Professor Mitchell show that impressions perceived in a pattern are more readily understood and recalled than unpatterned stimuli.

        B.   Your own experience demonstrates that you recall well-organized talks and forget confusing ones.

Conclusion

    For good thinking and better listening, try outlining.

NAME INDEX

SUBJECT INDEX

SCRIPTURE INDEX